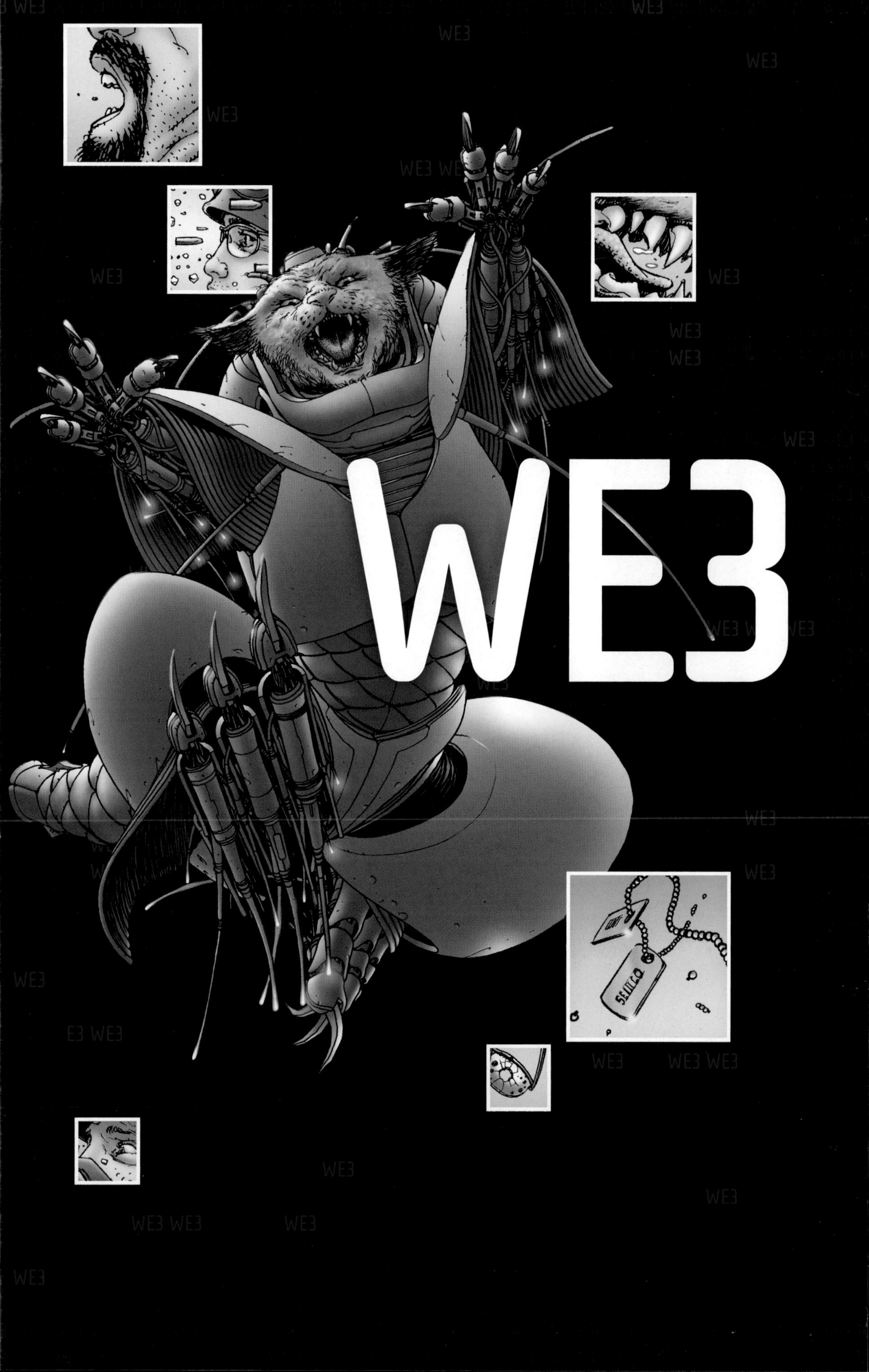
WE3

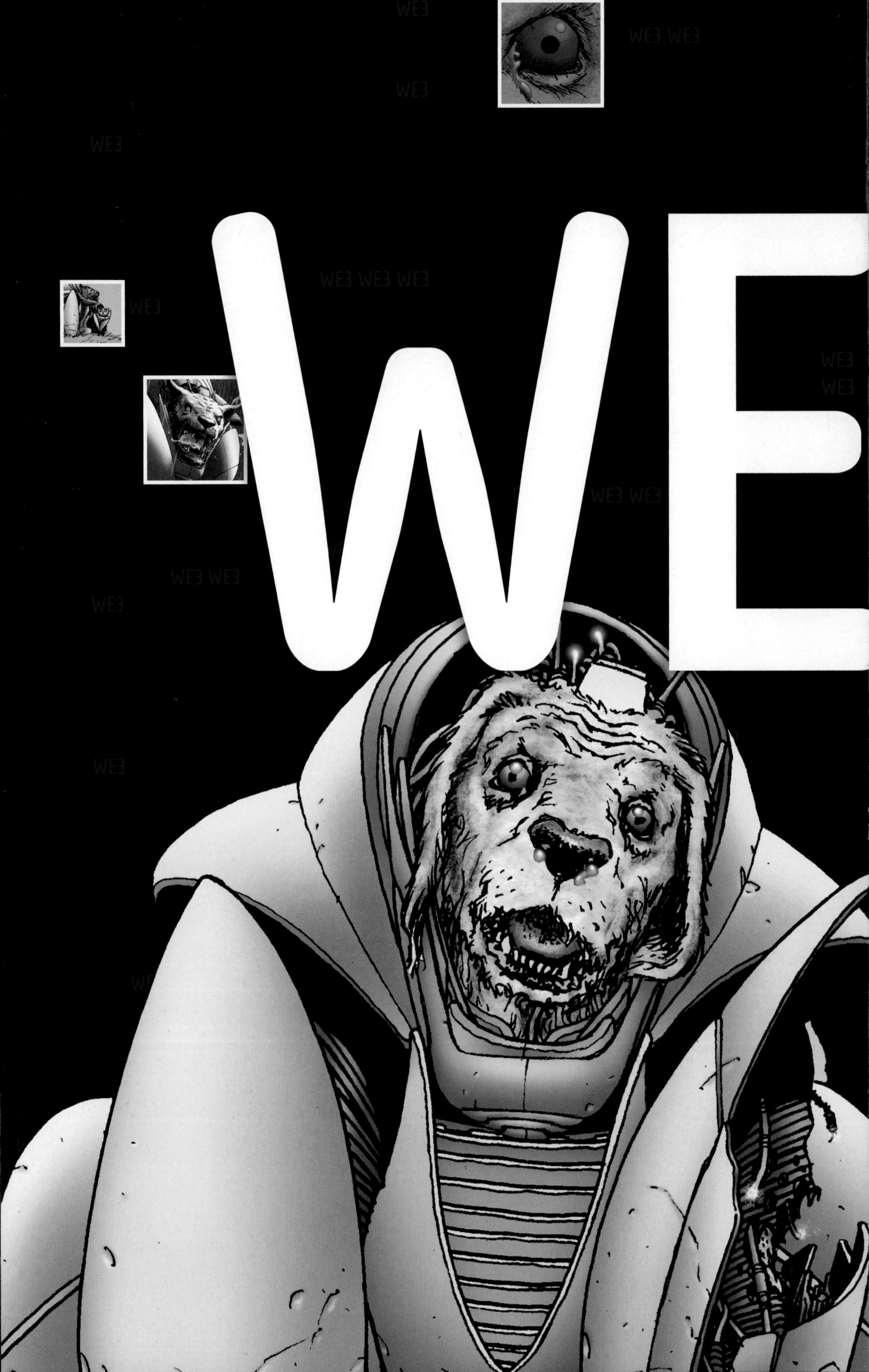

WE

THE DELUXE EDITION

GRANT MORRISON
writer

FRANK QUITELY
artist

JAMIE GRANT
colorist and digital inker

TODD KLEIN
letterer

WE3 created by
GRANT MORRISON AND FRANK QUITELY

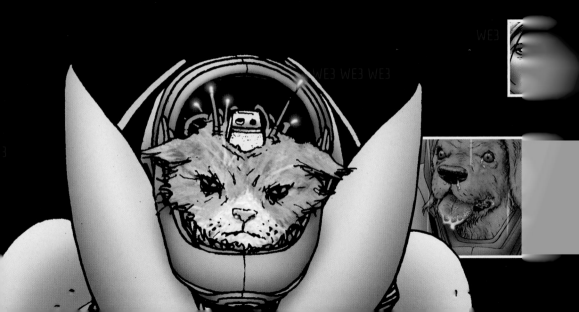

: THE DELUXE EDITION
ished by DC Comics. Cover and compilation Copyright © 2011 Grant Morrison and Frank Quitely. All Rights Reserved. Originally published in single magazine form as WE3 1-3. Copyright
004, 2005 Grant Morrison and Frank Quitely. All Rights Reserved. All characters, their distinctive likenesses and related elements featured in this publication are trademarks of Grant Morrison
Frank Quitely. VERTIGO is a trademark of DC Comics. The stories, characters and incidents featured in this publication are entirely fictional. DC Comics does not read or accept unsolicited
missions of ideas, stories or artwork.

Comics
0 Broadway, New York, NY 10019. A Warner Bros. Entertainment Company.
ted in the USA. Second Printing. ISBN: 978-1-4012-3067-8

ary of Congress Cataloging-in-Publication Data

rison, Grant.
3 : the deluxe edition / Grant Morrison, Frank Quitely.
p. cm.
riginally published in single magazine form as We3 1-3."
N 978-1-4012-3067-8 (alk. paper)
Cyborgs—Comic books, strips, etc. 2. Graphic novels. I. Quitely, Frank, 1968- II. Title. III. Title: We 3. IV. Title: We three.
6727.M677W44 2012
1.5'9411—dc23
                    2012037331

MISSING

MEDIUM SIZE DOG - BROWN LABRADOR MIXED
FRIENDLY & APPROACHABLE
ANSWERS TO 'BANDIT'
REWARD OFFERED FOR ANY INFORMATION
PHONE: 555-2314

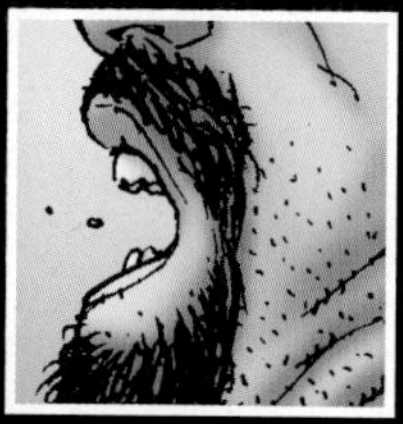

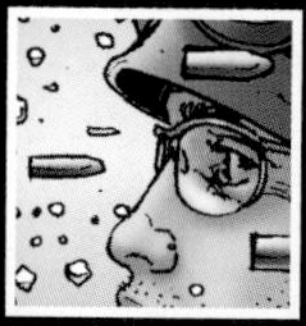

CHAPTER 1

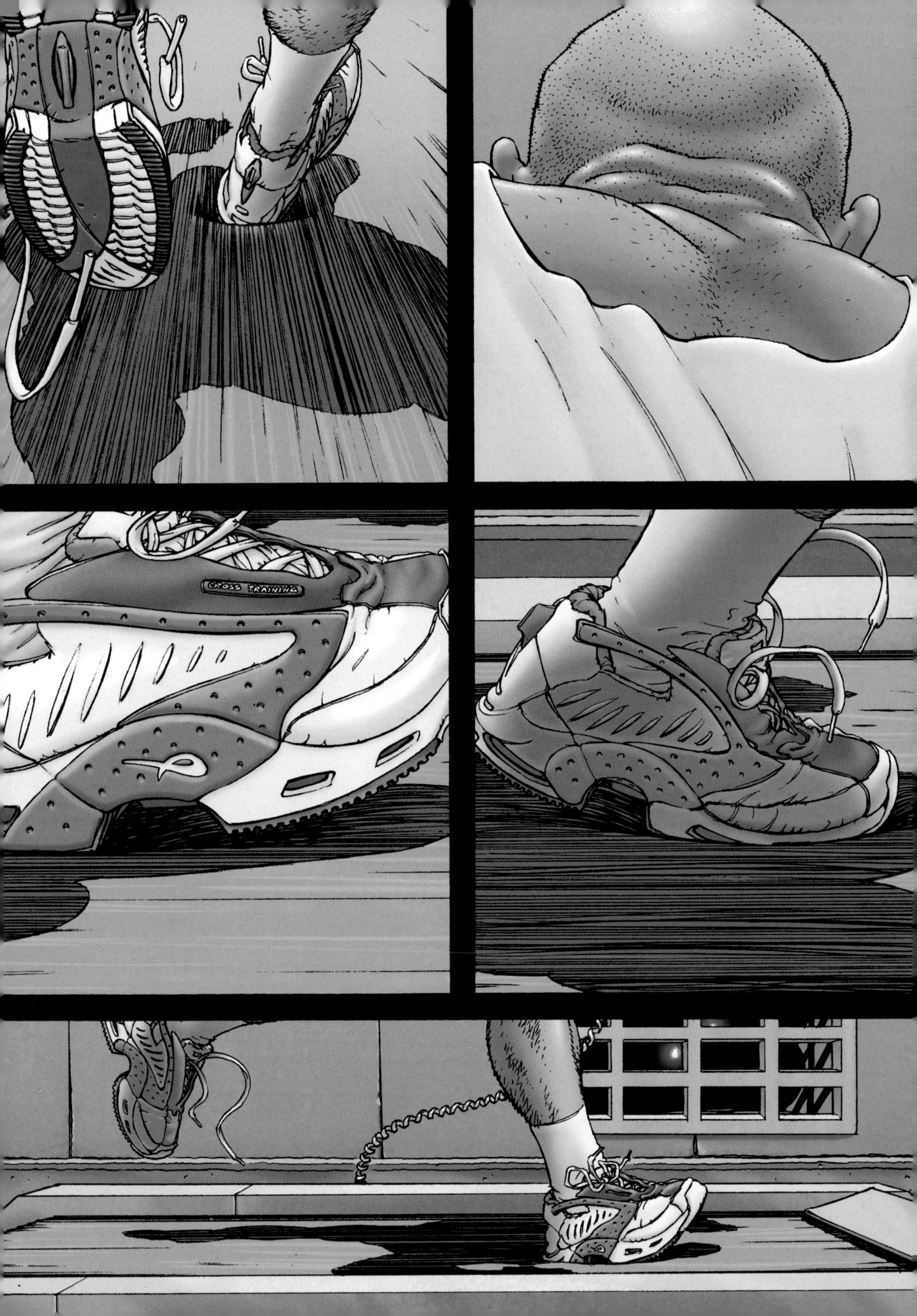
CROSS TRAINING

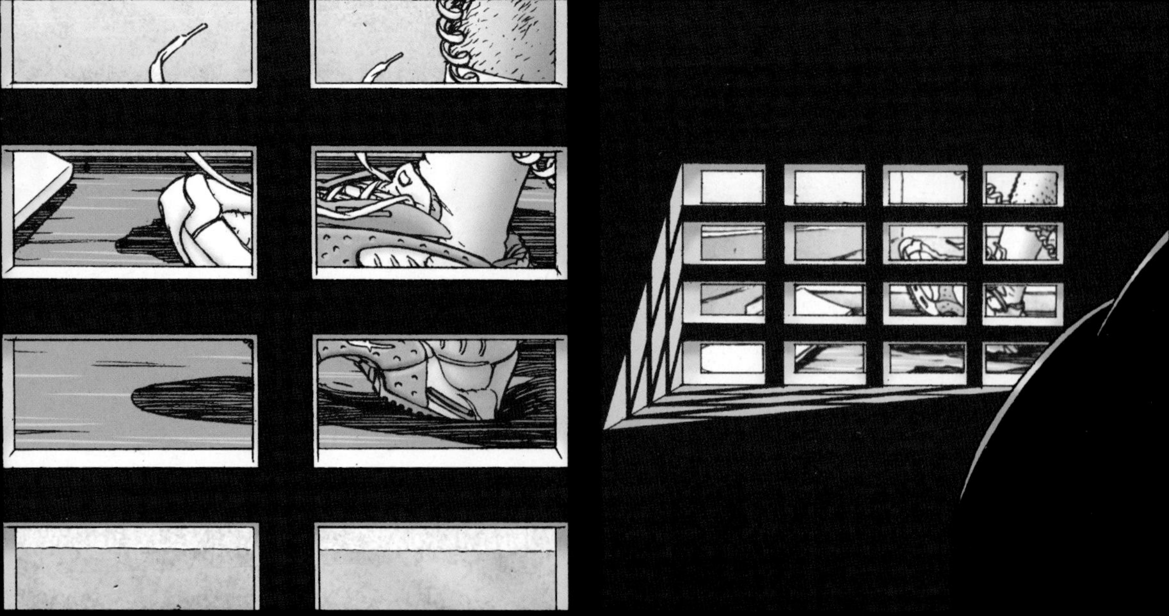

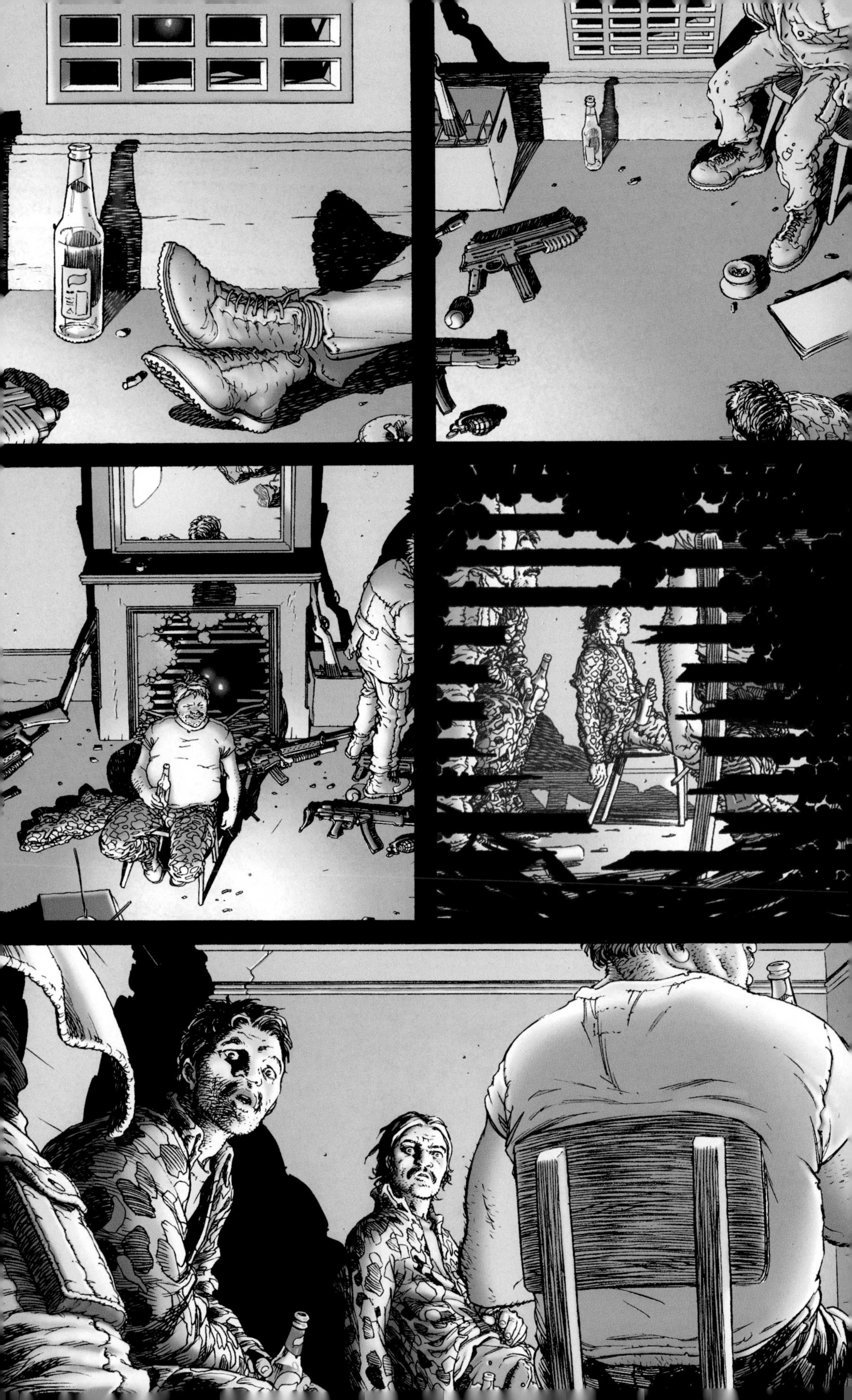

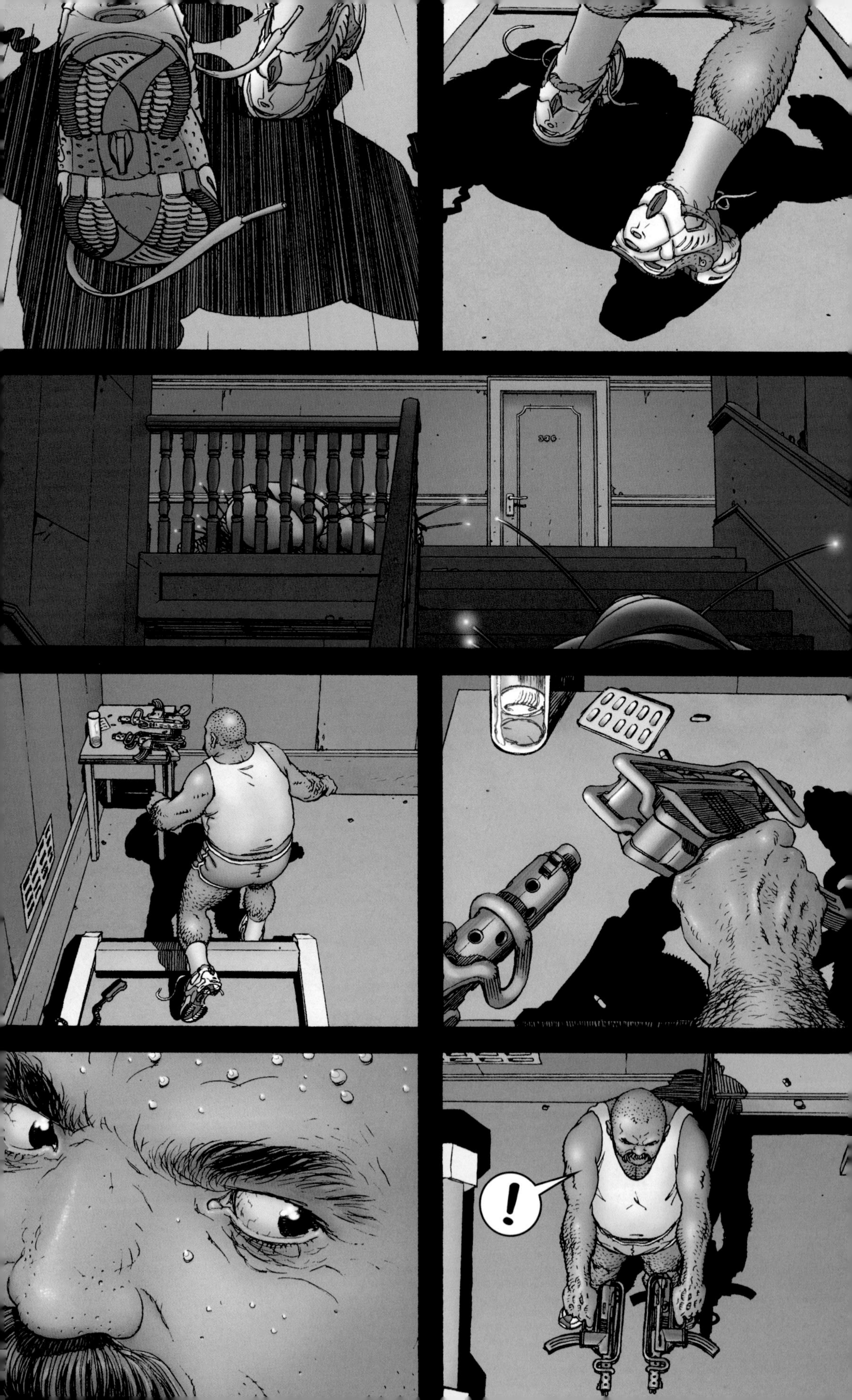
!

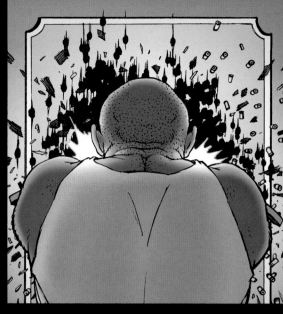

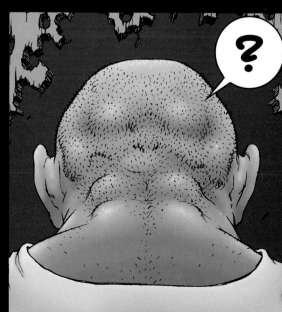

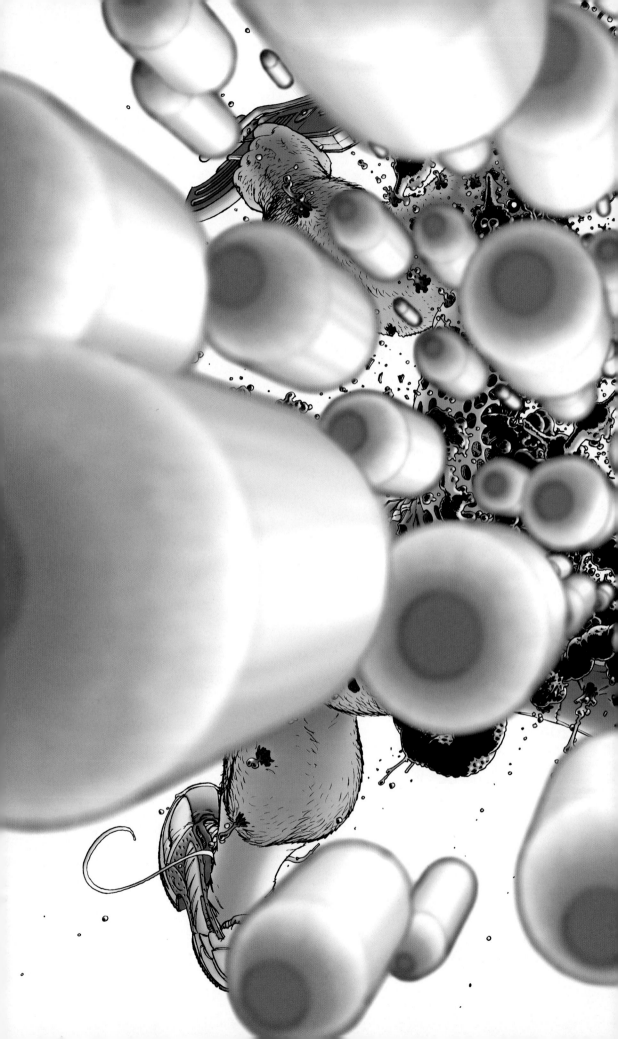

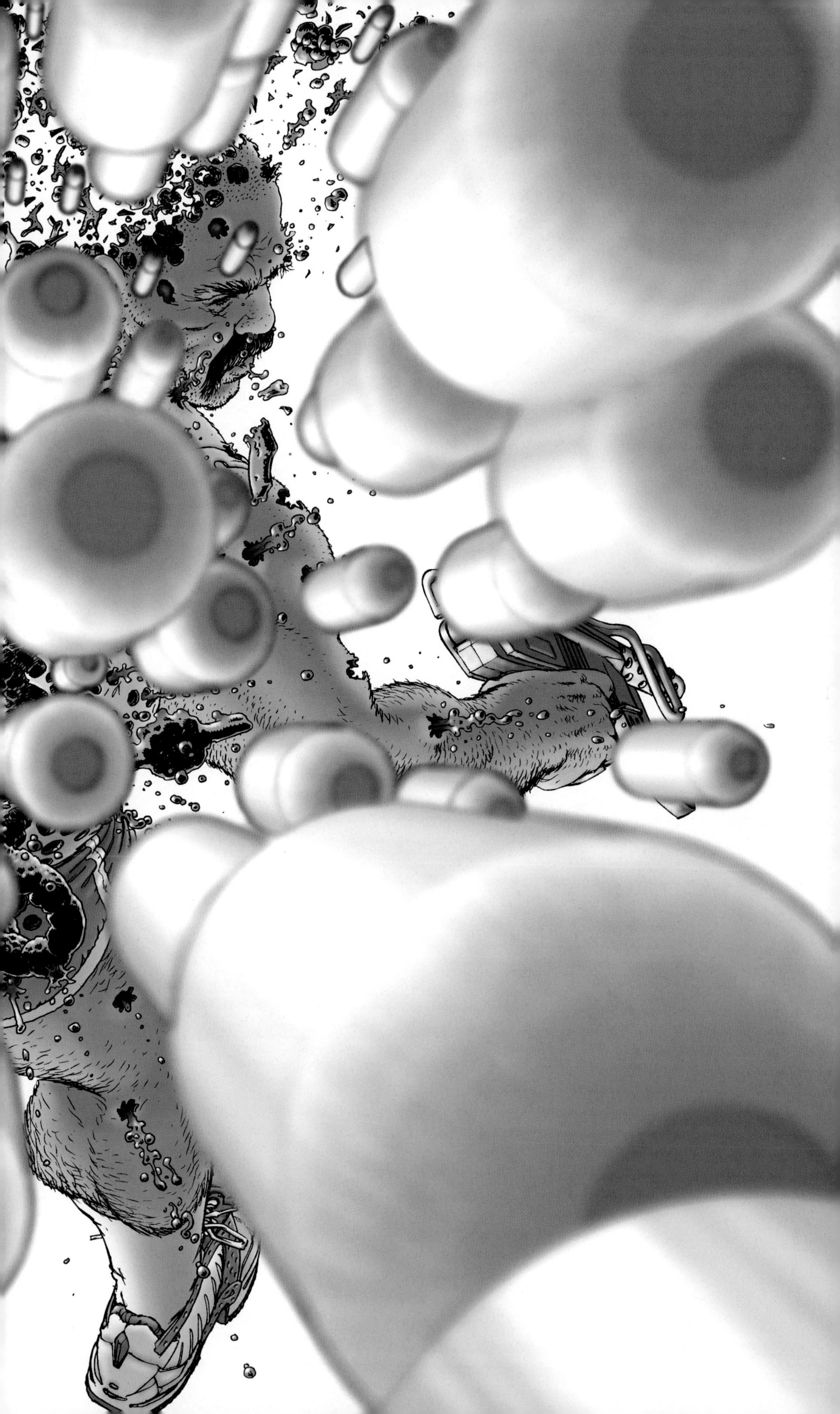

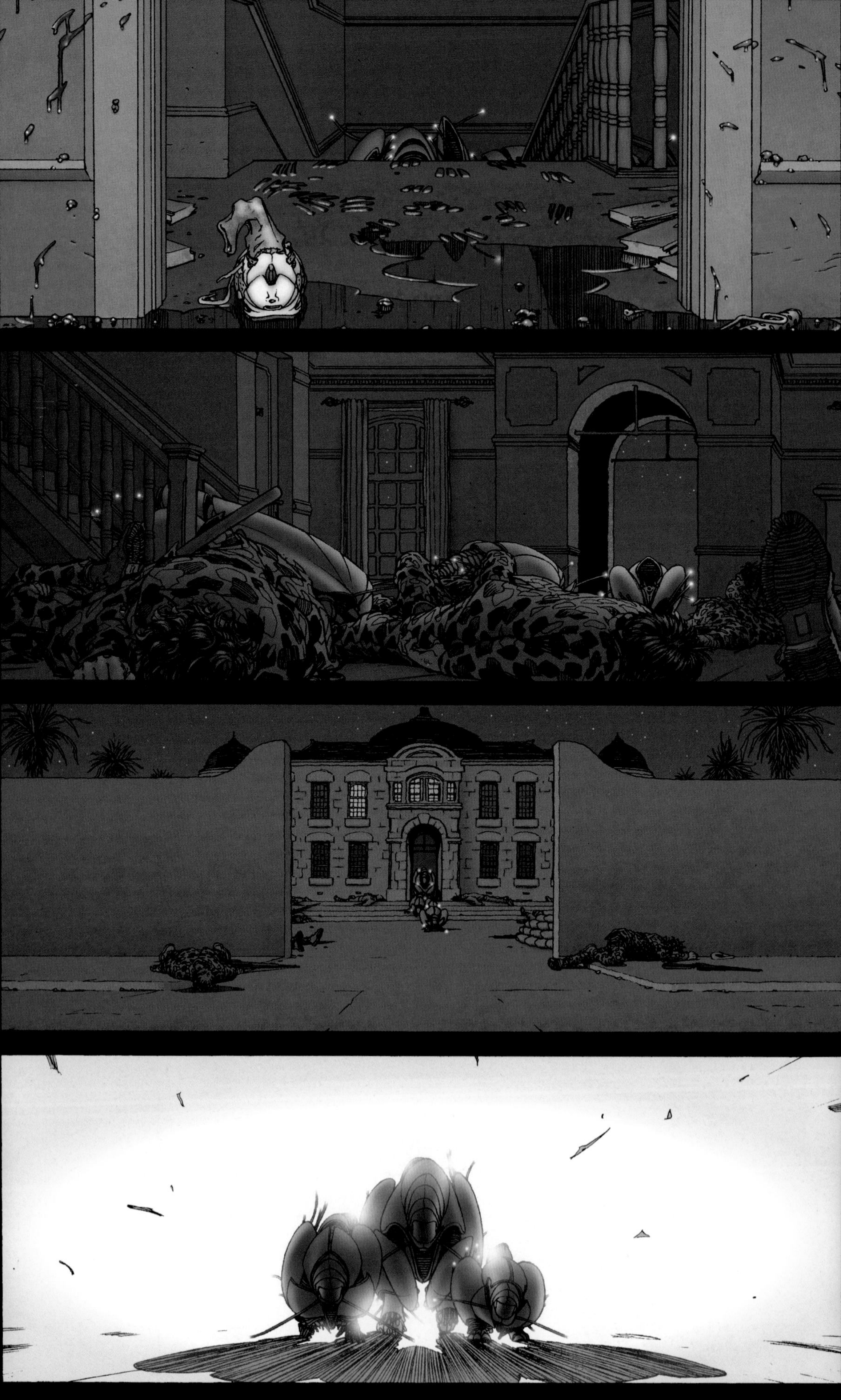

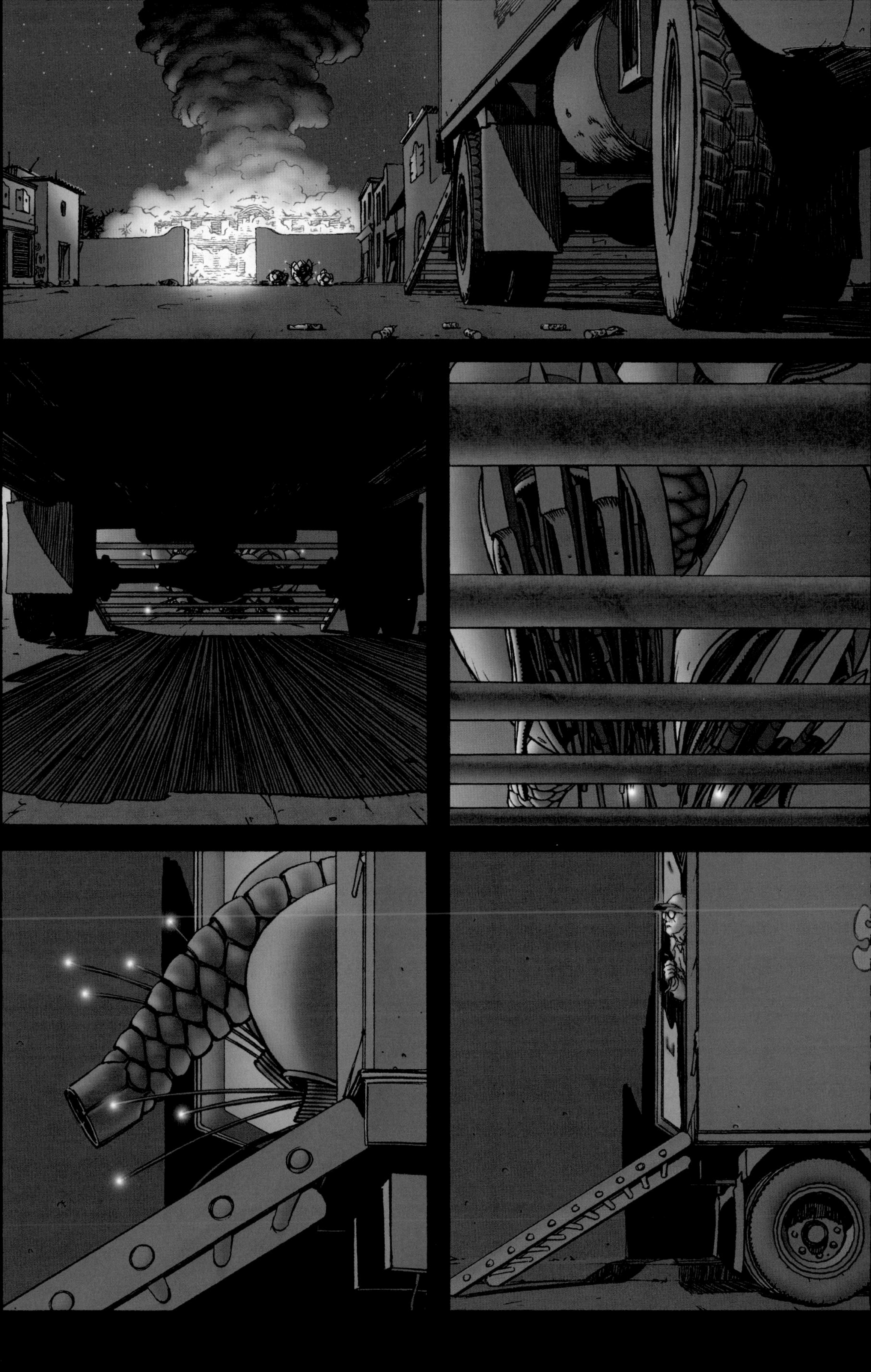

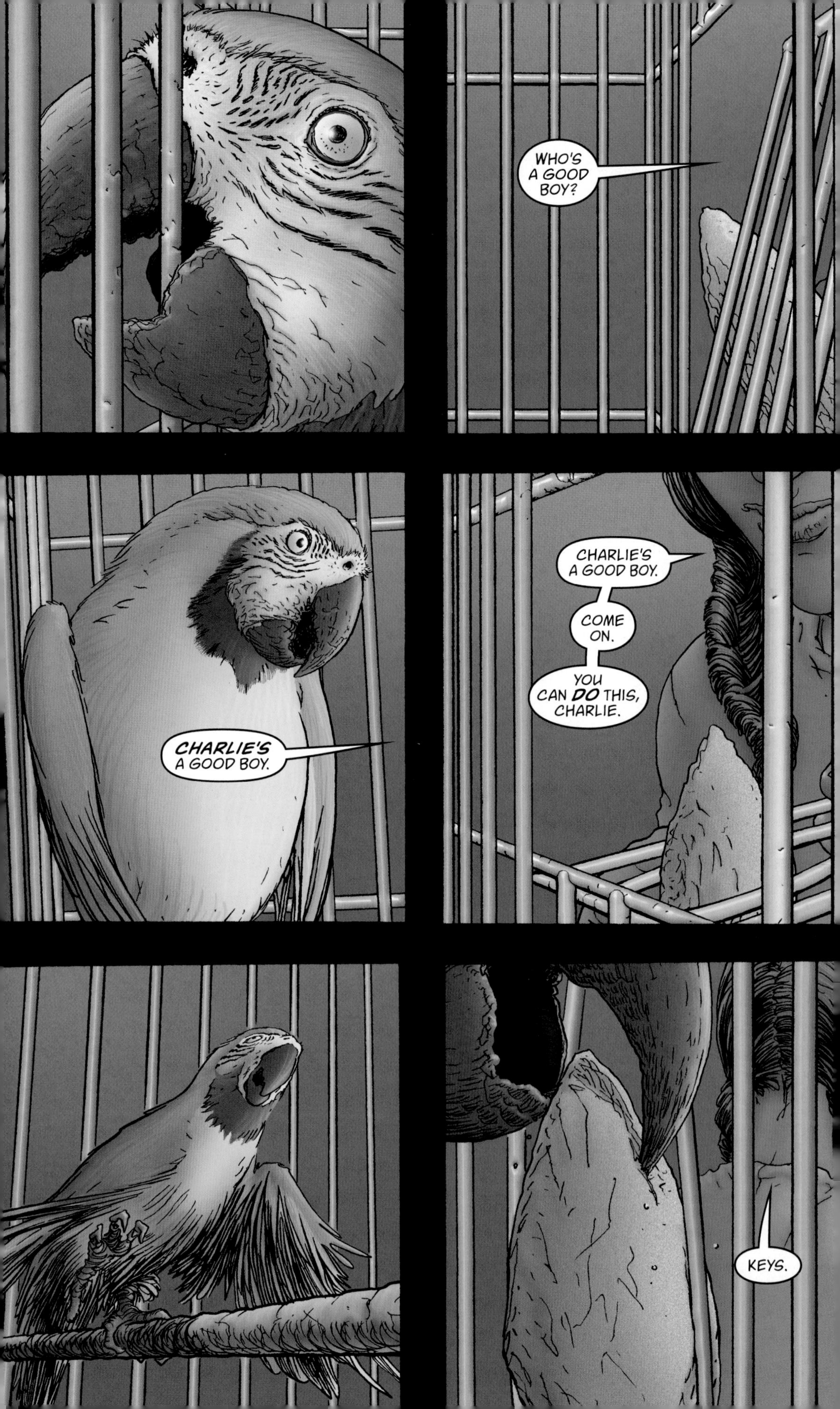
WHO'S A GOOD BOY?
CHARLIE'S A GOOD BOY.
CHARLIE'S A GOOD BOY.
COME ON.
YOU CAN DO THIS, CHARLIE.
KEYS.

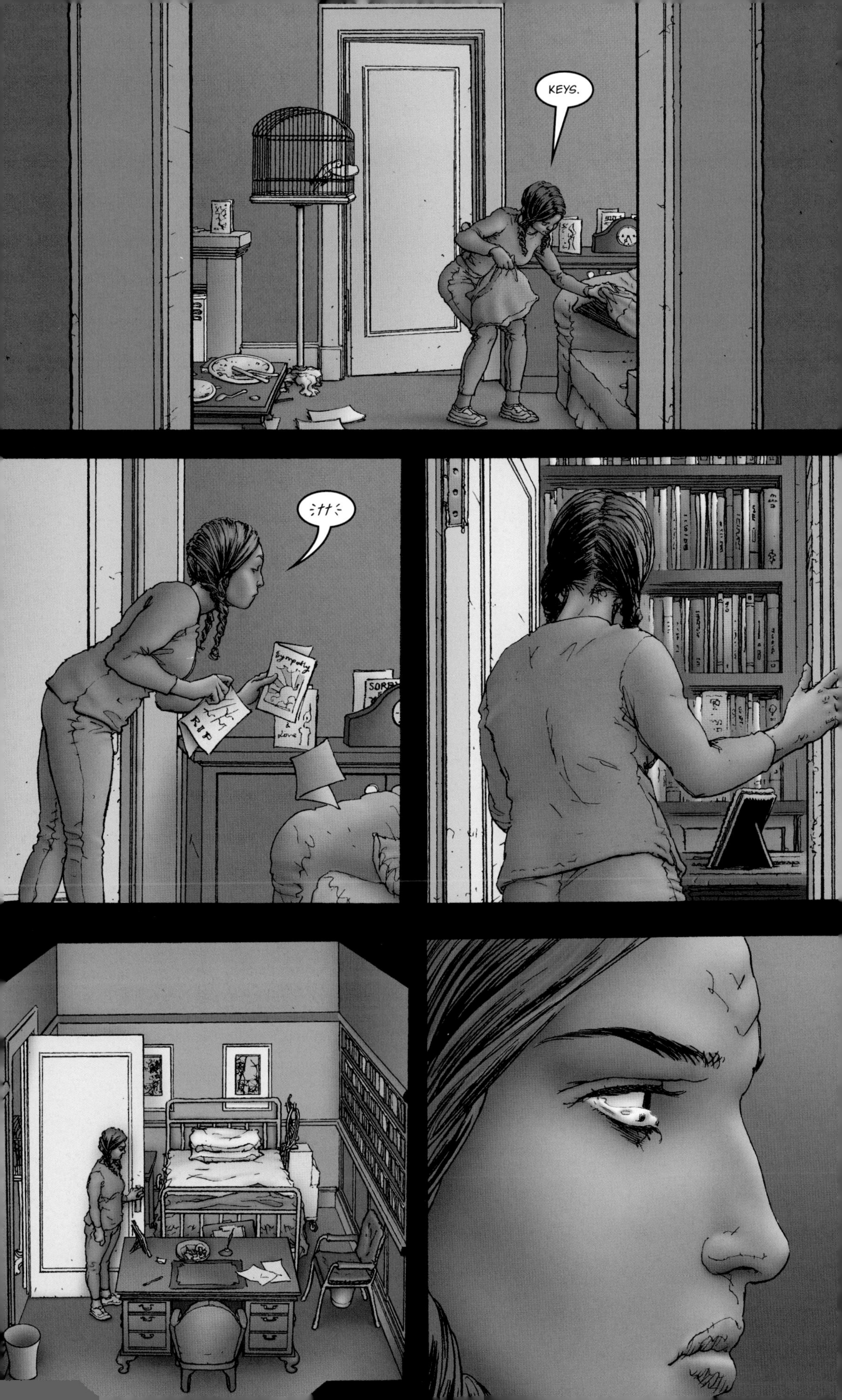
KEYS.
TT
Sympathy
RIP
& Love
SORR

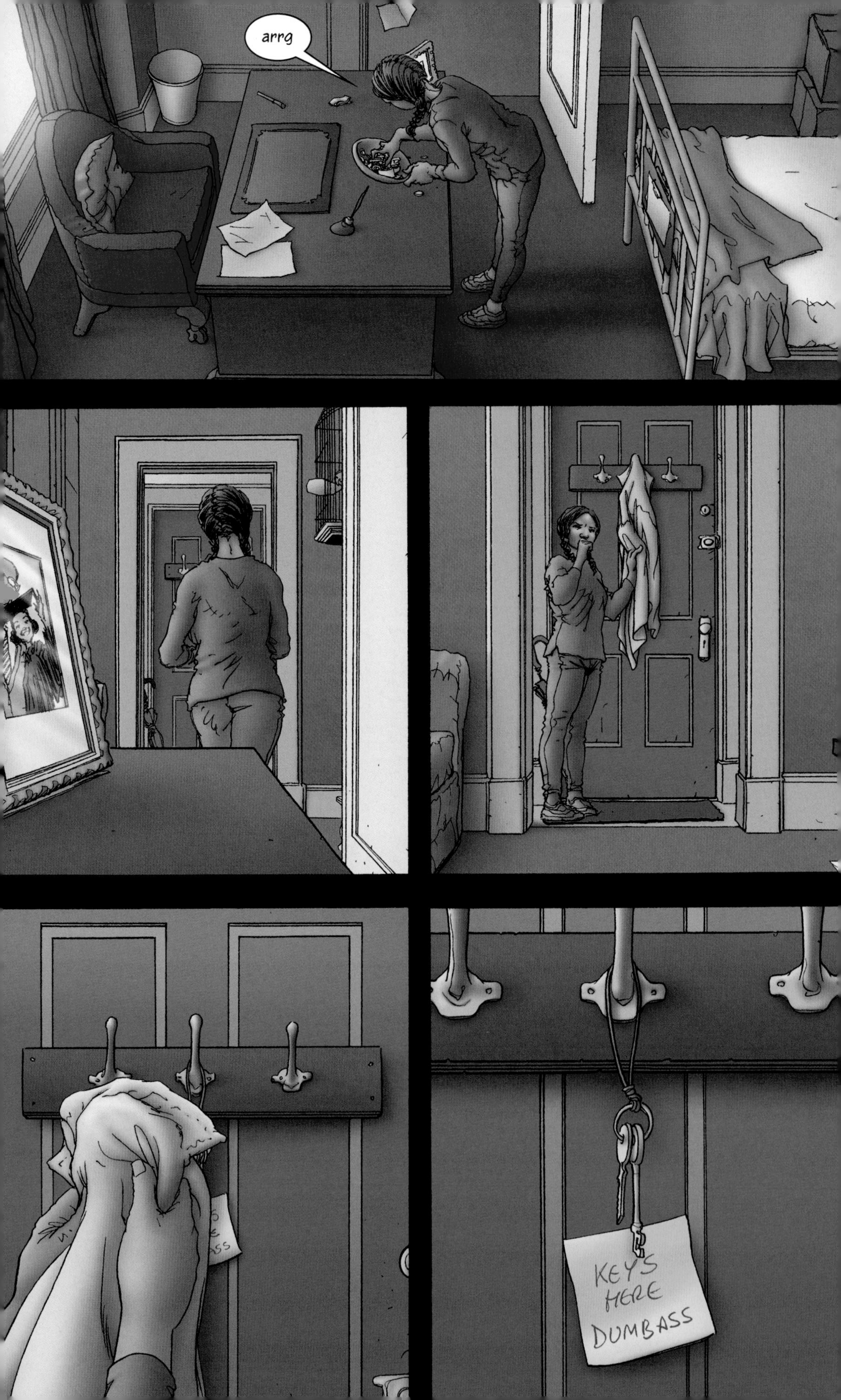
arrg
KEYS
HERE
DUMBASS

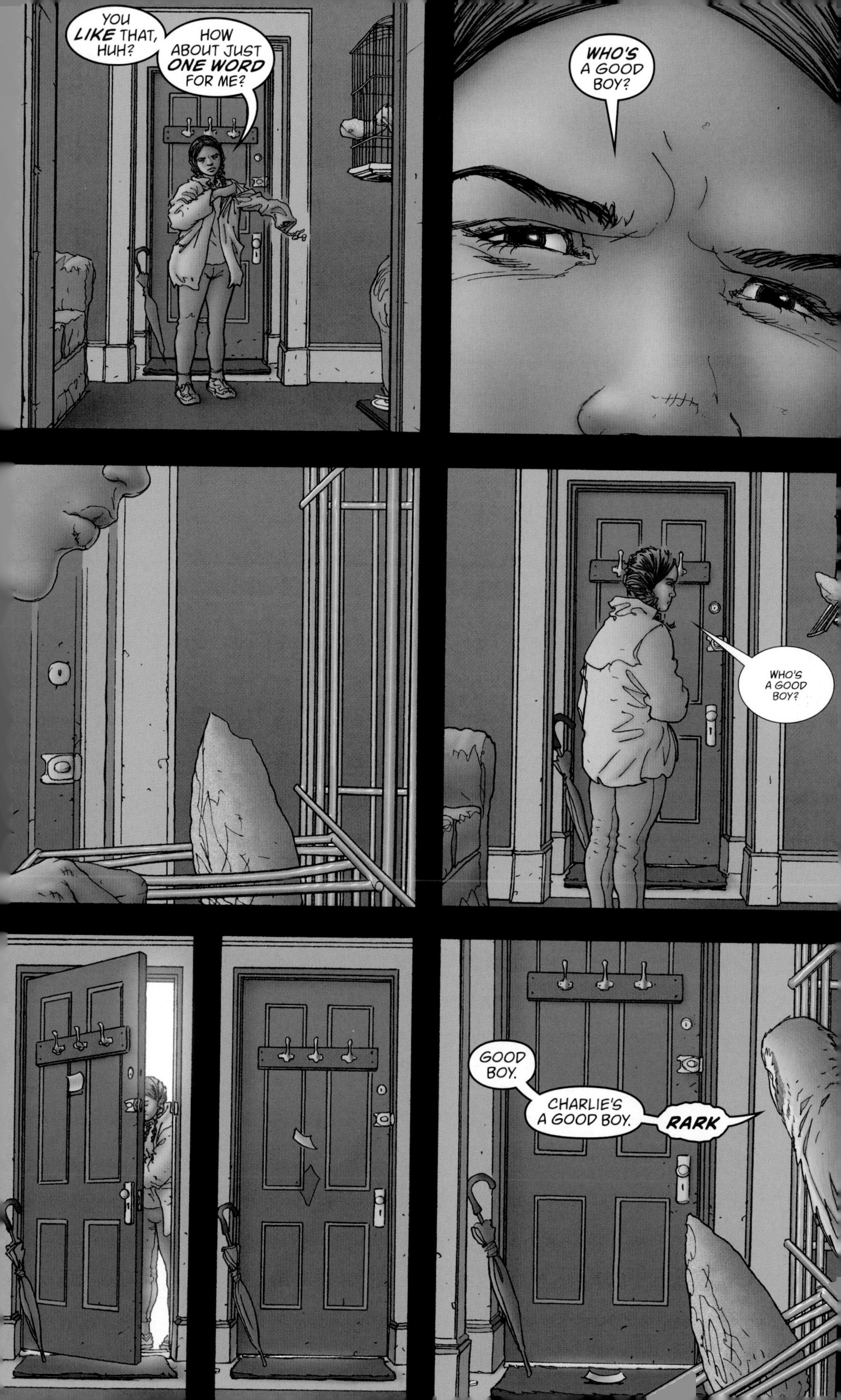
YOU LIKE THAT, HUH?
HOW ABOUT JUST ONE WORD FOR ME?
WHO'S A GOOD BOY?
WHO'S A GOOD BOY?
GOOD BOY.
CHARLIE'S A GOOD BOY.
RARK

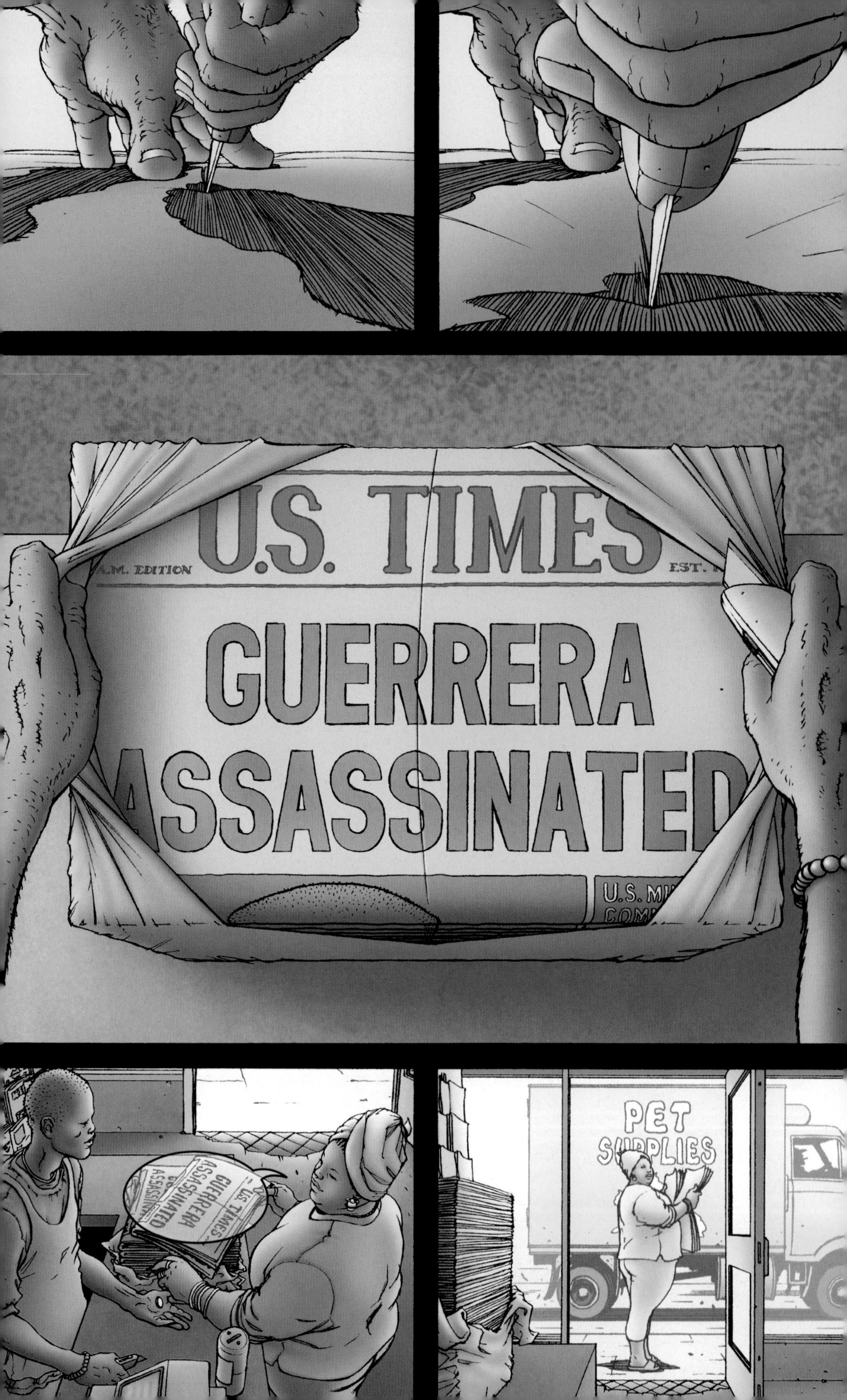
U.S. TIMES
GUERRERA
ASSASSINATED
U.S. TIMES
GUERRERA
ASSASSINATED
PET
SUPPLIES

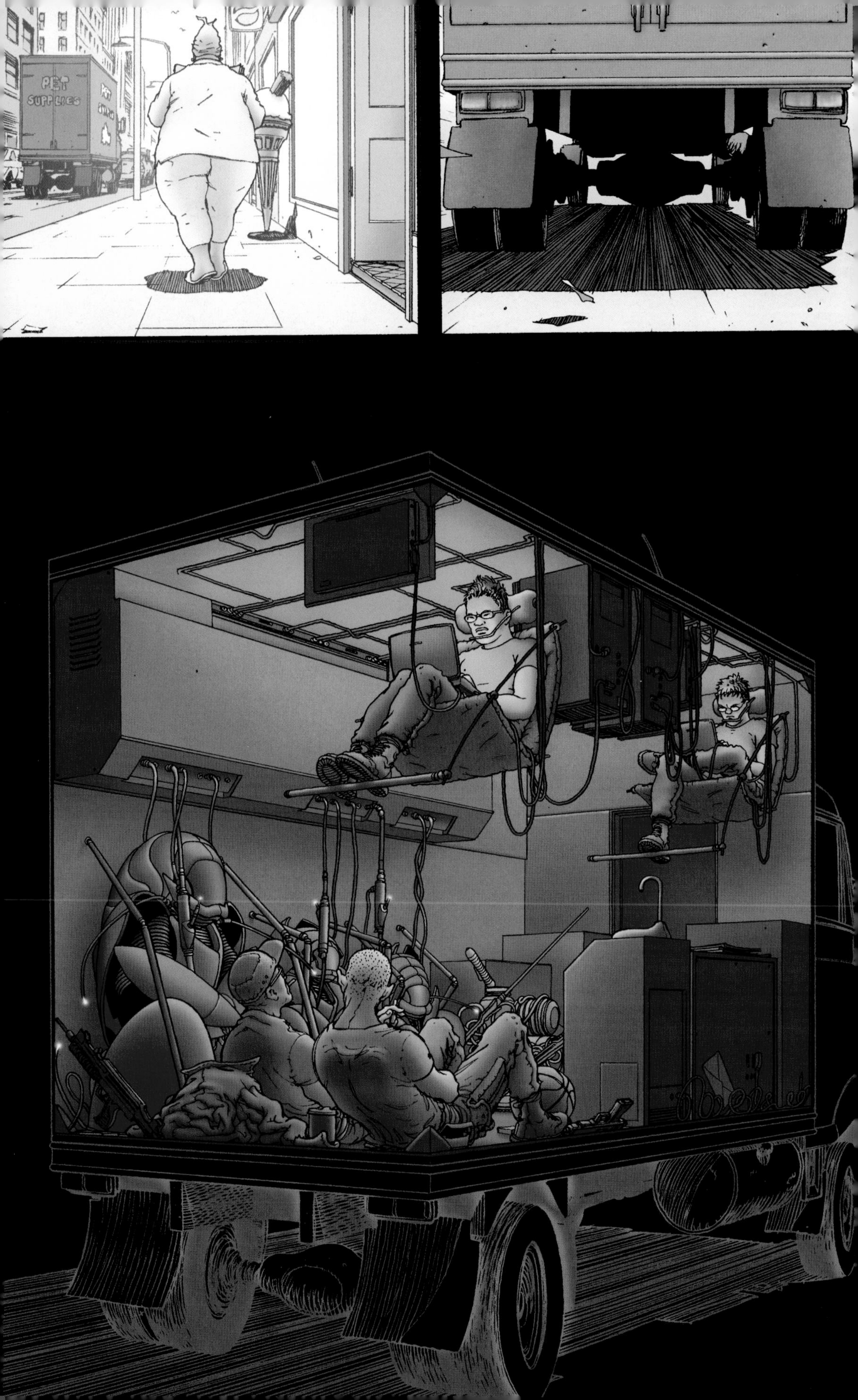
PET
SUPPLIES

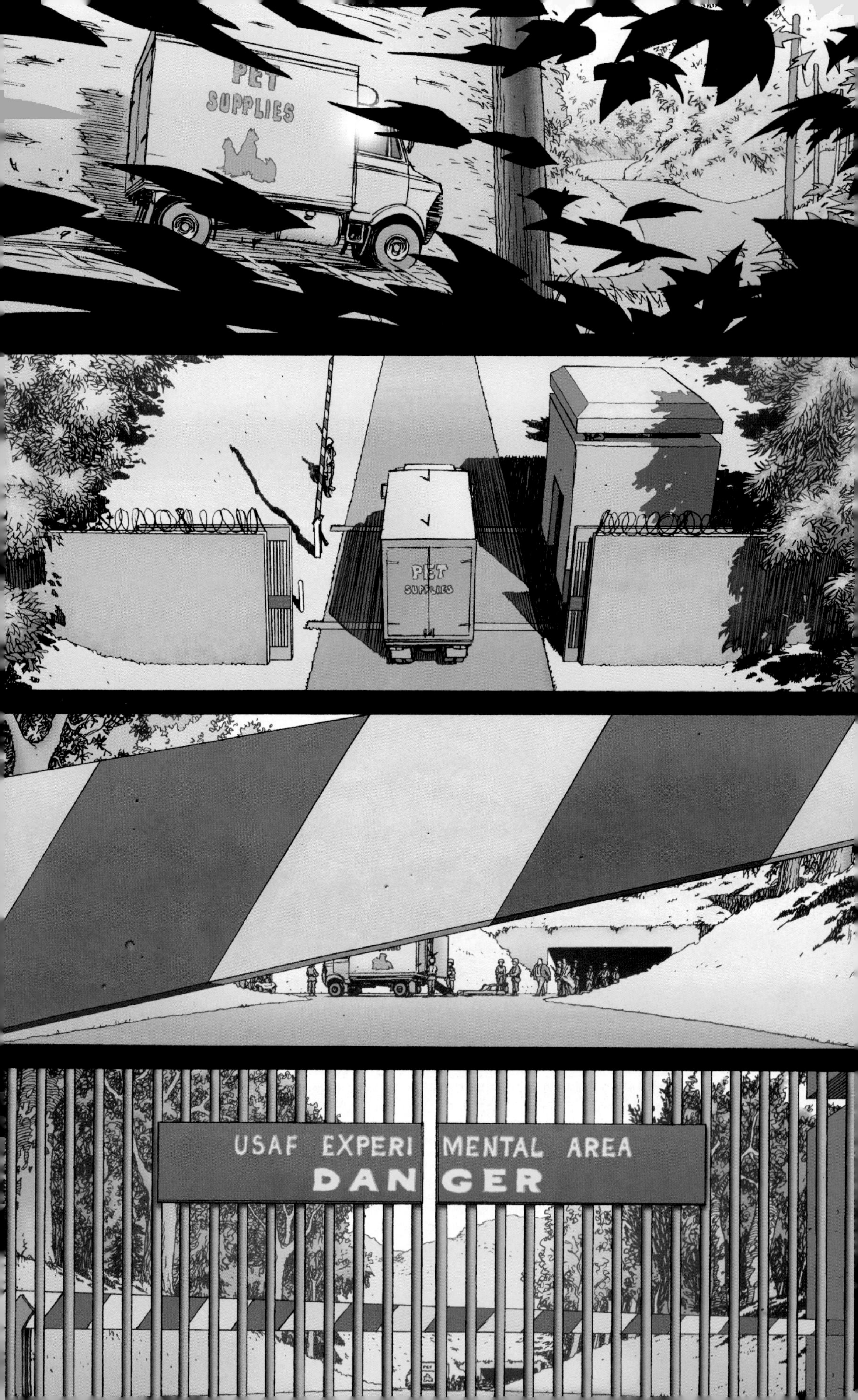
PET SUPPLIES
PET SUPPLIES
USAF EXPERIMENTAL AREA
DANGER

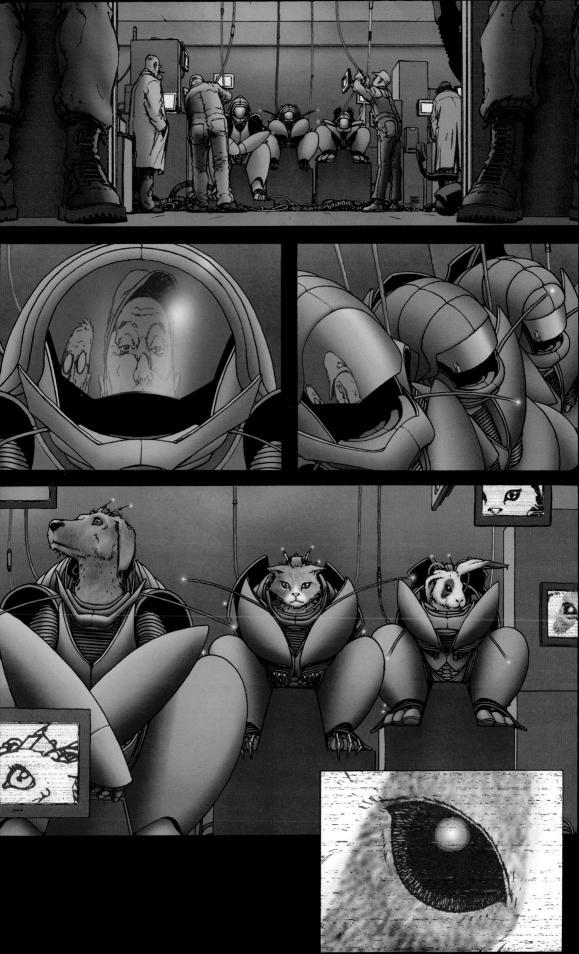

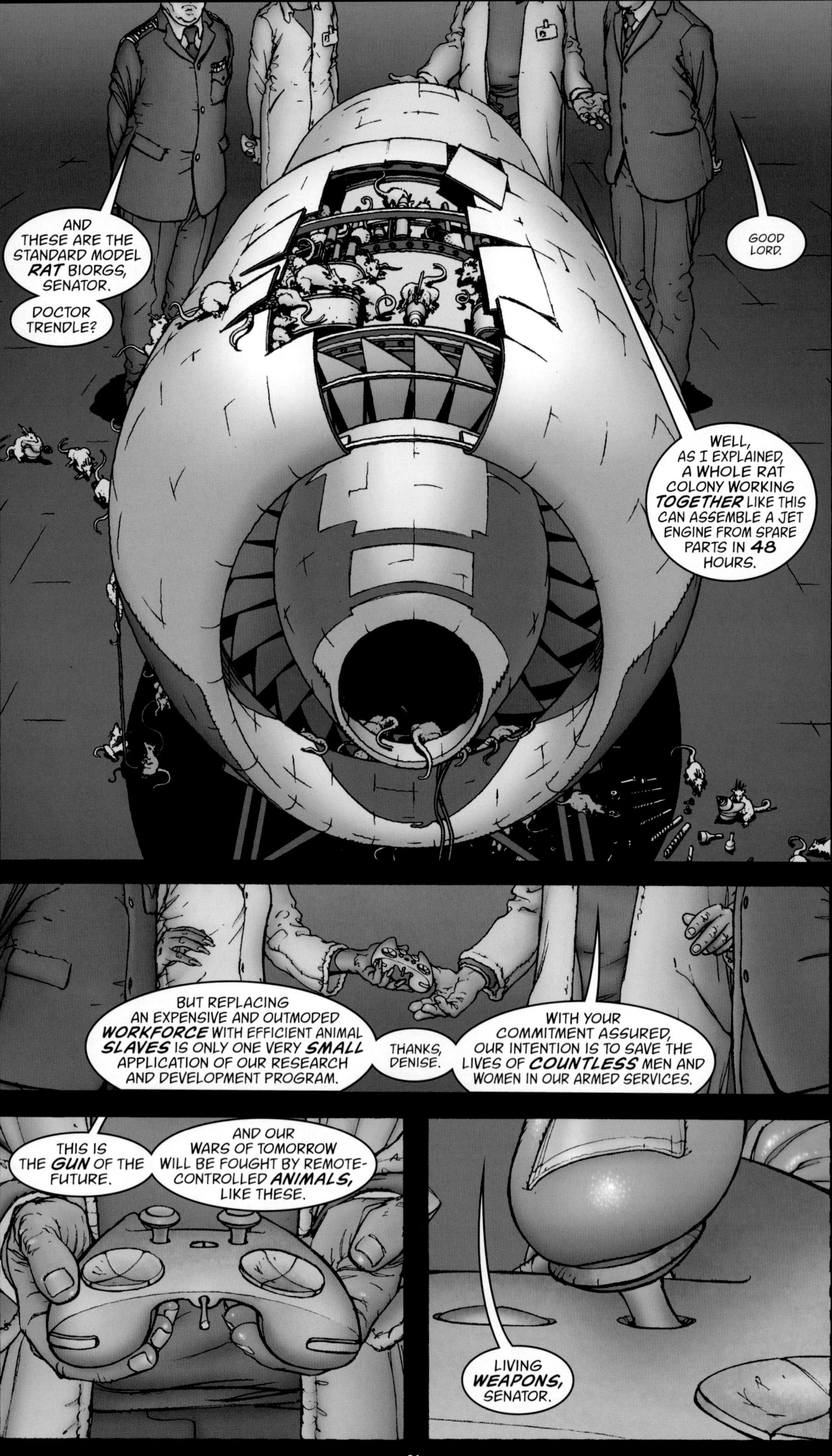
AND THESE ARE THE STANDARD MODEL RAT BIORGS, SENATOR.
DOCTOR TRENDLE?
GOOD LORD.
WELL, AS I EXPLAINED, A WHOLE RAT COLONY WORKING TOGETHER LIKE THIS CAN ASSEMBLE A JET ENGINE FROM SPARE PARTS IN 48 HOURS.
BUT REPLACING AN EXPENSIVE AND OUTMODED WORKFORCE WITH EFFICIENT ANIMAL SLAVES IS ONLY ONE VERY SMALL APPLICATION OF OUR RESEARCH AND DEVELOPMENT PROGRAM.
THANKS, DENISE.
WITH YOUR COMMITMENT ASSURED, OUR INTENTION IS TO SAVE THE LIVES OF COUNTLESS MEN AND WOMEN IN OUR ARMED SERVICES.
THIS IS THE GUN OF THE FUTURE.
AND OUR WARS OF TOMORROW WILL BE FOUGHT BY REMOTE-CONTROLLED ANIMALS, LIKE THESE.
LIVING WEAPONS, SENATOR.

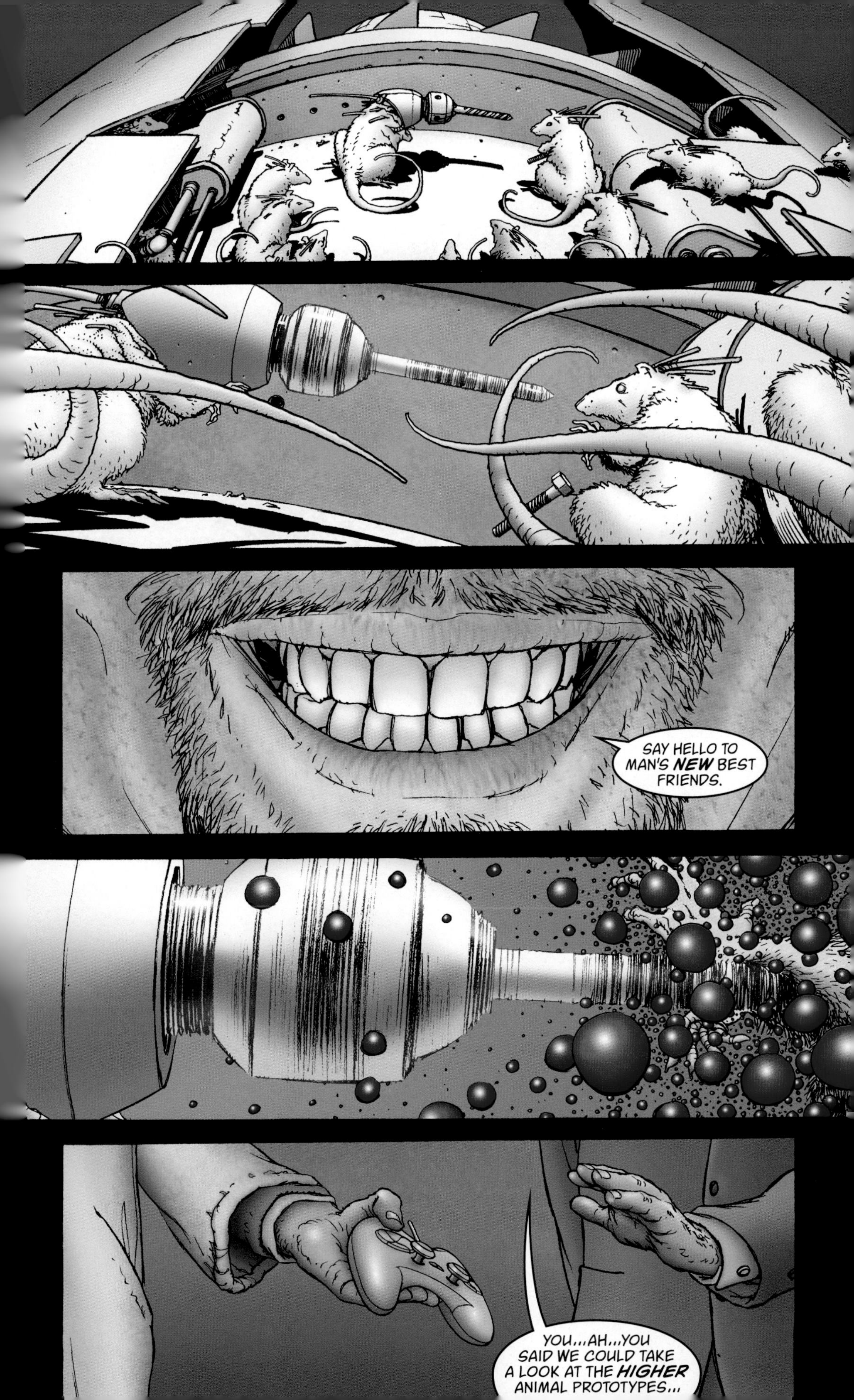
SAY HELLO TO MAN'S **NEW** BEST FRIENDS.
YOU...AH...YOU SAID WE COULD TAKE A LOOK AT THE **HIGHER** ANIMAL PROTOTYPES...

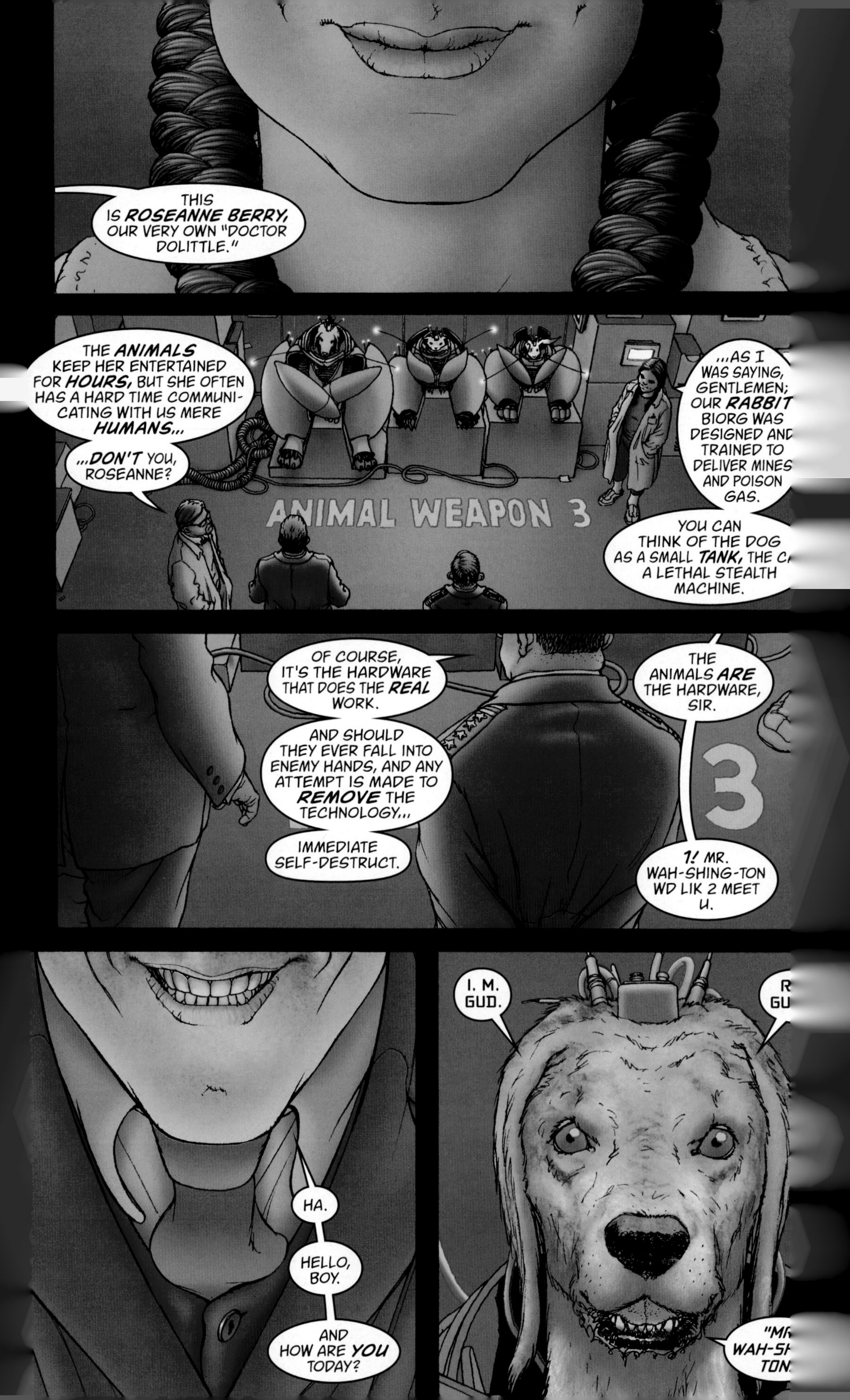
THIS IS ROSEANNE BERRY, OUR VERY OWN "DOCTOR DOLITTLE."
THE ANIMALS KEEP HER ENTERTAINED FOR HOURS, BUT SHE OFTEN HAS A HARD TIME COMMUNICATING WITH US MERE HUMANS...
...DON'T YOU, ROSEANNE?
ANIMAL WEAPON 3
...AS I WAS SAYING, GENTLEMEN; OUR RABBIT BIORG WAS DESIGNED AND TRAINED TO DELIVER MINES AND POISON GAS.
YOU CAN THINK OF THE DOG AS A SMALL TANK, THE C A LETHAL STEALTH MACHINE.
OF COURSE, IT'S THE HARDWARE THAT DOES THE REAL WORK.
AND SHOULD THEY EVER FALL INTO ENEMY HANDS, AND ANY ATTEMPT IS MADE TO REMOVE THE TECHNOLOGY...
IMMEDIATE SELF-DESTRUCT.
THE ANIMALS ARE THE HARDWARE, SIR.
3
1! MR. WAH-SHING-TON WD LIK 2 MEET U.
HA.
HELLO, BOY.
AND HOW ARE YOU TODAY?
I. M. GUD.
"MR WAH-SH TON

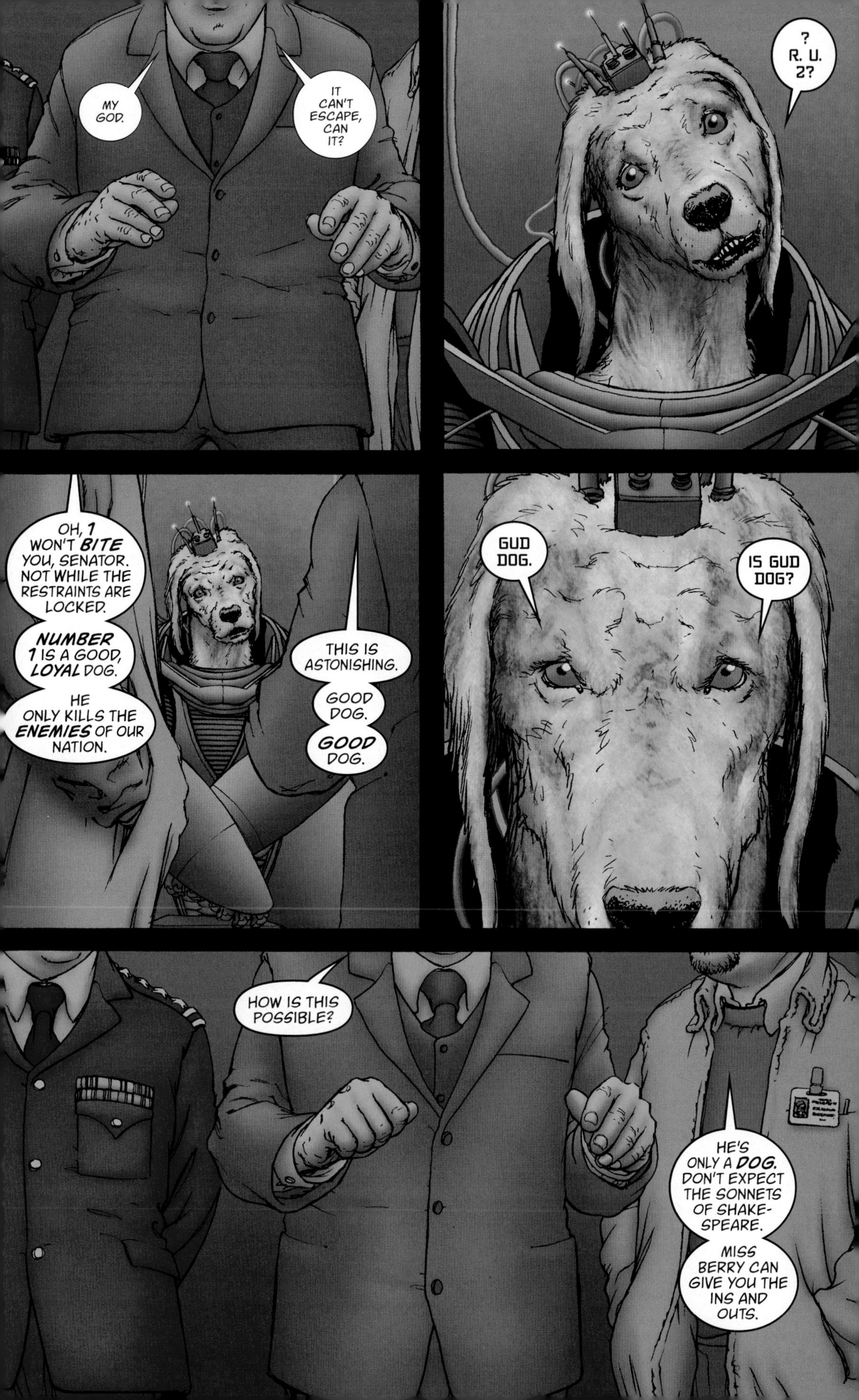
MY GOD.
IT CAN'T ESCAPE, CAN IT?
? R. U. 2?
OH, I WON'T BITE YOU, SENATOR. NOT WHILE THE RESTRAINTS ARE LOCKED.
NUMBER 1 IS A GOOD, LOYAL DOG.
HE ONLY KILLS THE ENEMIES OF OUR NATION.
THIS IS ASTONISHING.
GOOD DOG.
GOOD DOG.
GUD DOG.
IS GUD DOG?
HOW IS THIS POSSIBLE?
HE'S ONLY A DOG. DON'T EXPECT THE SONNETS OF SHAKE-SPEARE.
MISS BERRY CAN GIVE YOU THE INS AND OUTS.

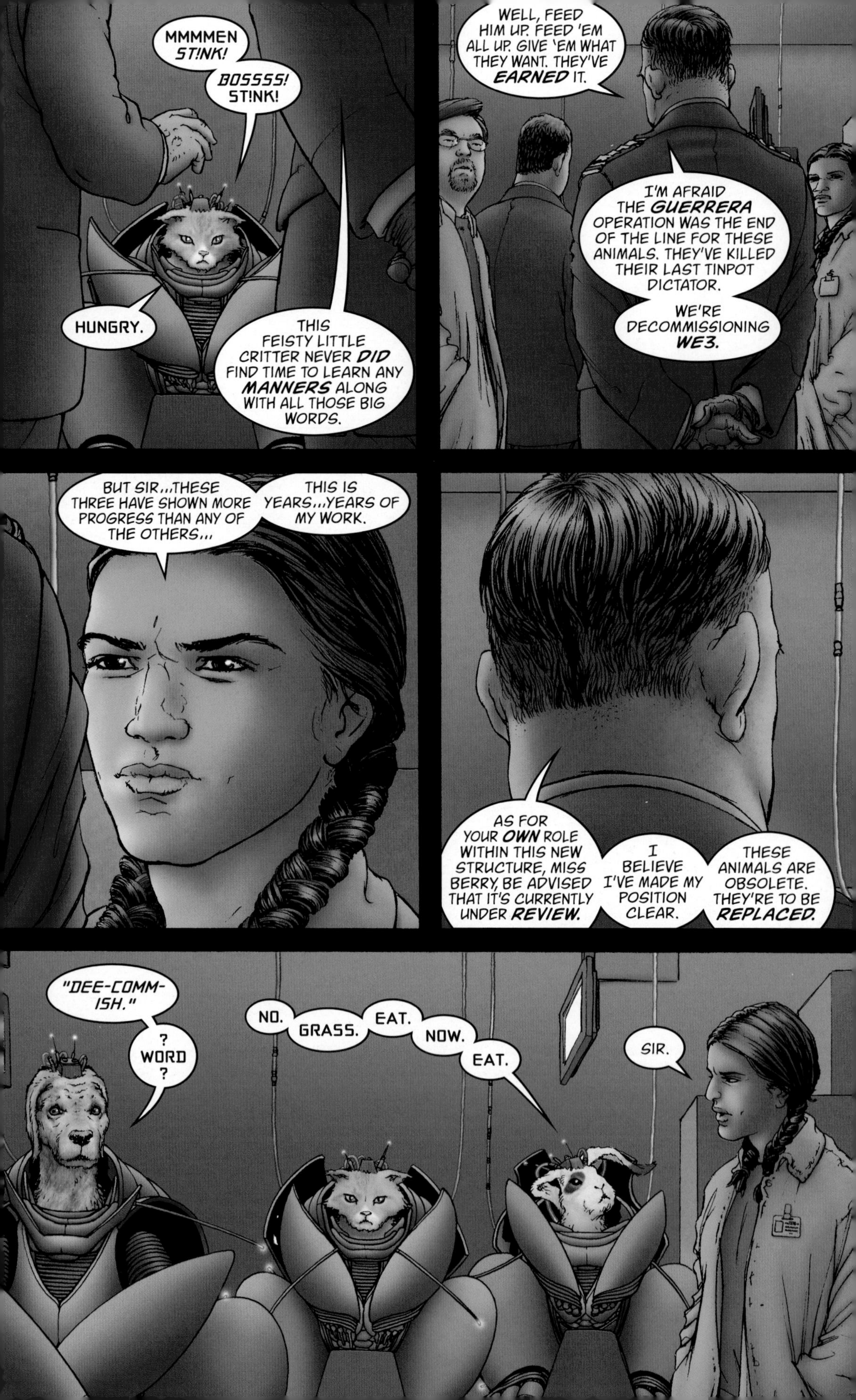
MMMMEN
ST!NK!
BOSSSS!
ST!NK!
HUNGRY.
THIS FEISTY LITTLE CRITTER NEVER DID FIND TIME TO LEARN ANY MANNERS ALONG WITH ALL THOSE BIG WORDS.
WELL, FEED HIM UP. FEED 'EM ALL UP. GIVE 'EM WHAT THEY WANT. THEY'VE EARNED IT.
I'M AFRAID THE GUERRERA OPERATION WAS THE END OF THE LINE FOR THESE ANIMALS. THEY'VE KILLED THEIR LAST TINPOT DICTATOR.
WE'RE DECOMMISSIONING WE3.
BUT SIR...THESE THREE HAVE SHOWN MORE PROGRESS THAN ANY OF THE OTHERS...
THIS IS YEARS...YEARS OF MY WORK.
AS FOR YOUR OWN ROLE WITHIN THIS NEW STRUCTURE, MISS BERRY, BE ADVISED THAT IT'S CURRENTLY UNDER REVIEW.
I BELIEVE I'VE MADE MY POSITION CLEAR.
THESE ANIMALS ARE OBSOLETE. THEY'RE TO BE REPLACED.
"DEE-COMM-ISH."
? WORD ?
NO.
GRASS.
EAT.
NOW.
EAT.
SIR.

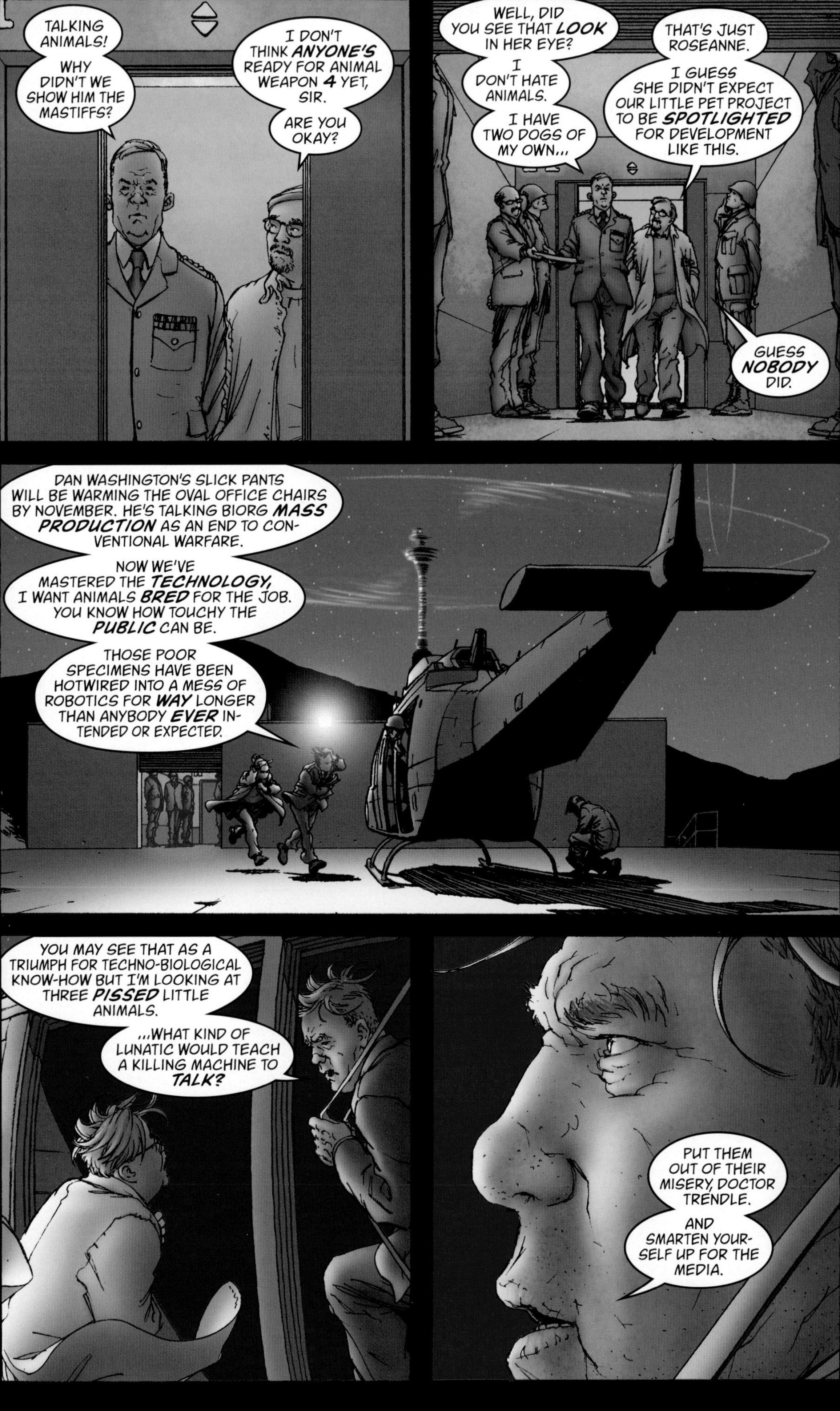
TALKING ANIMALS!
WHY DIDN'T WE SHOW HIM THE MASTIFFS?
I DON'T THINK ANYONE'S READY FOR ANIMAL WEAPON 4 YET, SIR.
ARE YOU OKAY?
WELL, DID YOU SEE THAT LOOK IN HER EYE?
I DON'T HATE ANIMALS.
I HAVE TWO DOGS OF MY OWN...
THAT'S JUST ROSEANNE.
I GUESS SHE DIDN'T EXPECT OUR LITTLE PET PROJECT TO BE SPOTLIGHTED FOR DEVELOPMENT LIKE THIS.
GUESS NOBODY DID.
DAN WASHINGTON'S SLICK PANTS WILL BE WARMING THE OVAL OFFICE CHAIRS BY NOVEMBER. HE'S TALKING BIORG MASS PRODUCTION AS AN END TO CONVENTIONAL WARFARE.
NOW WE'VE MASTERED THE TECHNOLOGY, I WANT ANIMALS BRED FOR THE JOB. YOU KNOW HOW TOUCHY THE PUBLIC CAN BE.
THOSE POOR SPECIMENS HAVE BEEN HOTWIRED INTO A MESS OF ROBOTICS FOR WAY LONGER THAN ANYBODY EVER INTENDED OR EXPECTED.
YOU MAY SEE THAT AS A TRIUMPH FOR TECHNO-BIOLOGICAL KNOW-HOW BUT I'M LOOKING AT THREE PISSED LITTLE ANIMALS.
...WHAT KIND OF LUNATIC WOULD TEACH A KILLING MACHINE TO TALK?
PUT THEM OUT OF THEIR MISERY, DOCTOR TRENDLE.
AND SMARTEN YOURSELF UP FOR THE MEDIA.

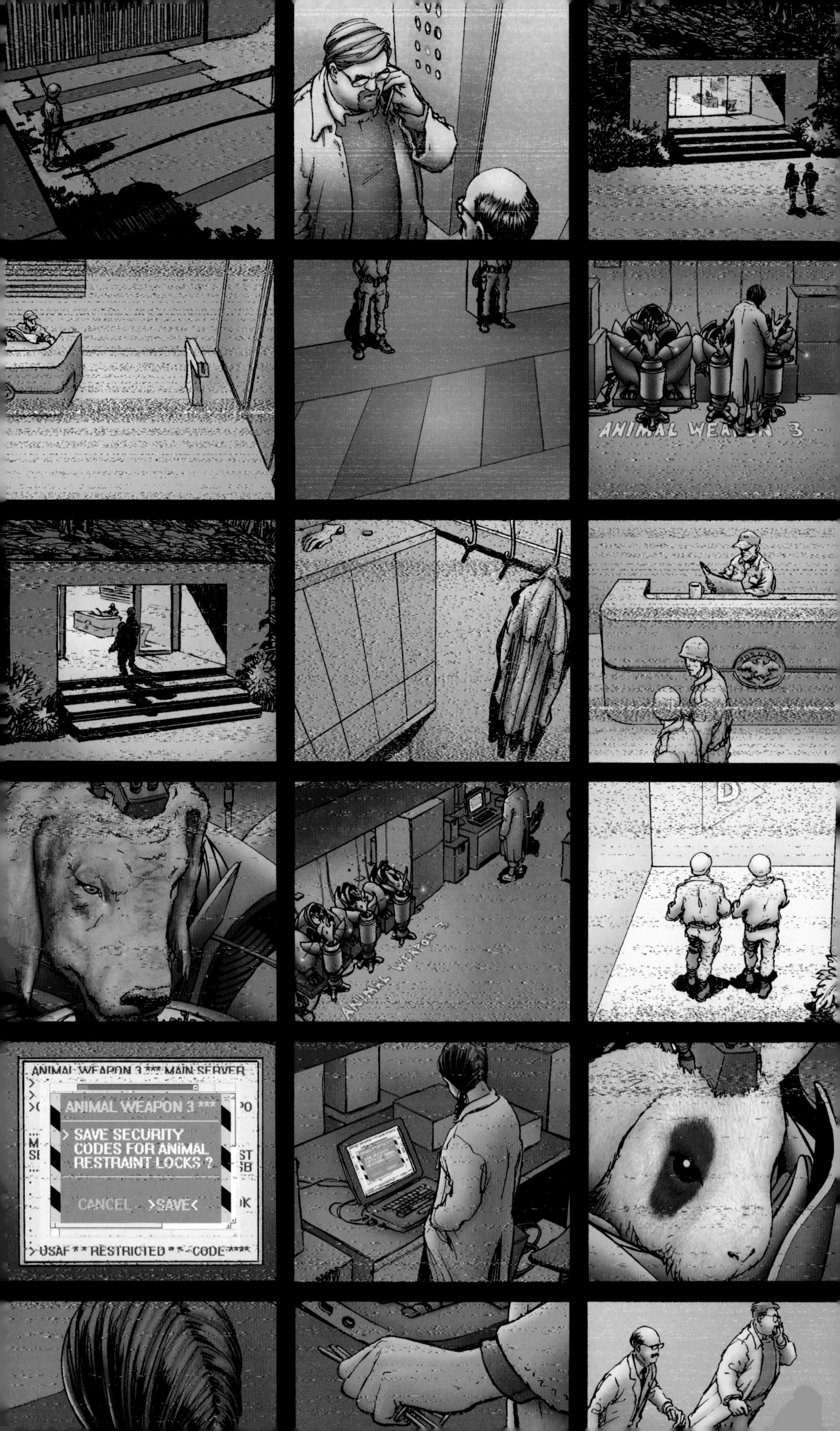
ANIMAL WEAPON 3
ANIMAL WEAPON 3
ANIMAL WEAPON 3 *** MAIN SERVER
ANIMAL WEAPON 3 ***
> SAVE SECURITY CODES FOR ANIMAL RESTRAINT LOCKS ?
CANCEL >SAVE<
>USAF * * RESTRICTED * * CODE ****

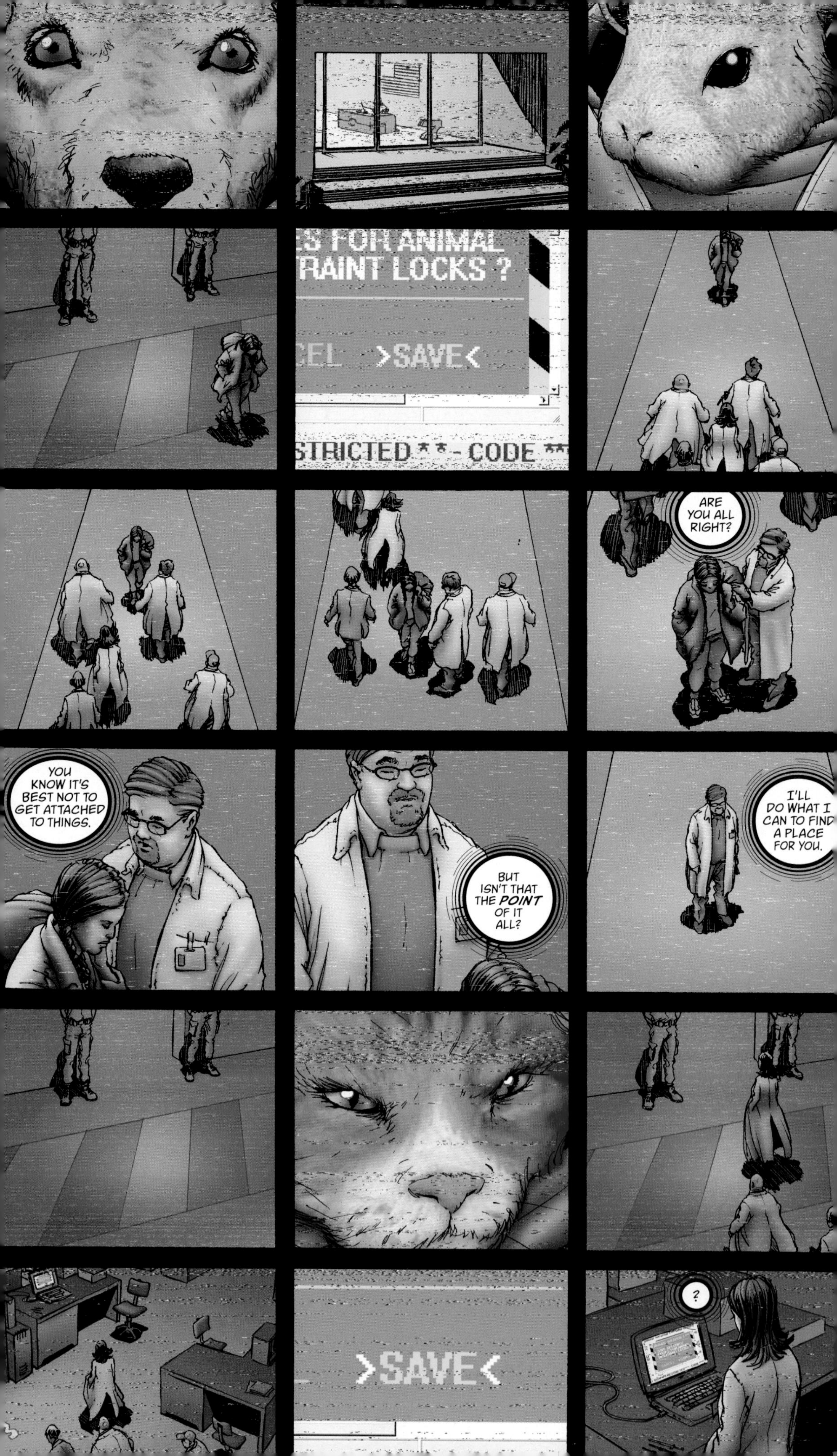

ES FOR ANIMAL
RAINT LOCKS ?
CEL >SAVE<
STRICTED ** - CODE **
ARE YOU ALL RIGHT?
YOU KNOW IT'S BEST NOT TO GET ATTACHED TO THINGS.
BUT ISN'T THAT THE *POINT* OF IT ALL?
I'LL DO WHAT I CAN TO FIND A PLACE FOR YOU.
>SAVE<
?

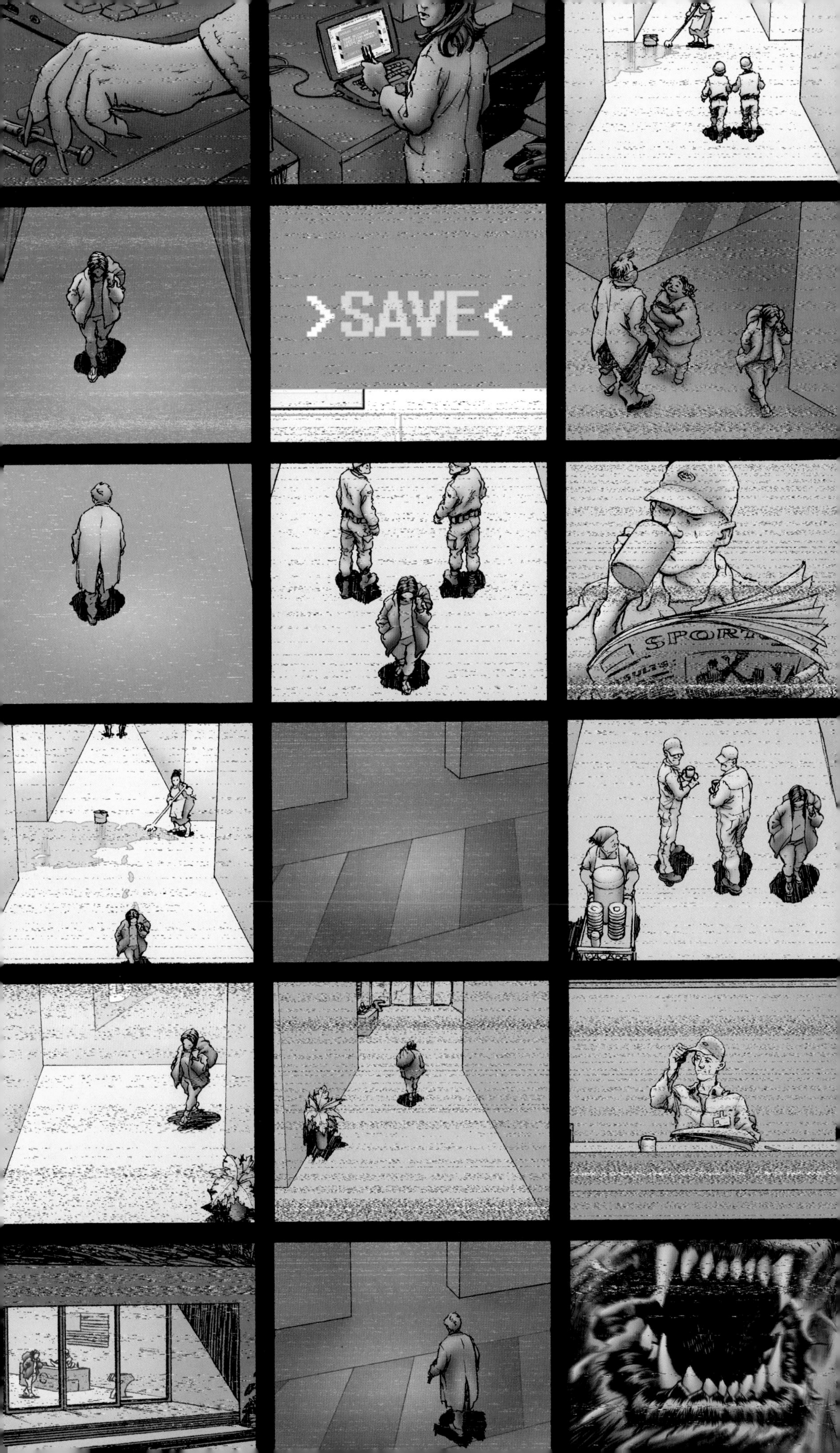

>SAVE<
SPORT

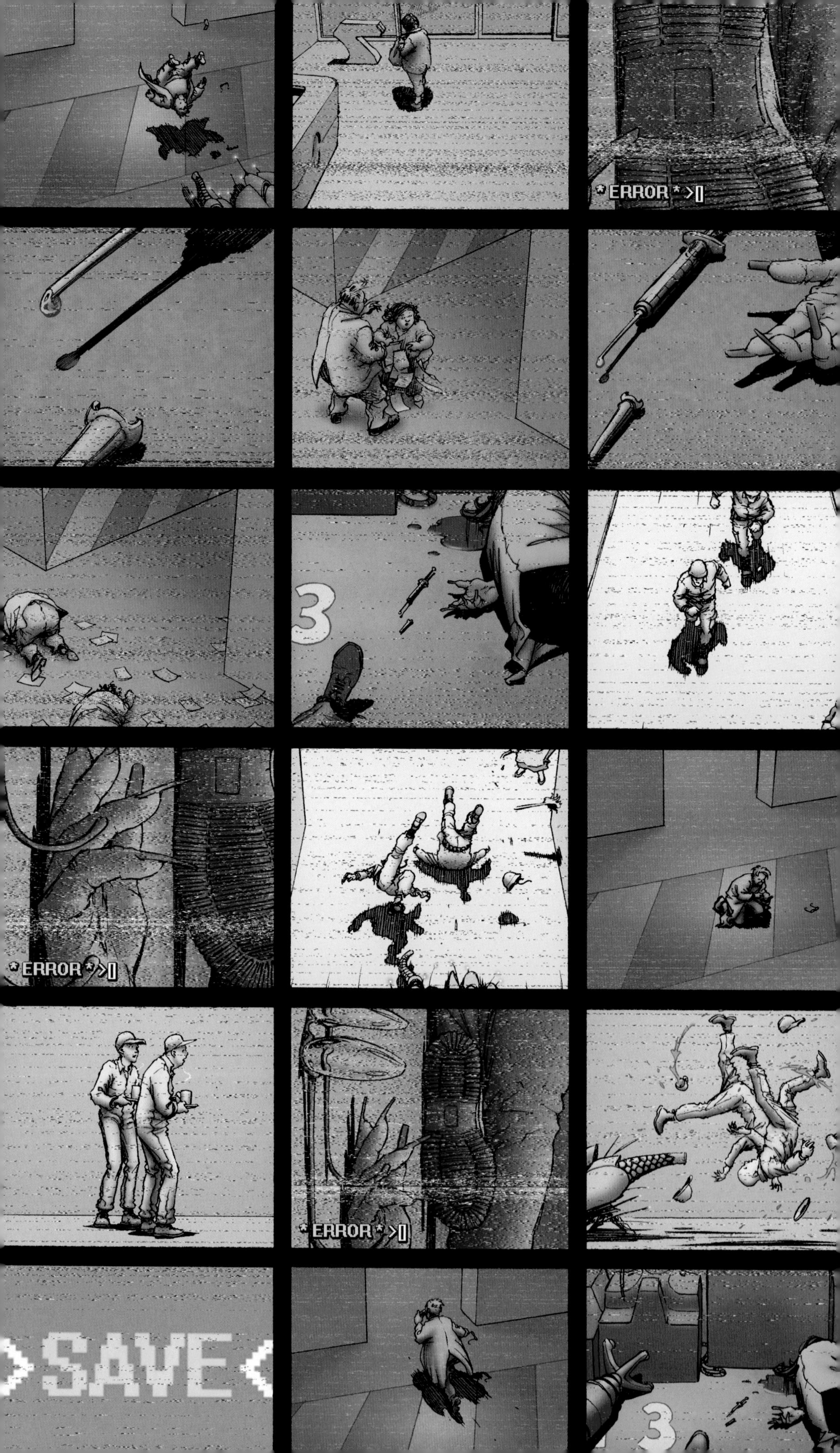

* ERROR * >[]
3
* ERROR * >[]
* ERROR * >[]
>SAVE<
3

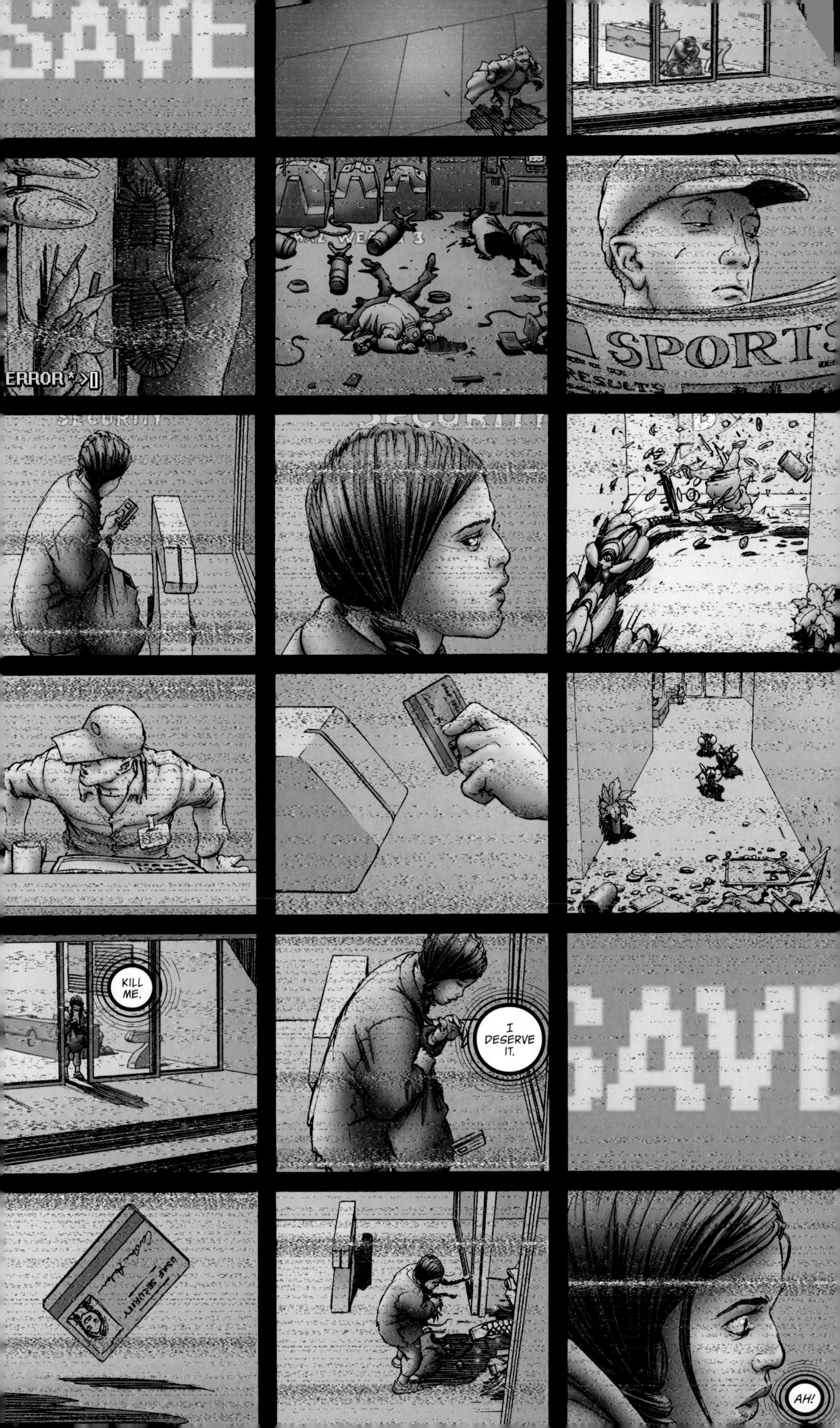

SAVE
ERROR*>
SPORTS
RESULTS
KILL ME.
I DESERVE IT.
SAVE
USAF SECURITY
AH!

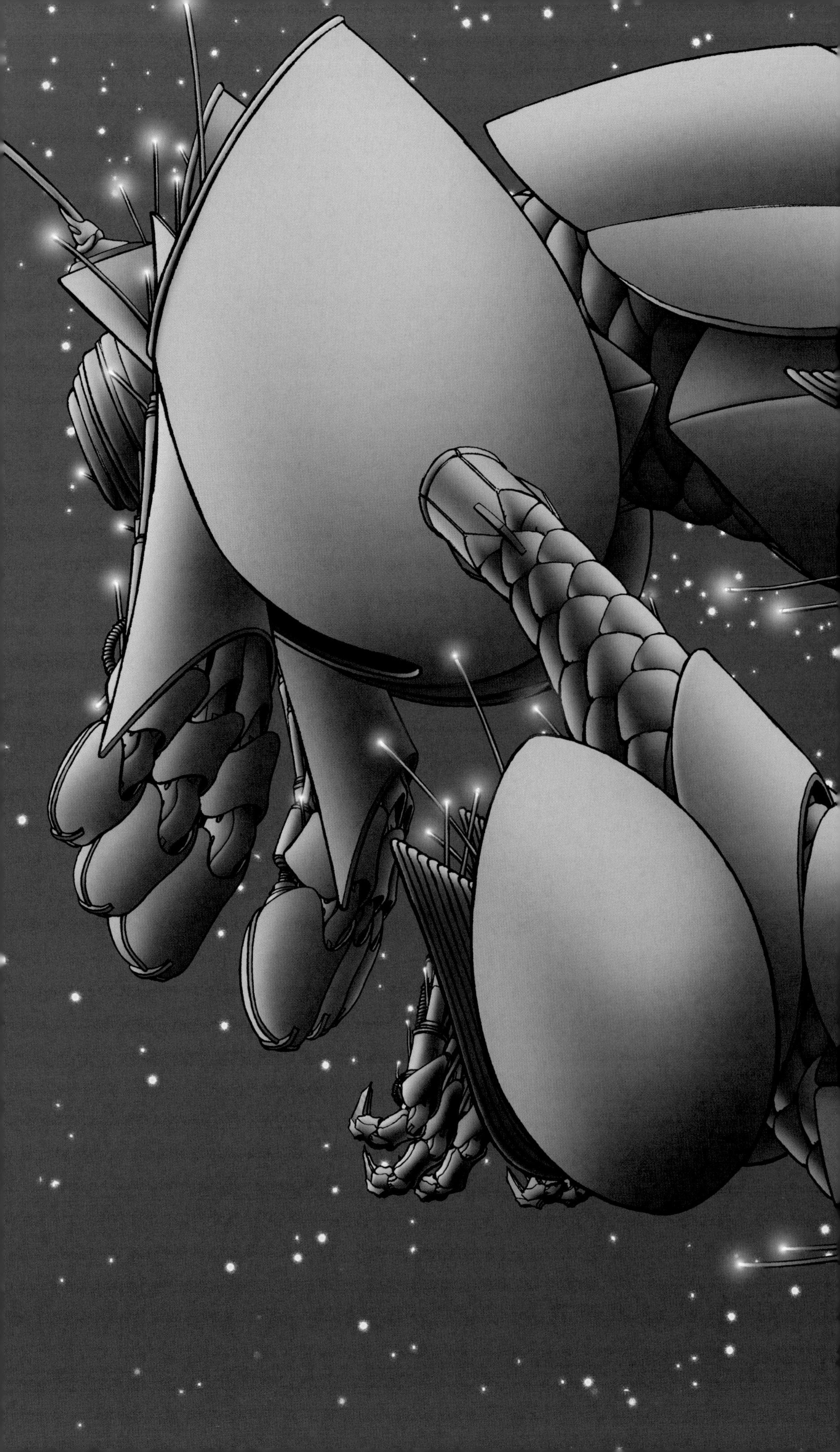

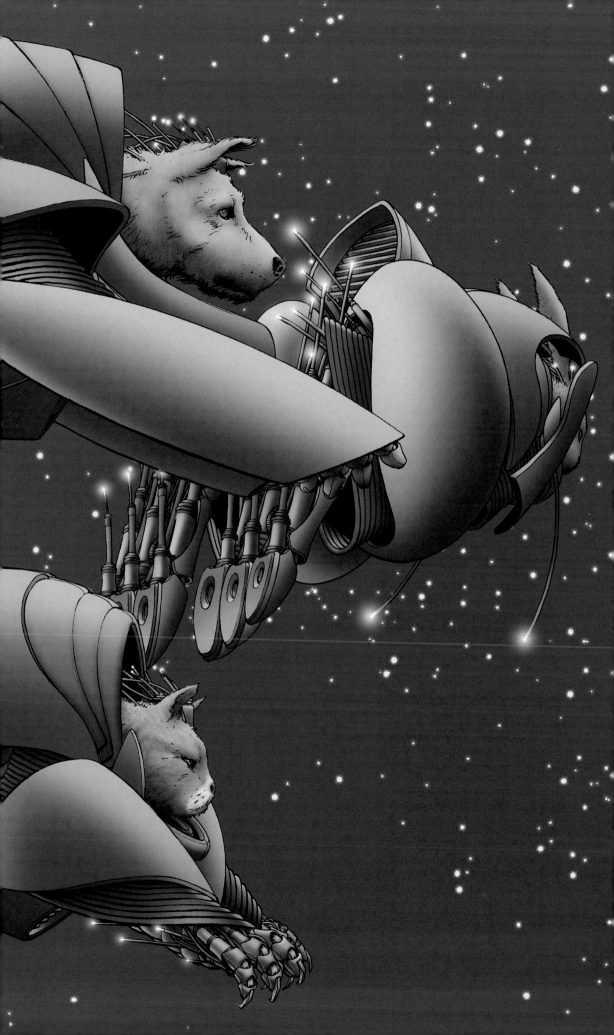

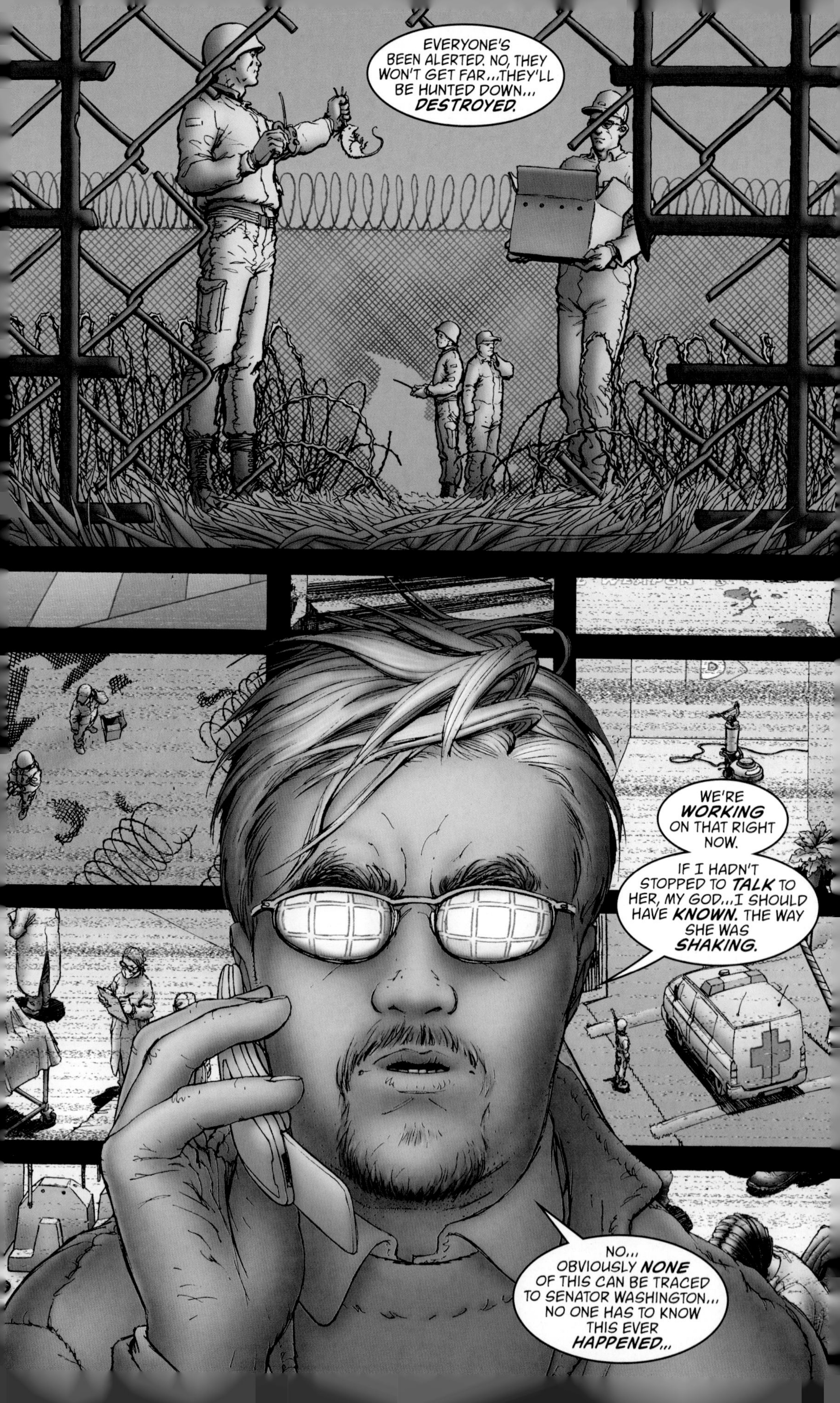
EVERYONE'S BEEN ALERTED. NO, THEY WON'T GET FAR...THEY'LL BE HUNTED DOWN... DESTROYED.
WE'RE WORKING ON THAT RIGHT NOW.
IF I HADN'T STOPPED TO TALK TO HER, MY GOD...I SHOULD HAVE KNOWN. THE WAY SHE WAS SHAKING.
NO... OBVIOUSLY NONE OF THIS CAN BE TRACED TO SENATOR WASHINGTON... NO ONE HAS TO KNOW THIS EVER HAPPENED...

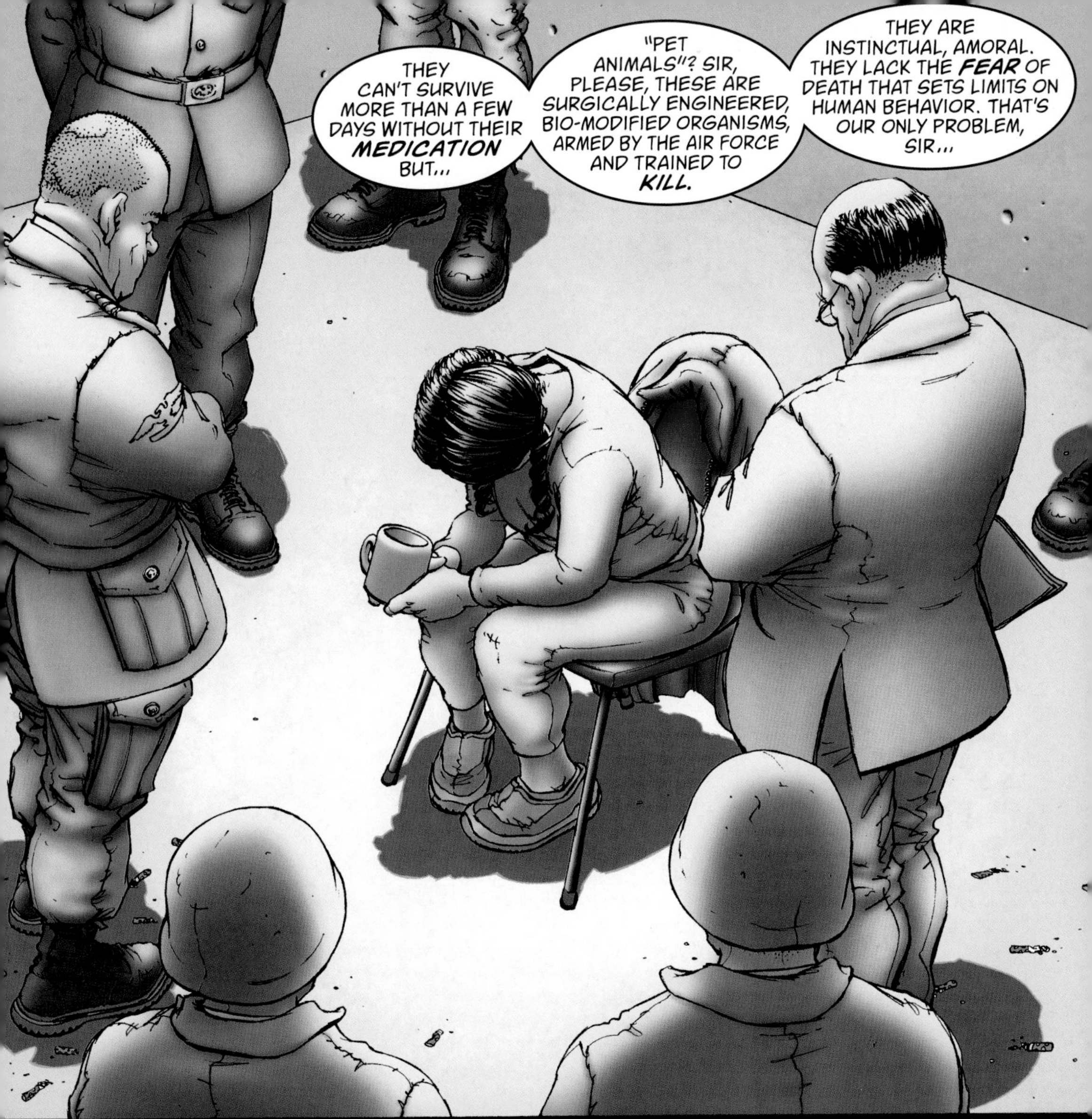
THEY CAN'T SURVIVE MORE THAN A FEW DAYS WITHOUT THEIR MEDICATION BUT...
"PET ANIMALS"? SIR, PLEASE, THESE ARE SURGICALLY ENGINEERED, BIO-MODIFIED ORGANISMS, ARMED BY THE AIR FORCE AND TRAINED TO KILL.
THEY ARE INSTINCTUAL, AMORAL. THEY LACK THE FEAR OF DEATH THAT SETS LIMITS ON HUMAN BEHAVIOR. THAT'S OUR ONLY PROBLEM, SIR...

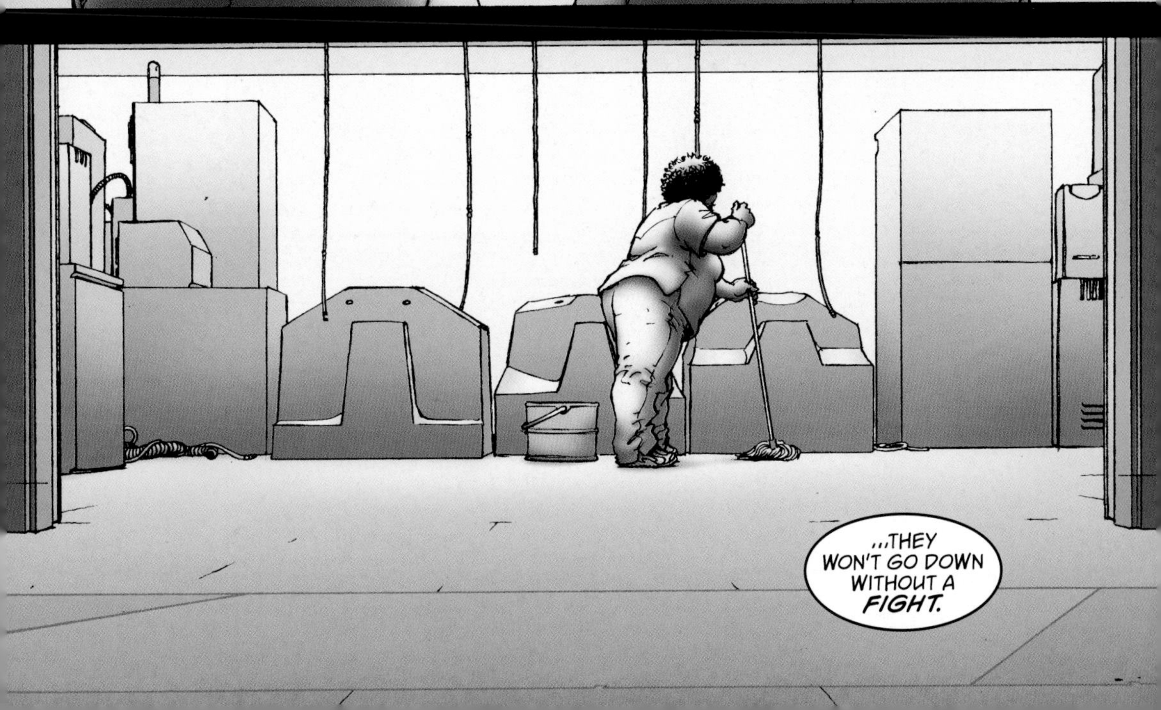
...THEY WON'T GO DOWN WITHOUT A FIGHT.

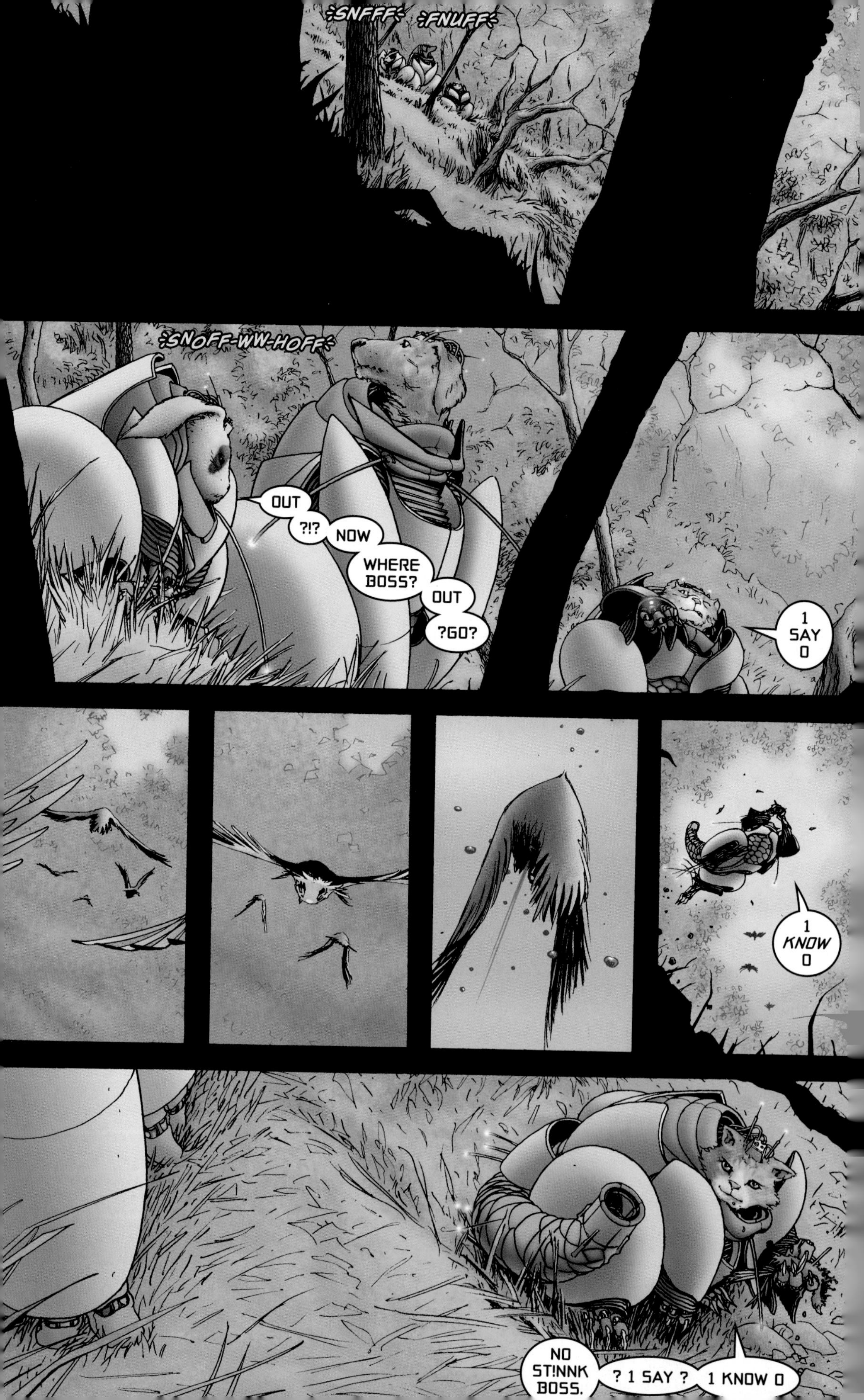
SNFFF
FNUFF
SNOFF-WW-HOFF
OUT
?!?
NOW
WHERE BOSS?
OUT
?GO?
1 SAY 0
1 KNOW 0
NO ST!NNK BOSS.
? 1 SAY ?
1 KNOW 0

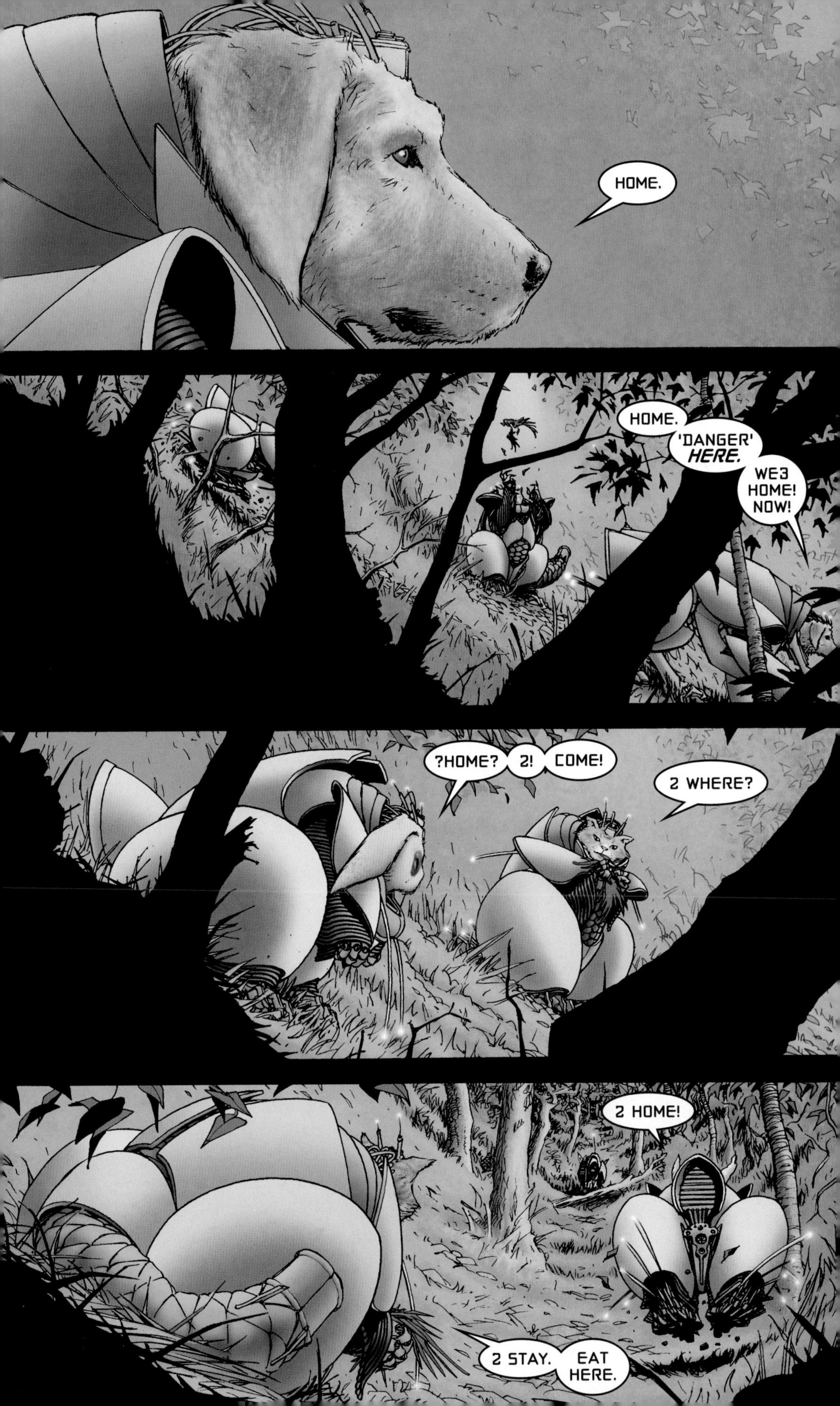
HOME.
HOME.
'DANGER' HERE.
WE3 HOME! NOW!
?HOME?
2!
COME!
2 WHERE?
2 HOME!
2 STAY.
EAT HERE.

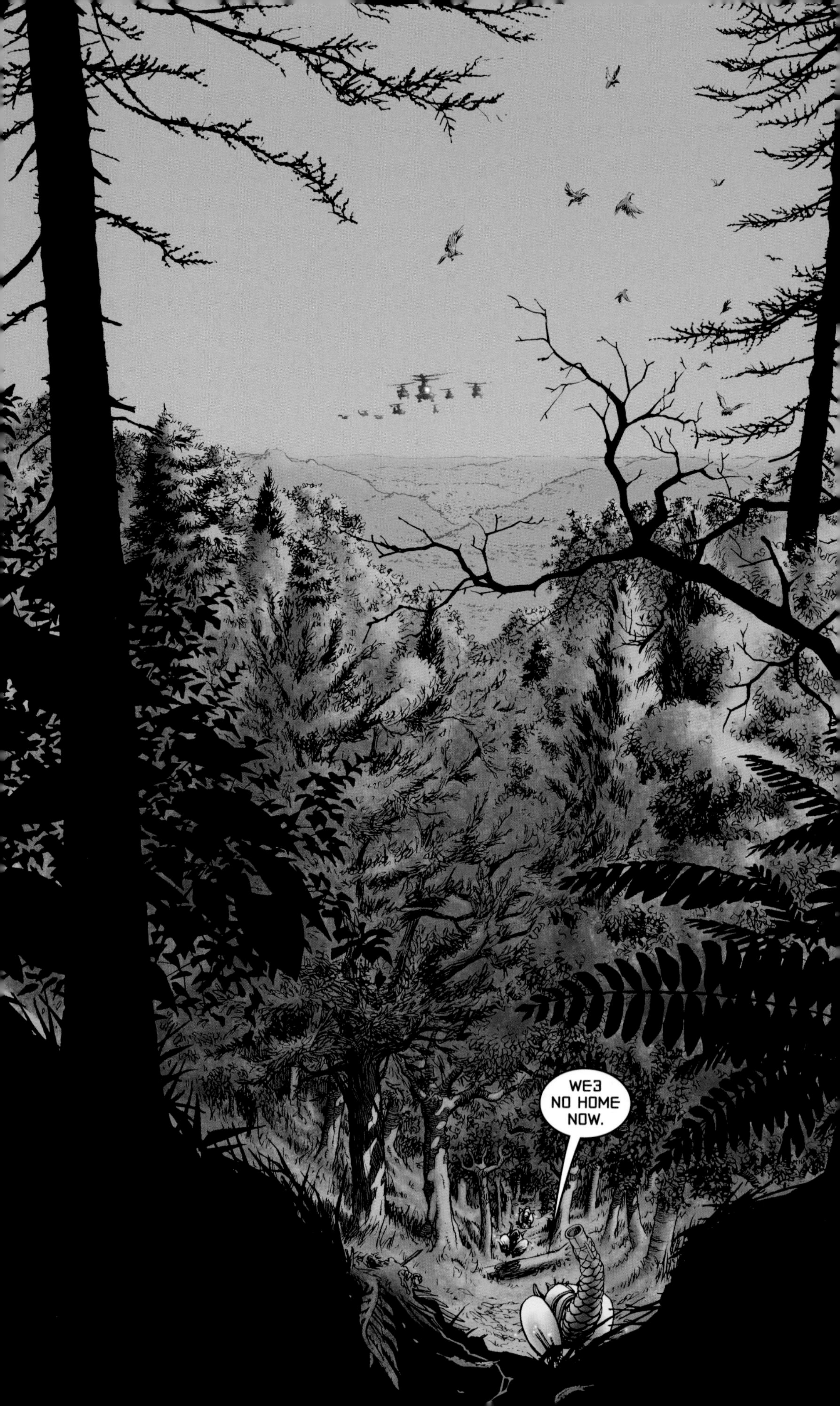
WE3 NO HOME NOW.

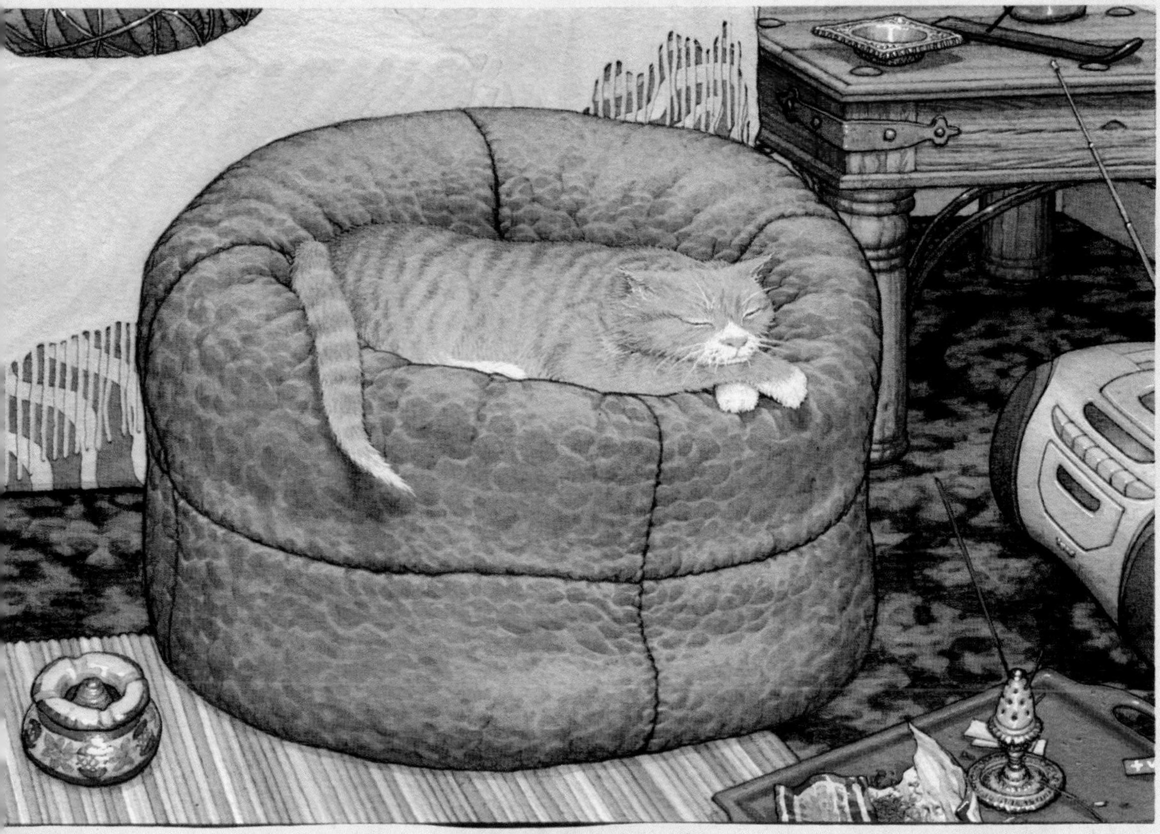

LOST

TINKER IS A GINGER-STRIPED CAT
WITH A WHITE NOSE & WHITE TIP OF HER TAIL.
LAST SEEN OUTSIDE THE LAUNDROMAT ON BELLTOWER STREET.
PLEASE CALL **CARLA** WITH ANY INFO AT 555-3899. **THANKS.**

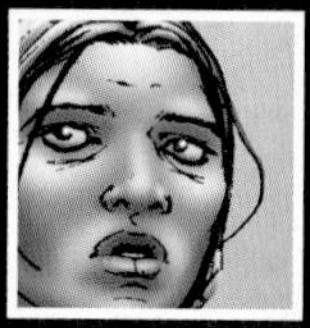

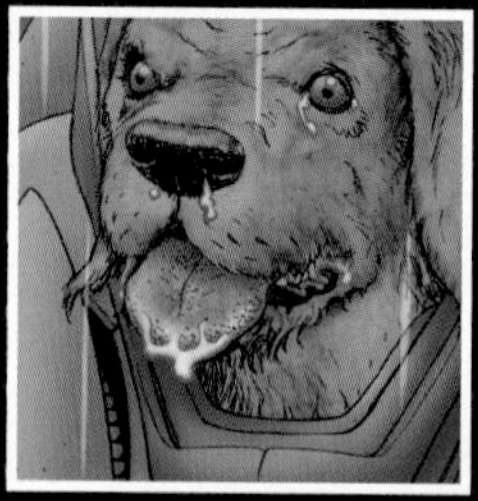

CHAPTER 2

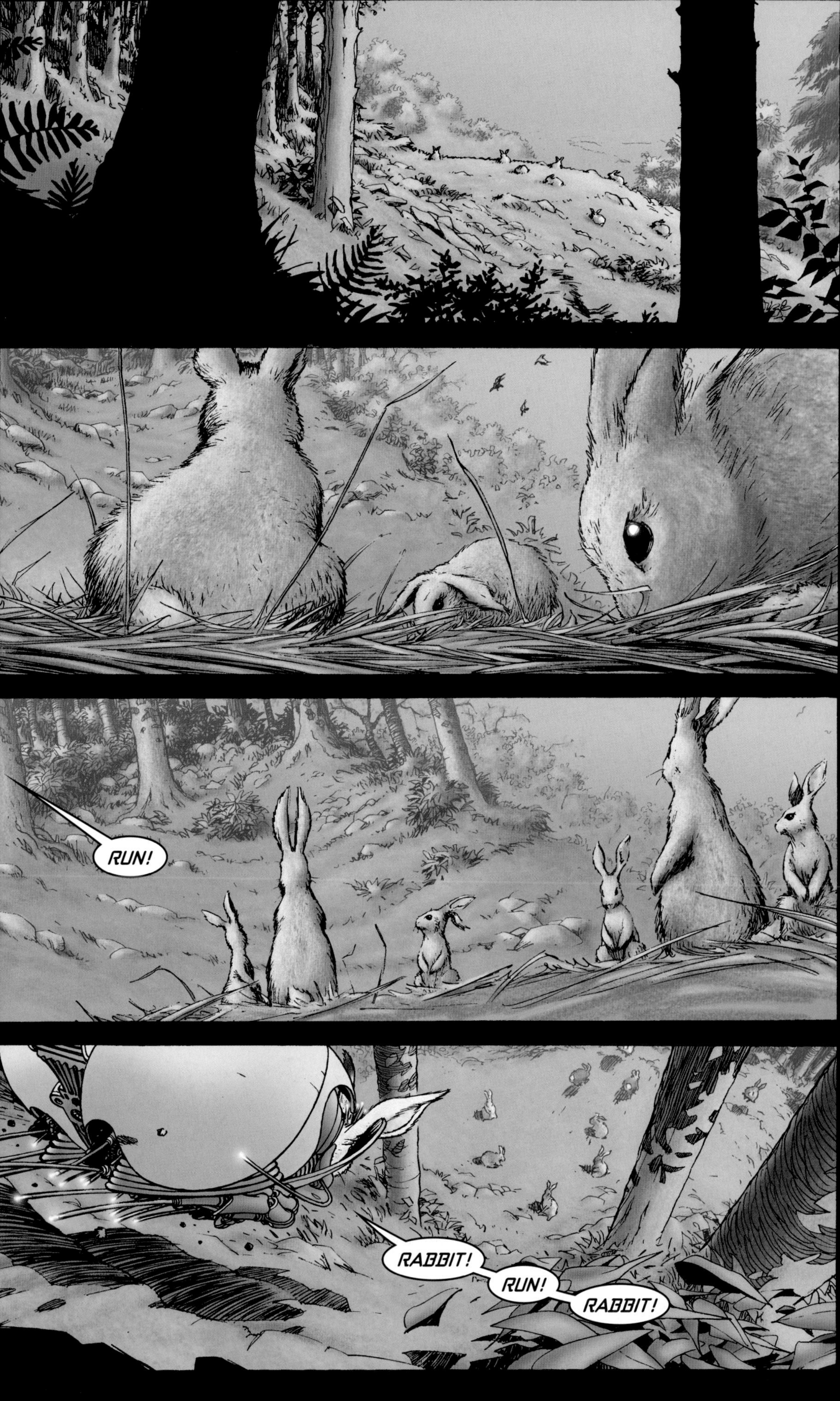
RUN!
RABBIT!
RUN!
RABBIT!

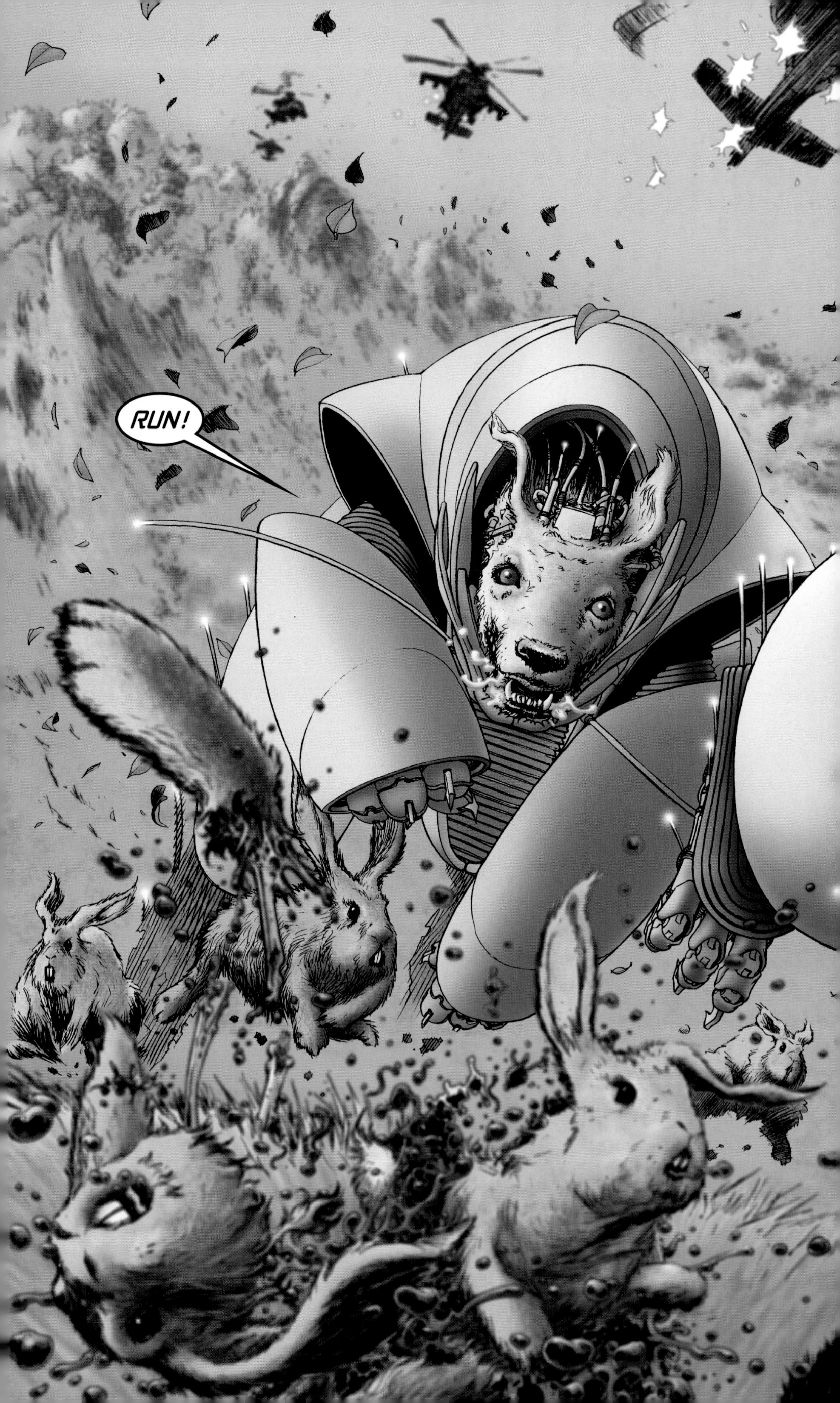
RUN!

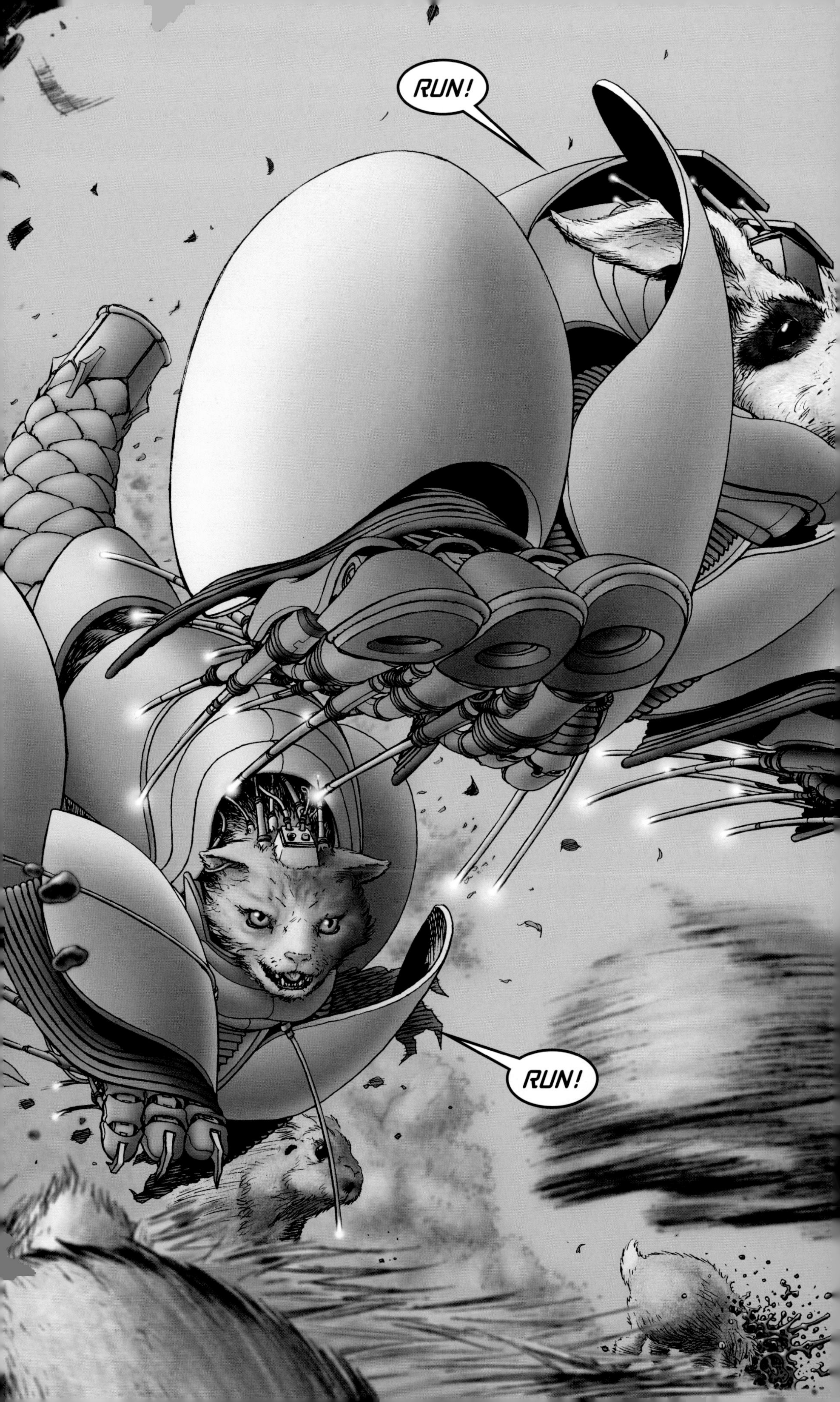
RUN!
RUN!

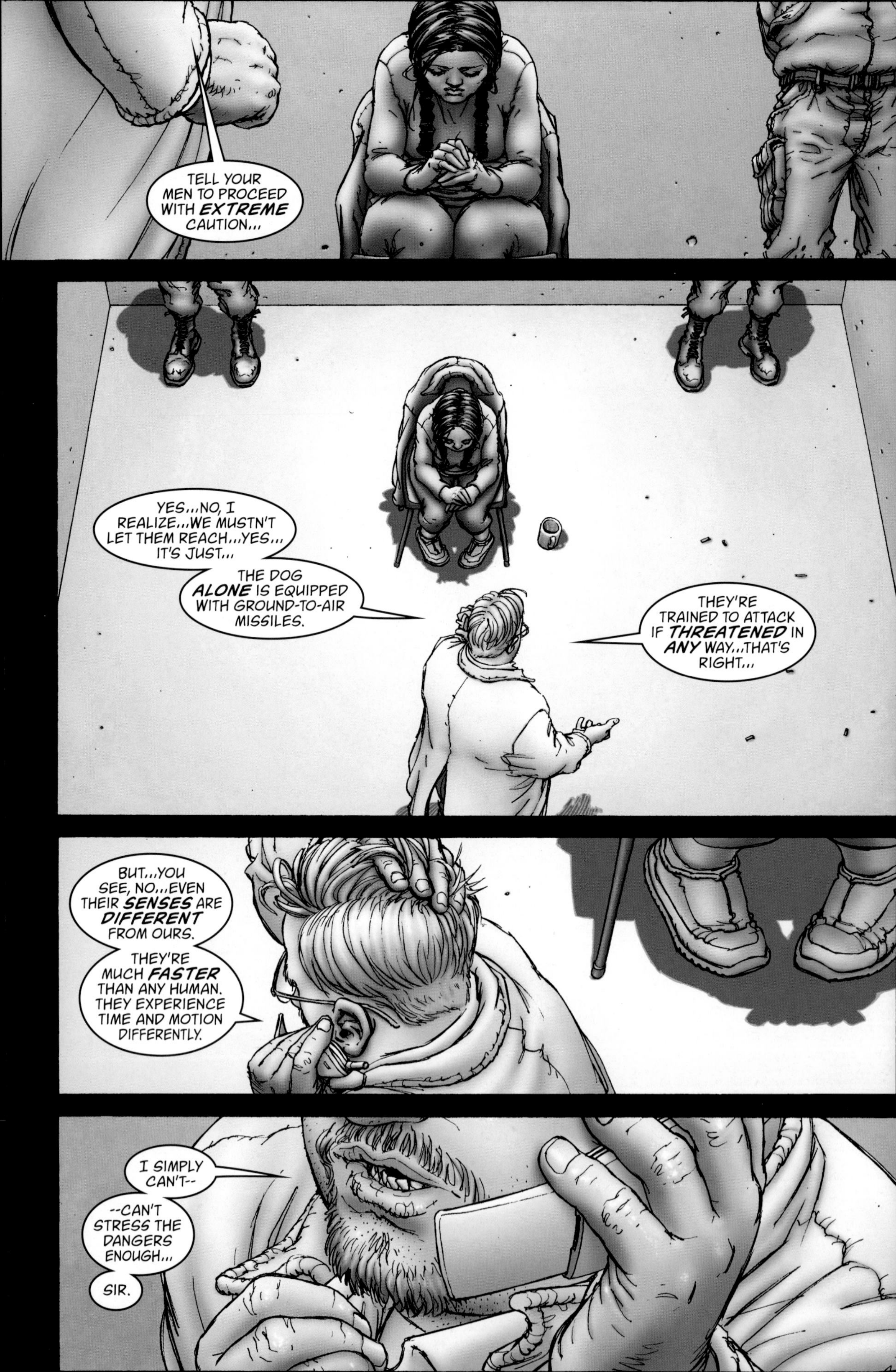
TELL YOUR MEN TO PROCEED WITH EXTREME CAUTION...
YES...NO, I REALIZE...WE MUSTN'T LET THEM REACH...YES... IT'S JUST...
THE DOG ALONE IS EQUIPPED WITH GROUND-TO-AIR MISSILES.
THEY'RE TRAINED TO ATTACK IF THREATENED IN ANY WAY...THAT'S RIGHT...
BUT...YOU SEE, NO...EVEN THEIR SENSES ARE DIFFERENT FROM OURS.
THEY'RE MUCH FASTER THAN ANY HUMAN. THEY EXPERIENCE TIME AND MOTION DIFFERENTLY.
I SIMPLY CAN'T--
--CAN'T STRESS THE DANGERS ENOUGH...
SIR.

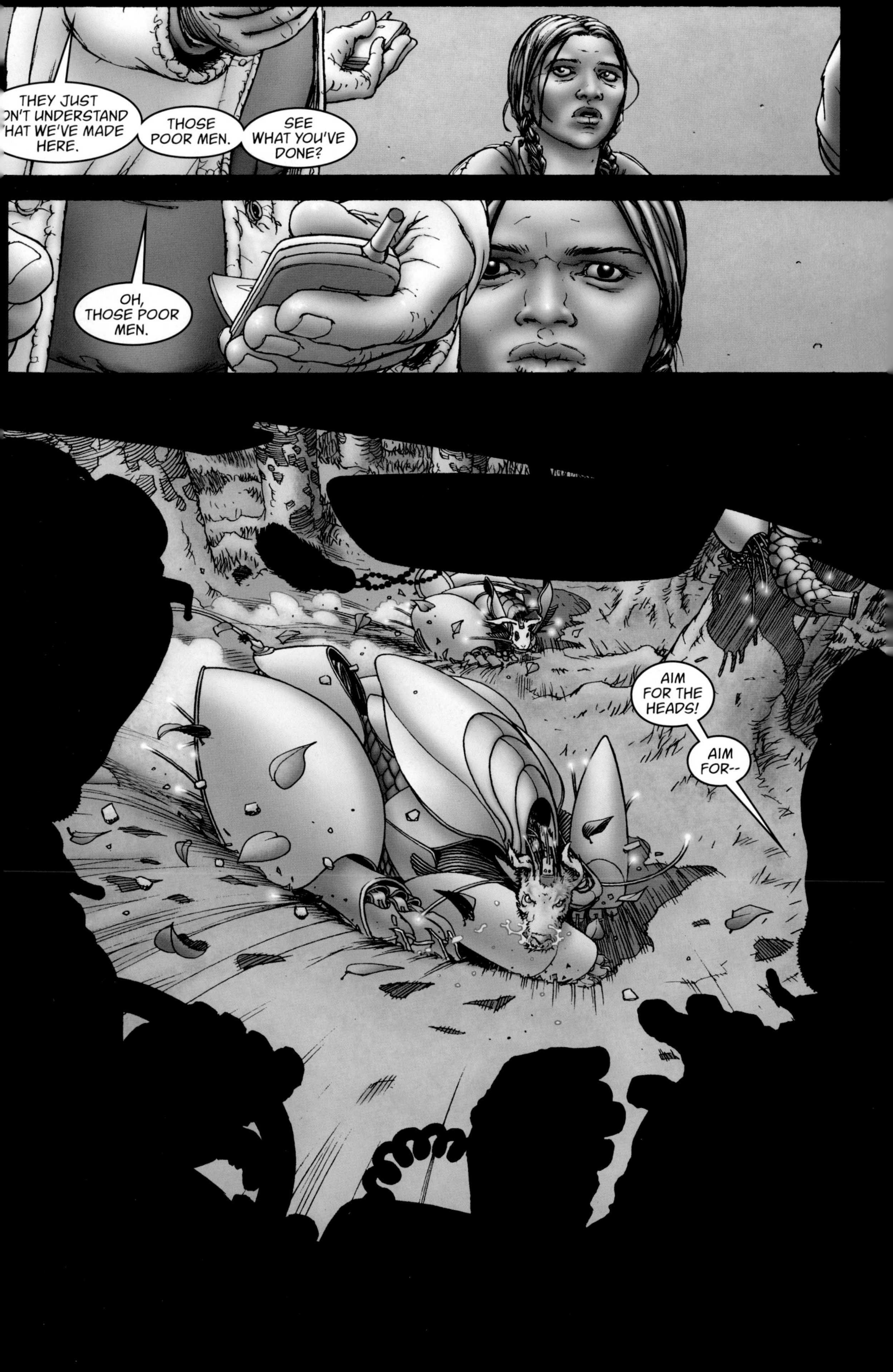
THEY JUST
N'T UNDERSTAND
HAT WE'VE MADE
HERE.
THOSE
POOR MEN.
SEE
WHAT YOU'VE
DONE?
OH,
THOSE POOR
MEN.
AIM
FOR THE
HEADS!
AIM
FOR--

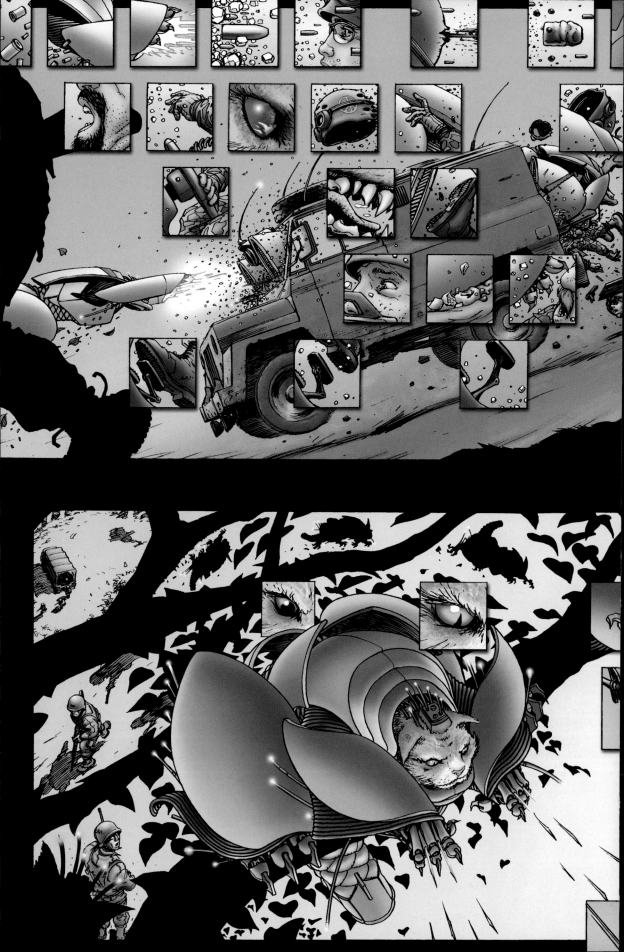

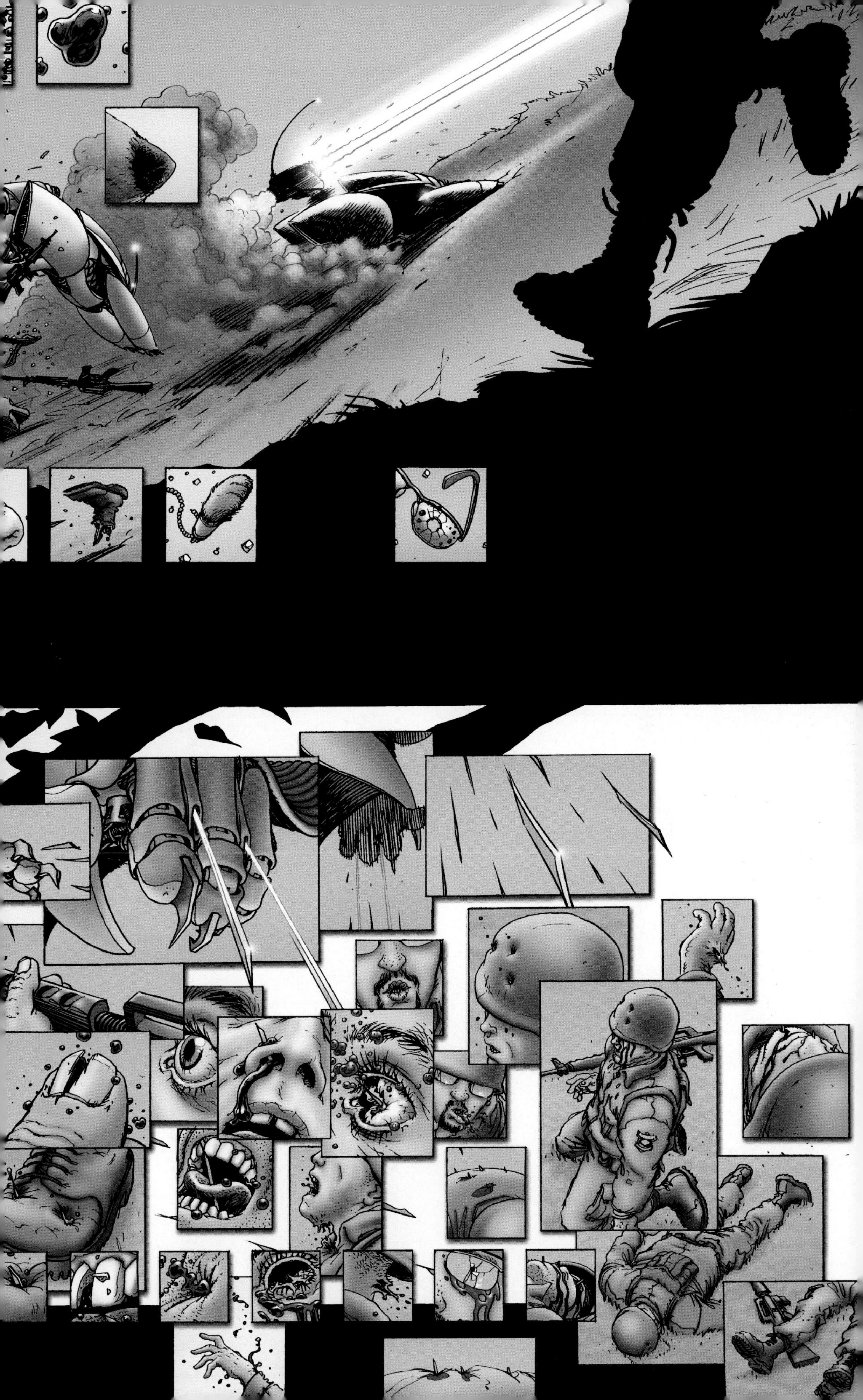

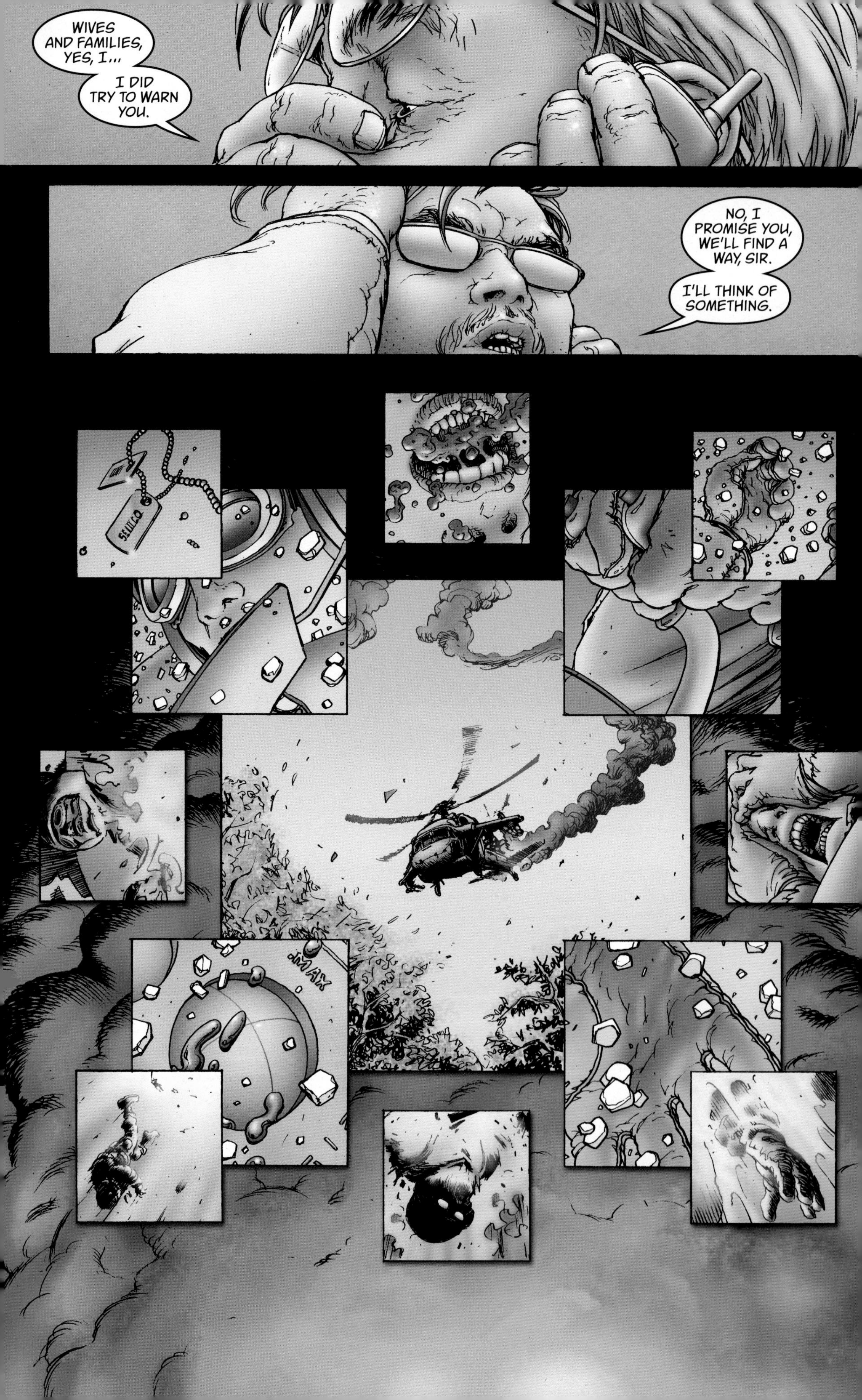
WIVES AND FAMILIES, YES, I...
I DID TRY TO WARN YOU.
NO, I PROMISE YOU, WE'LL FIND A WAY, SIR.
I'LL THINK OF SOMETHING.

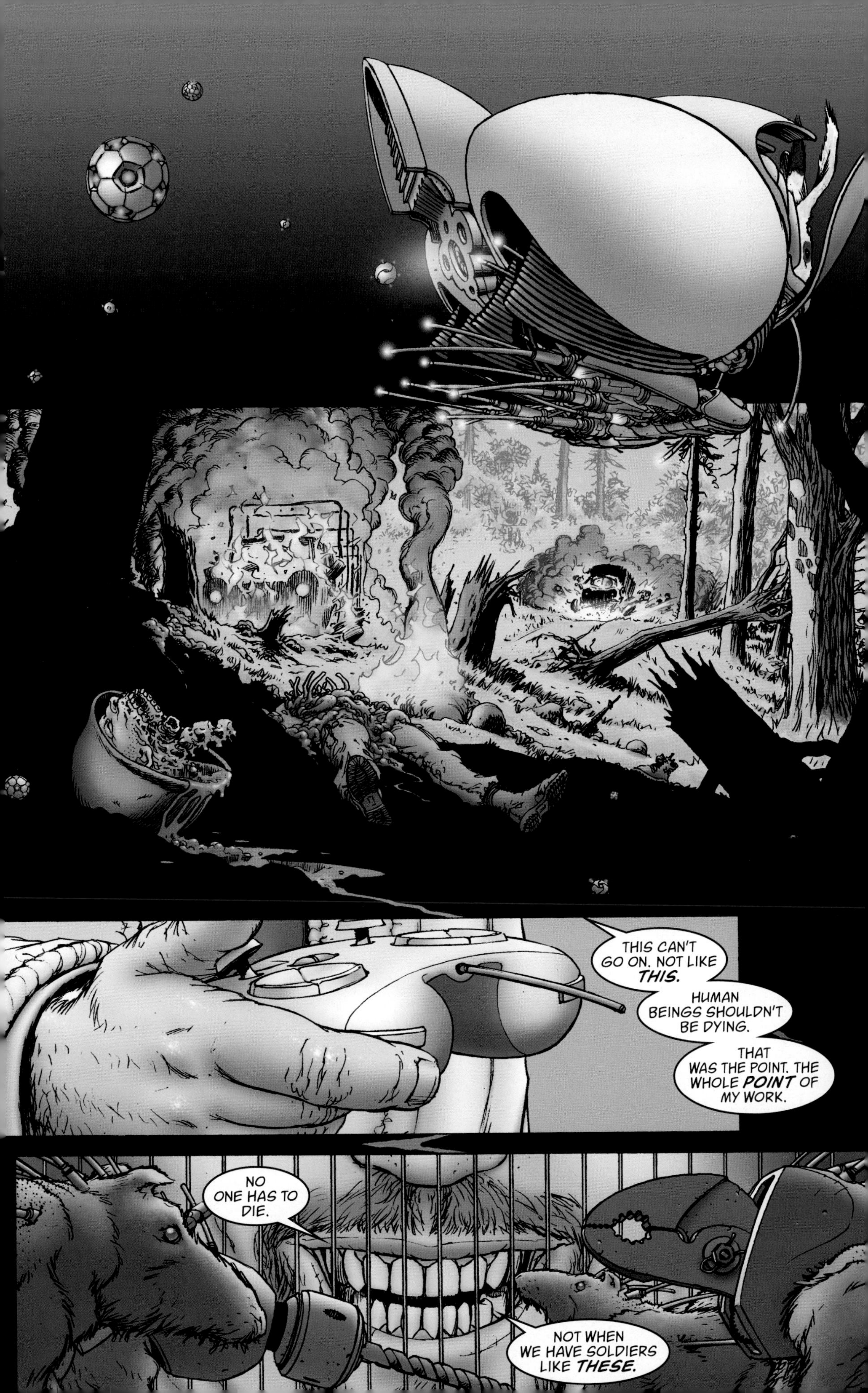
THIS CAN'T GO ON. NOT LIKE *THIS.*
HUMAN BEINGS SHOULDN'T BE DYING.
THAT WAS THE POINT. THE WHOLE *POINT* OF MY WORK.
NO ONE HAS TO DIE.
NOT WHEN WE HAVE SOLDIERS LIKE *THESE.*

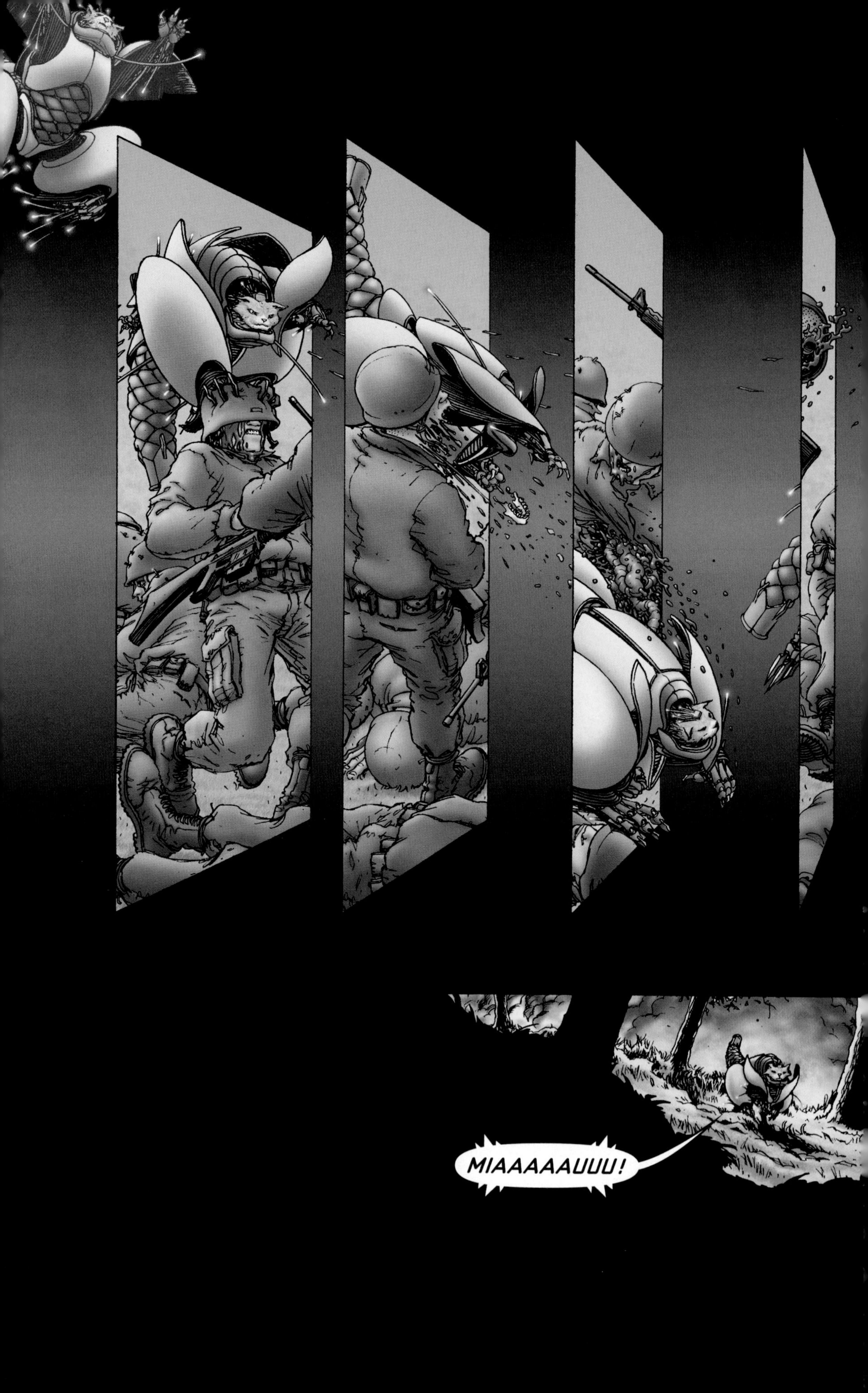
MIAAAAAUUU!

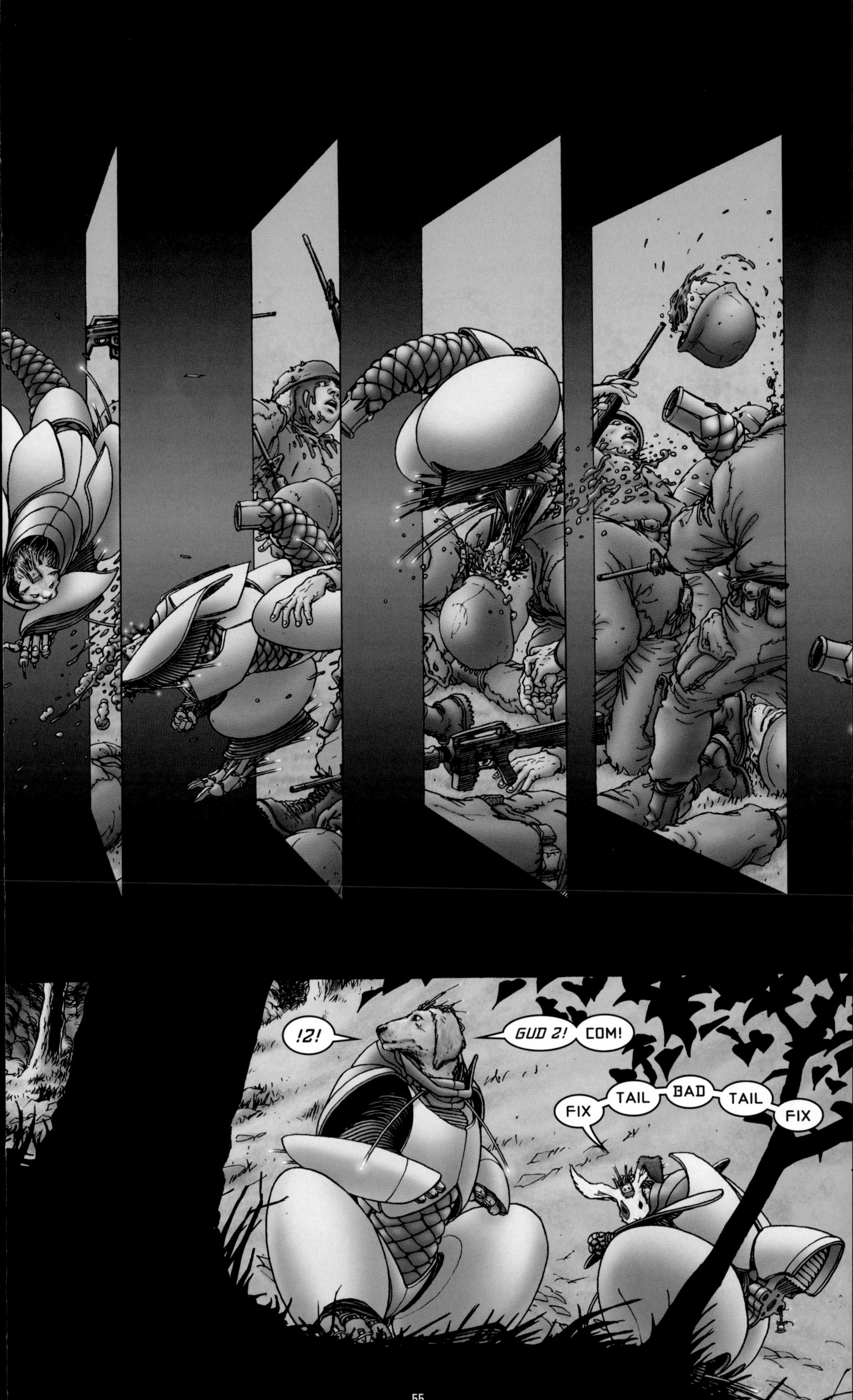
!Z!
GUD Z! COM!
FIX TAIL BAD TAIL FIX

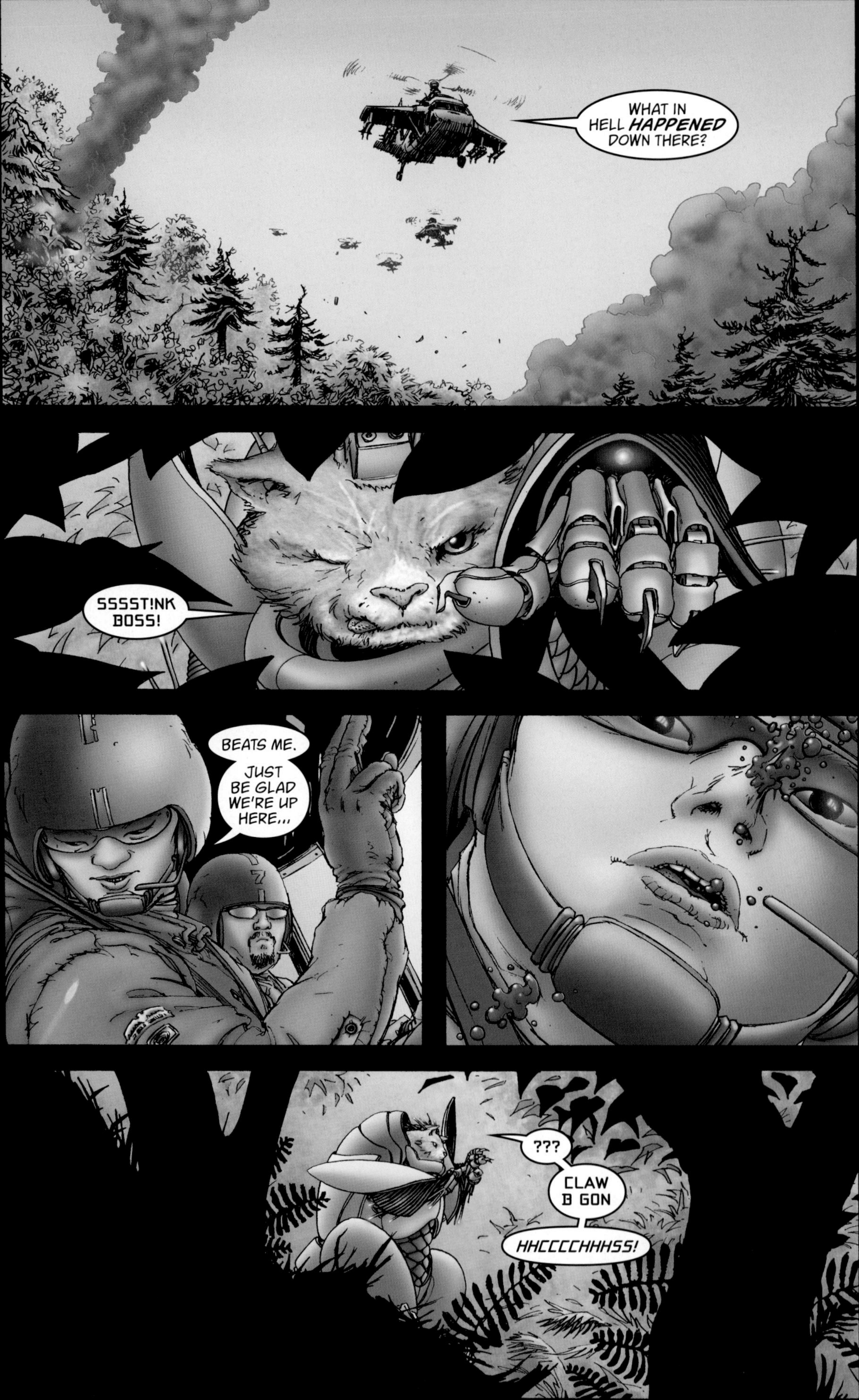
WHAT IN HELL *HAPPENED* DOWN THERE?
SSSST!NK BOSS!
BEATS ME.
JUST BE GLAD WE'RE UP HERE...
???
CLAW B GON
HHCCCCHHHSS!

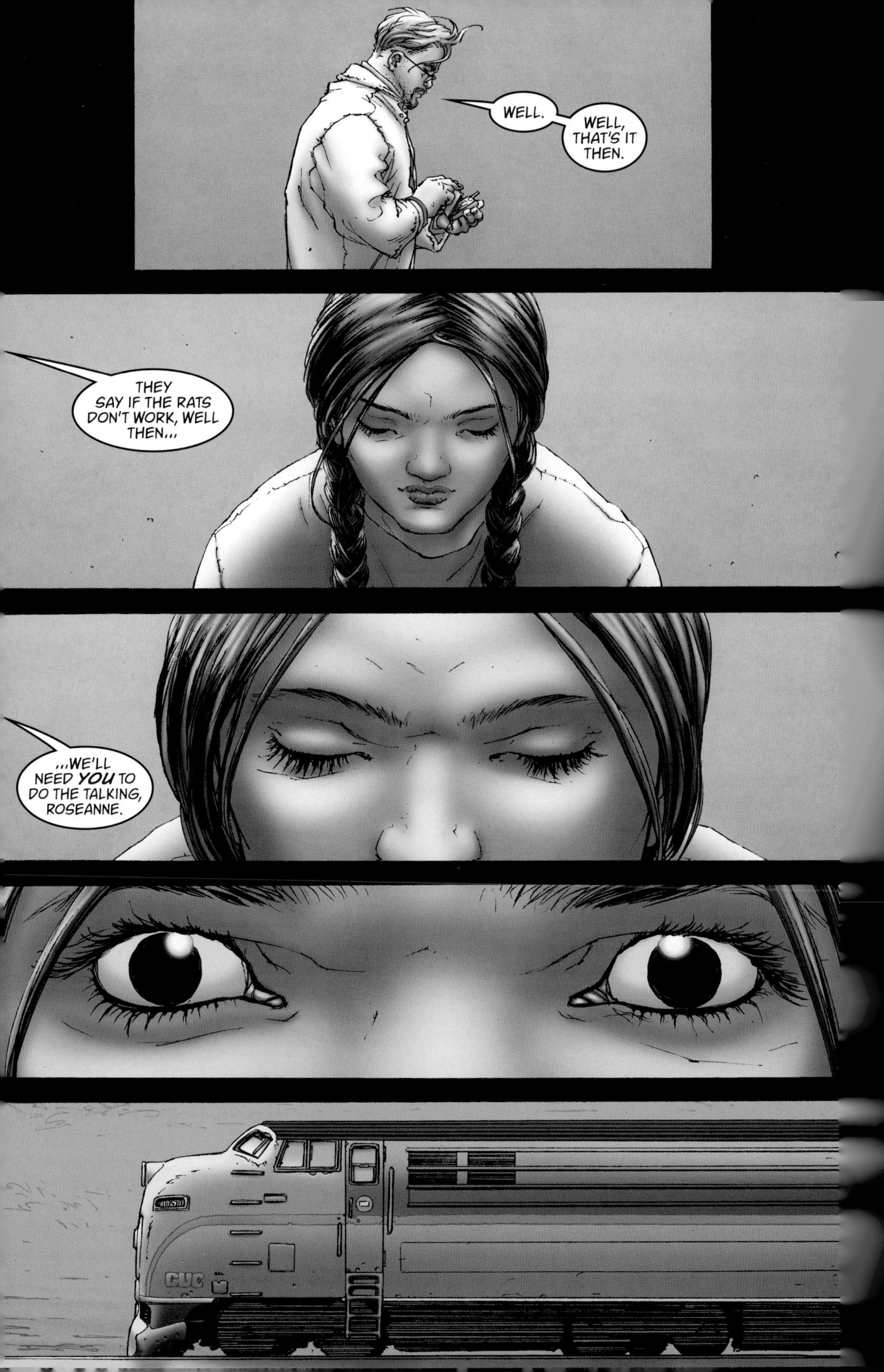

WELL.
WELL, THAT'S IT THEN.
THEY SAY IF THE RATS DON'T WORK, WELL THEN...
...WE'LL NEED **YOU** TO DO THE TALKING, ROSEANNE.

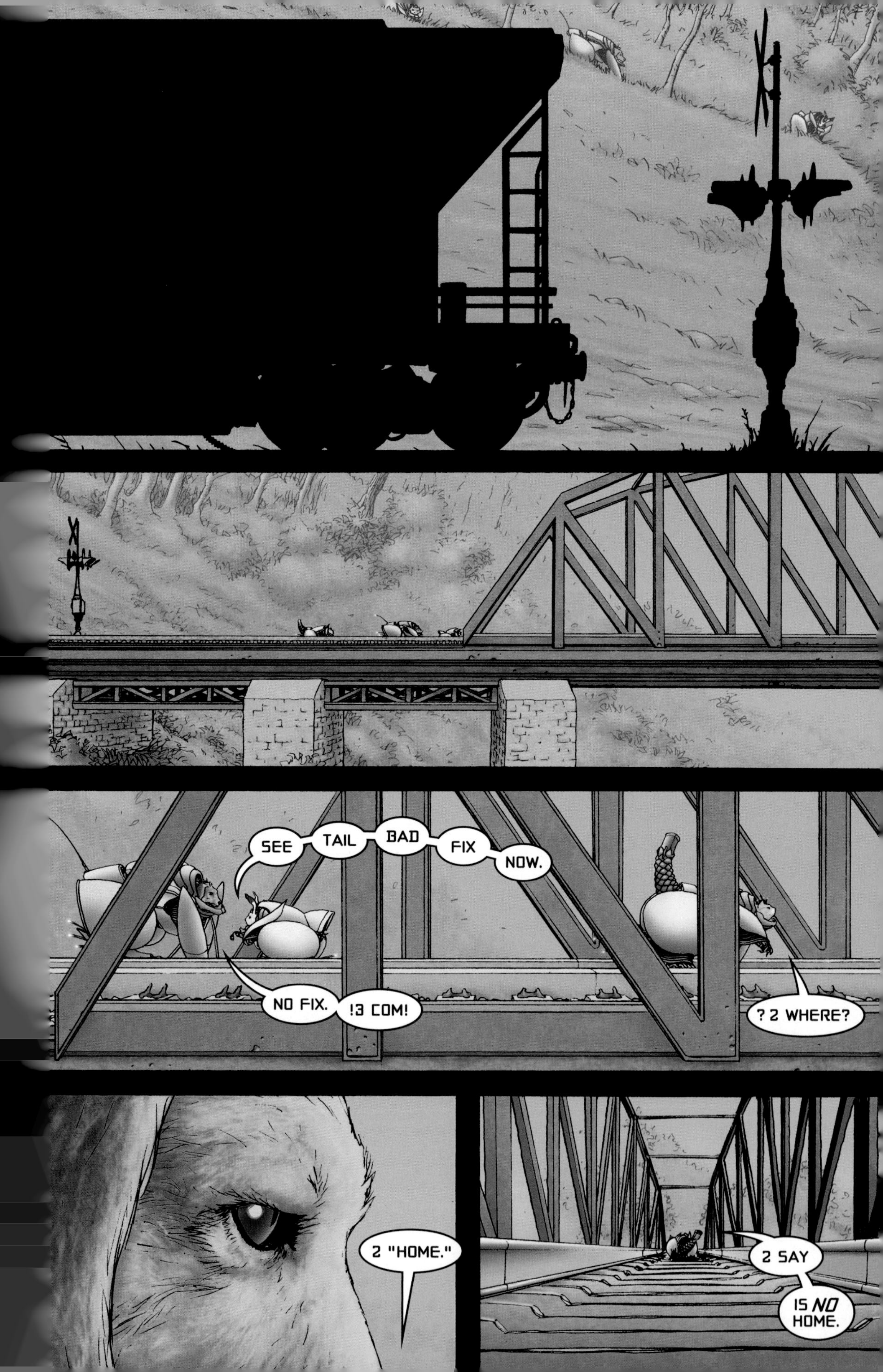
SEE
TAIL
BAD
FIX
NOW.
NO FIX.
!3 COM!
? 2 WHERE?
2 "HOME."
2 SAY
IS NO HOME.

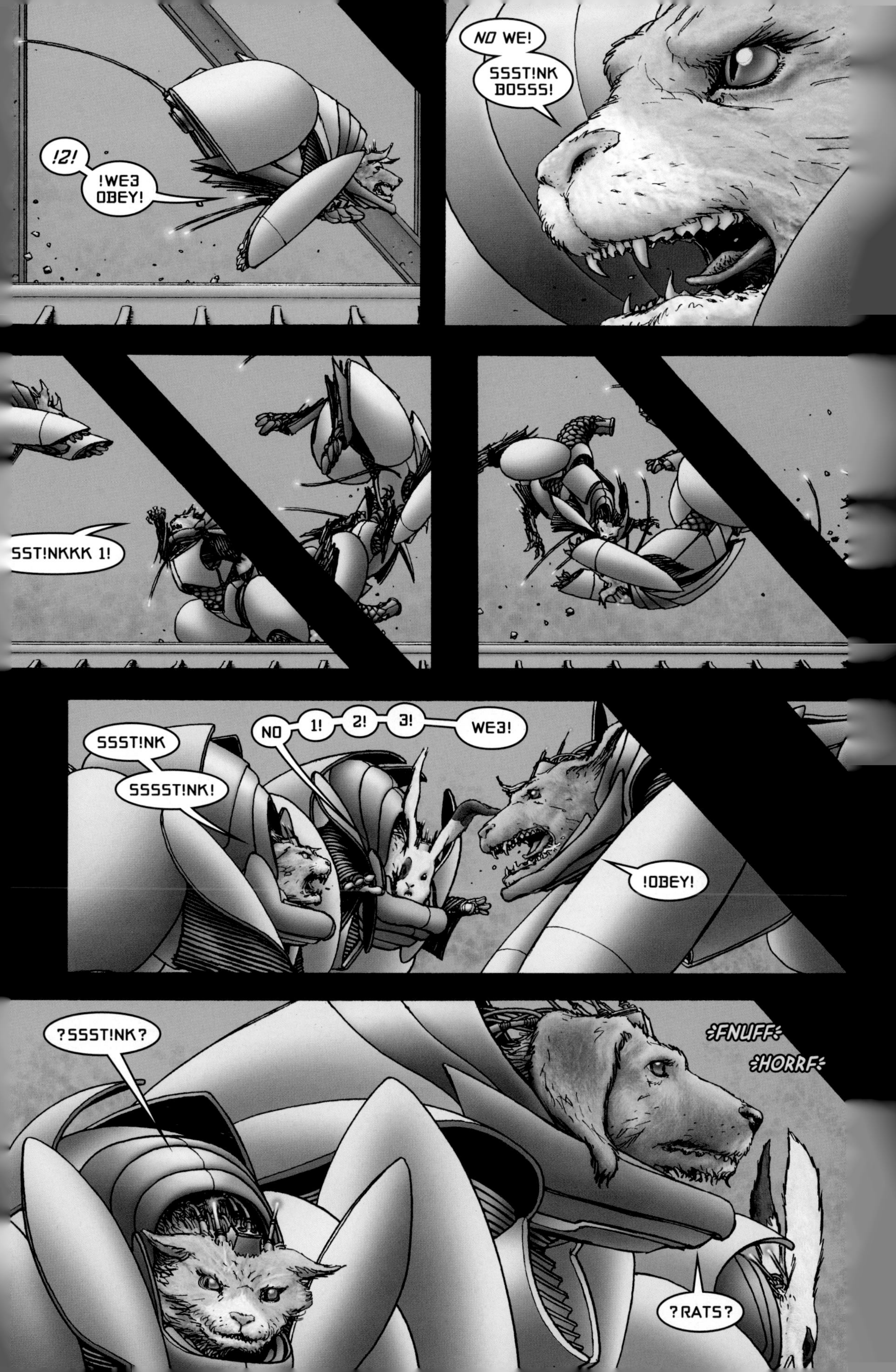
!2!
!WE3 OBEY!
NO WE!
SSST!NK BOSSS!
SST!NKKK 1!
SSST!NK
SSSST!NK!
NO
1!
2!
3!
WE3!
!OBEY!
?SSST!NK?
FNUFF
HORRF
?RATS?

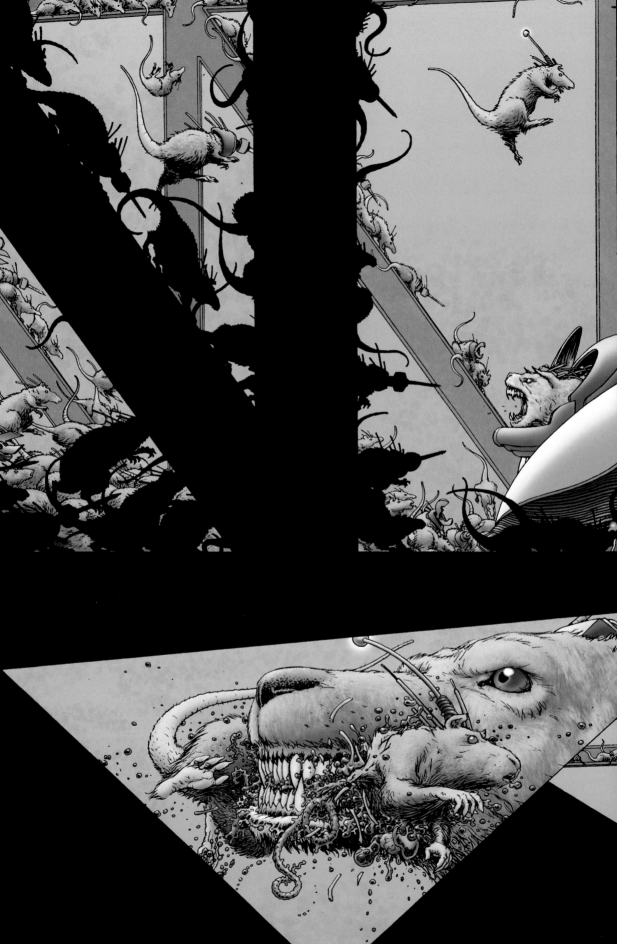

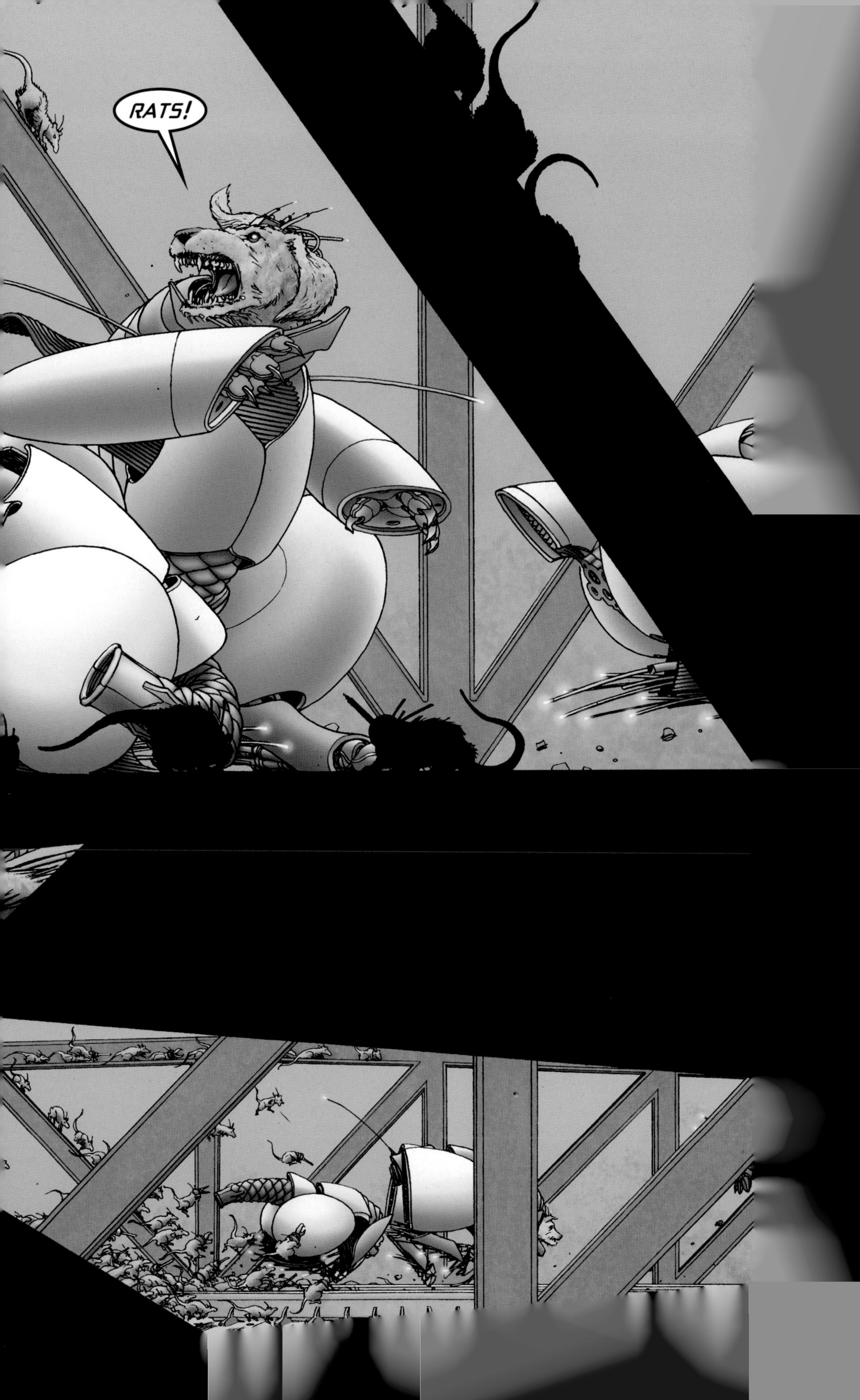
RATS!

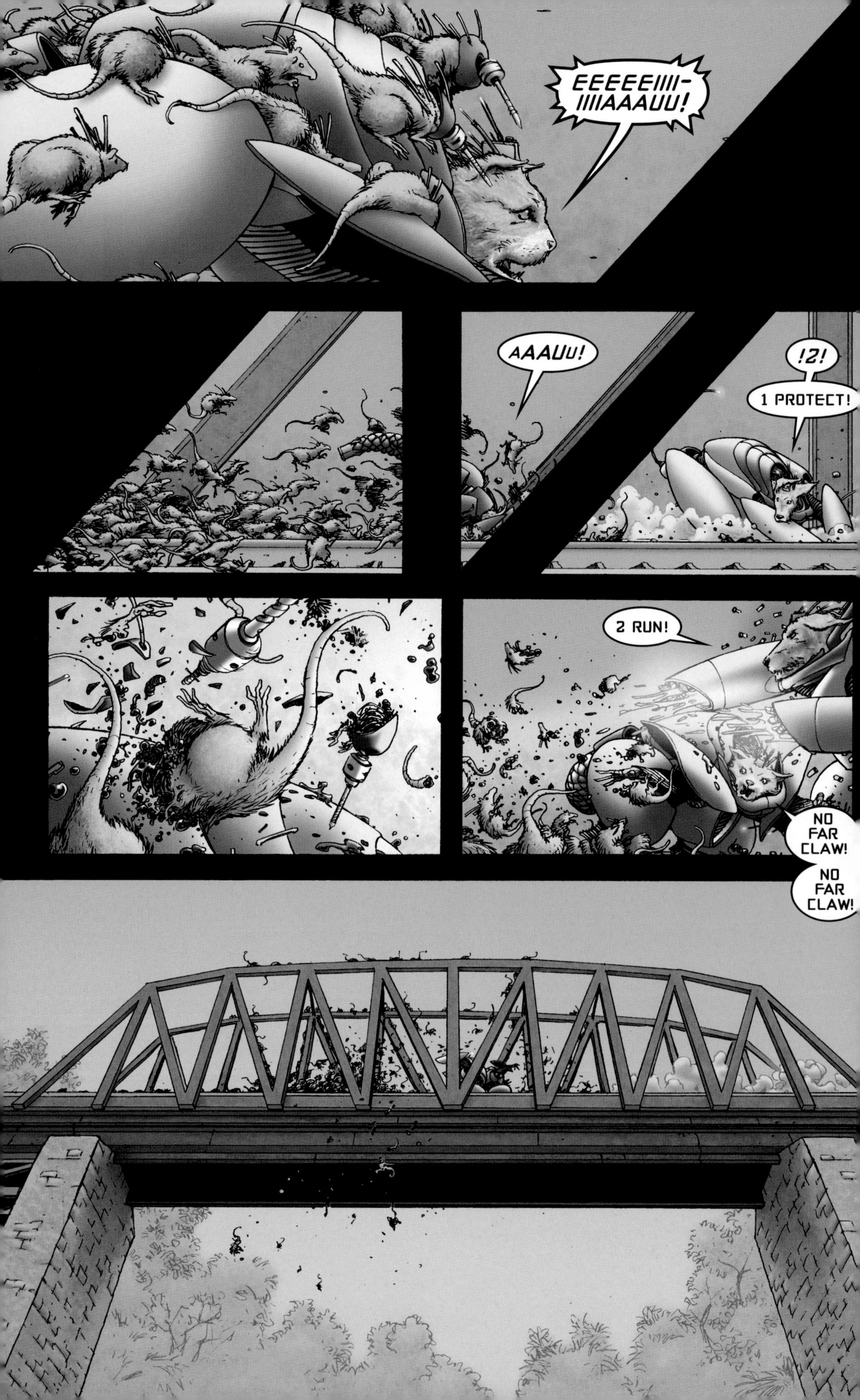
EEEEEIIII-
IIIIAAAAUU!
AAAUU!
!2!
1 PROTECT!
2 RUN!
NO
FAR
CLAW!
NO
FAR
CLAW!

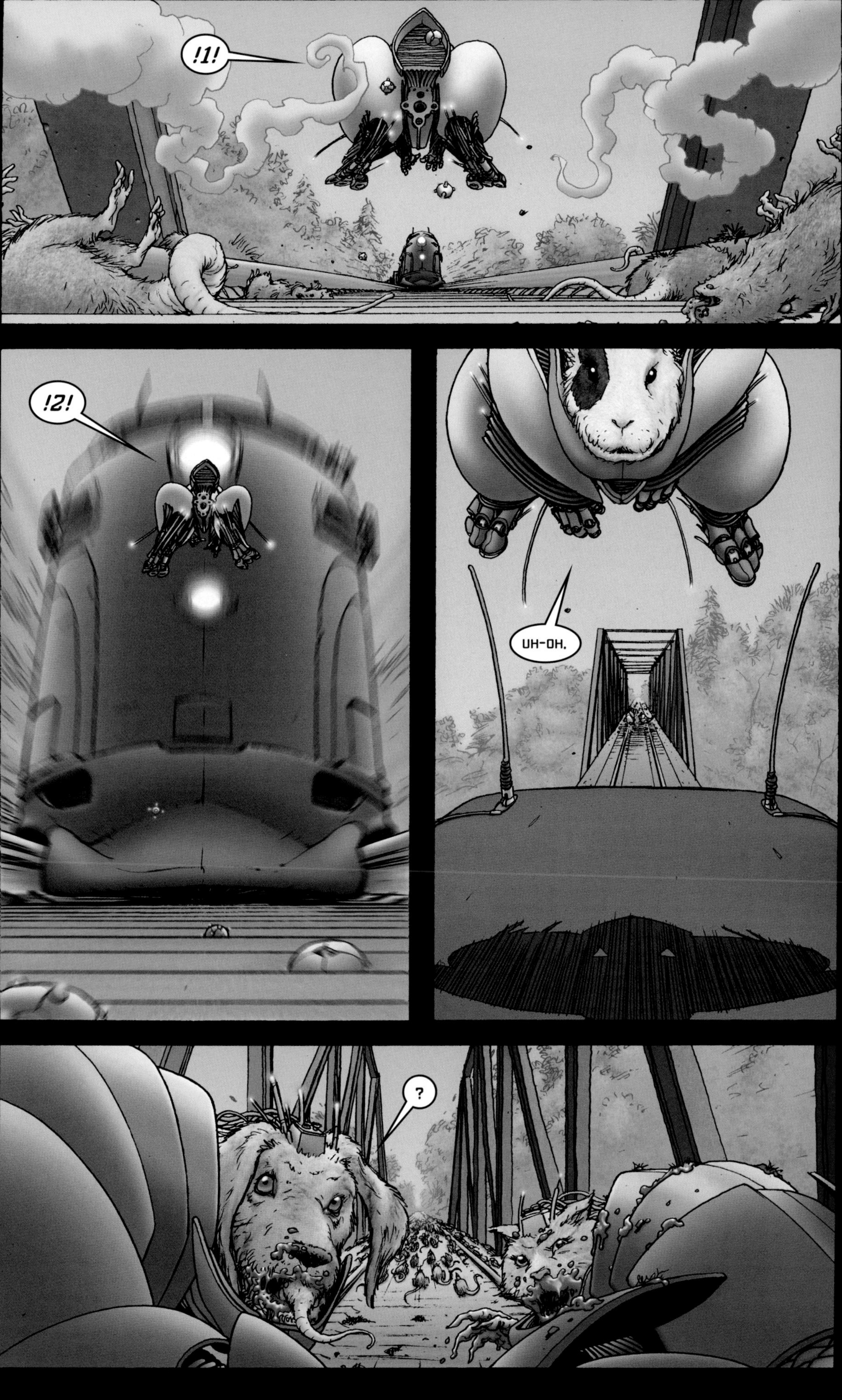
!1!
!2!
UH-OH.
?

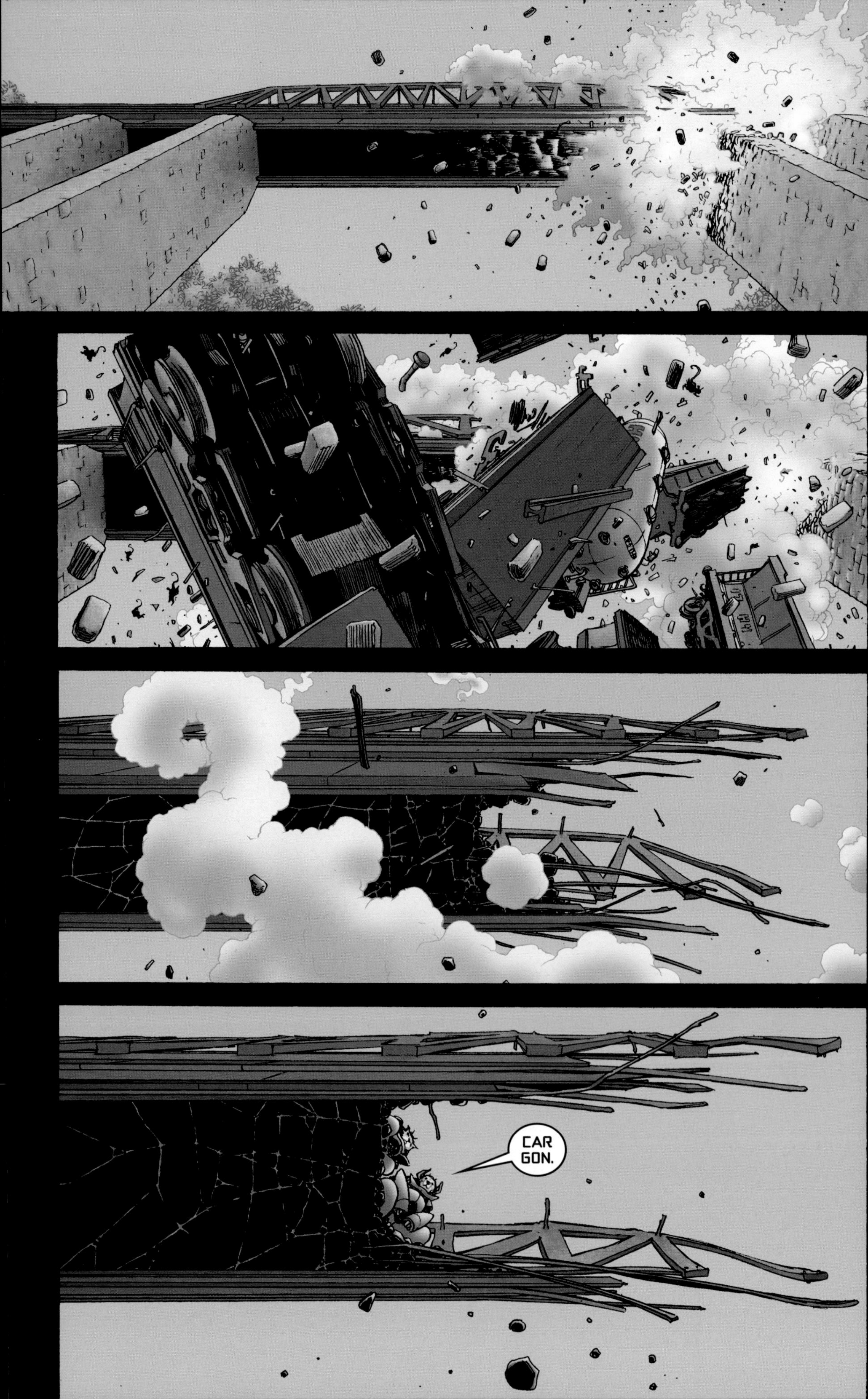
CAR GON.

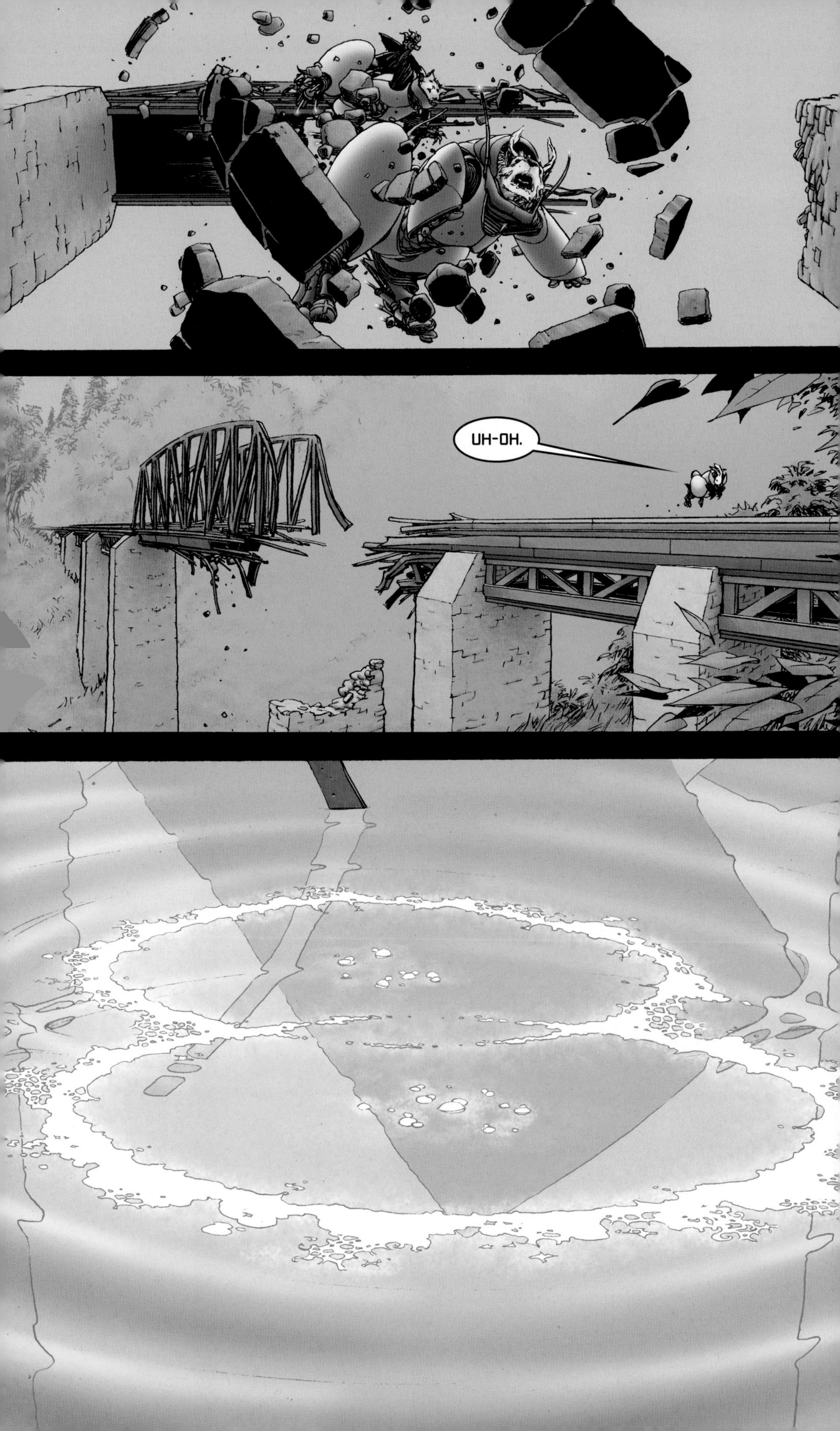
UH-OH.

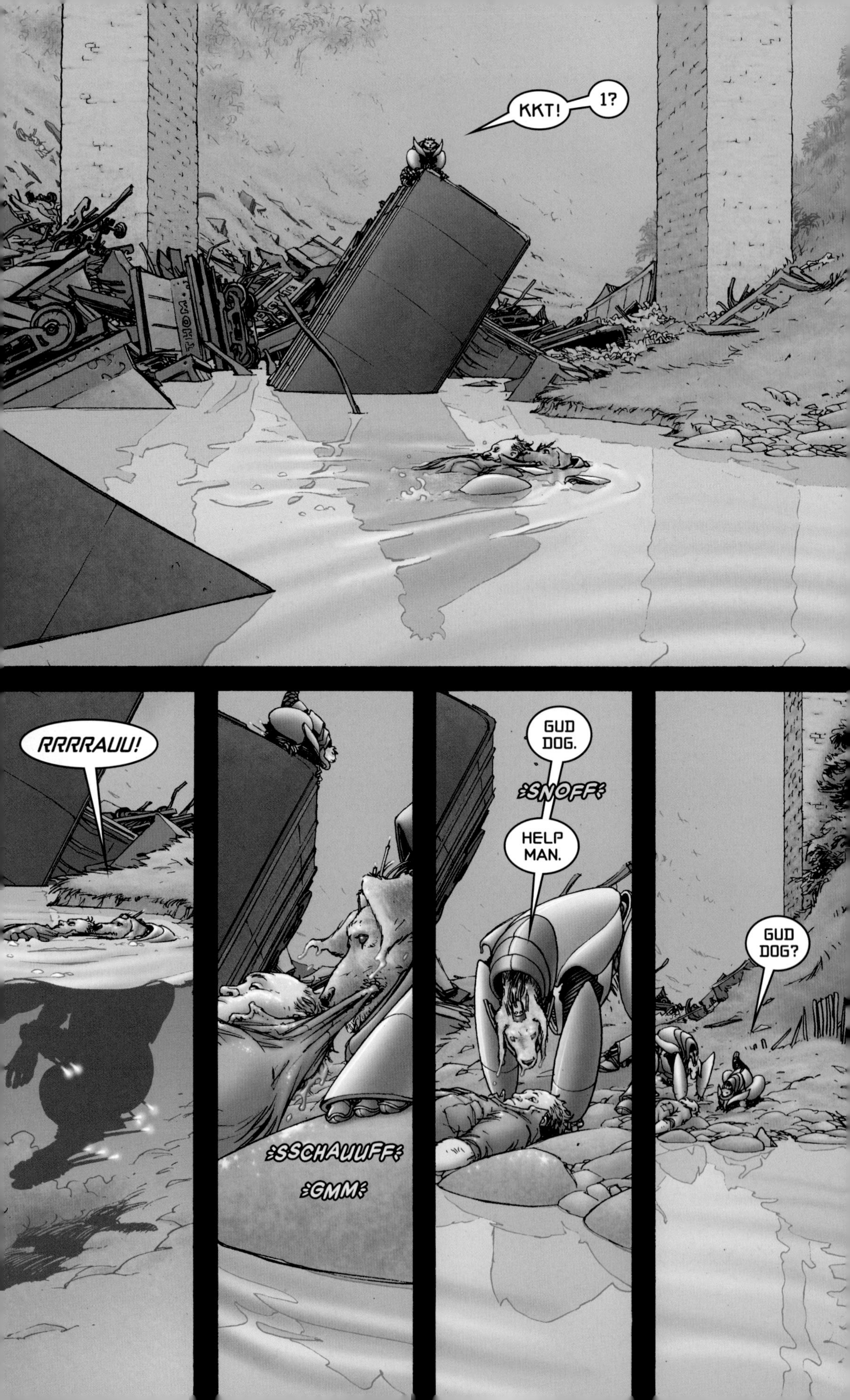
KKT!
1?
RRRRAUU!
SSCHAUUFF
GMM
GUD DOG.
SNOFF
HELP MAN.
GUD DOG?

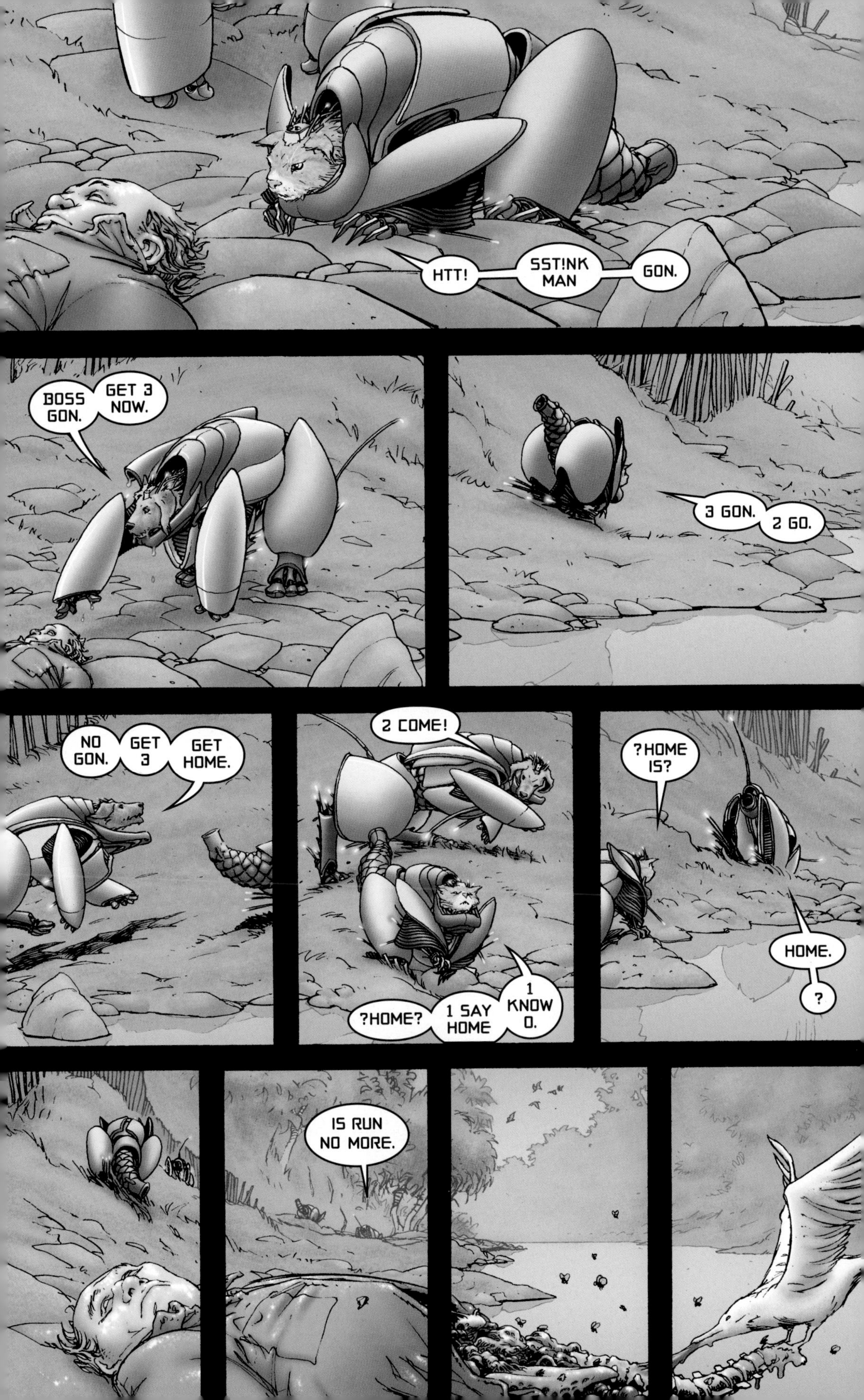
HTT!
SST!NK MAN
GON.
BOSS GON.
GET 3 NOW.
3 GON.
2 GO.
NO GON.
GET 3
GET HOME.
2 COME!
1 KNOW 0.
1 SAY HOME
?HOME?
?HOME IS?
HOME.
?
IS RUN NO MORE.

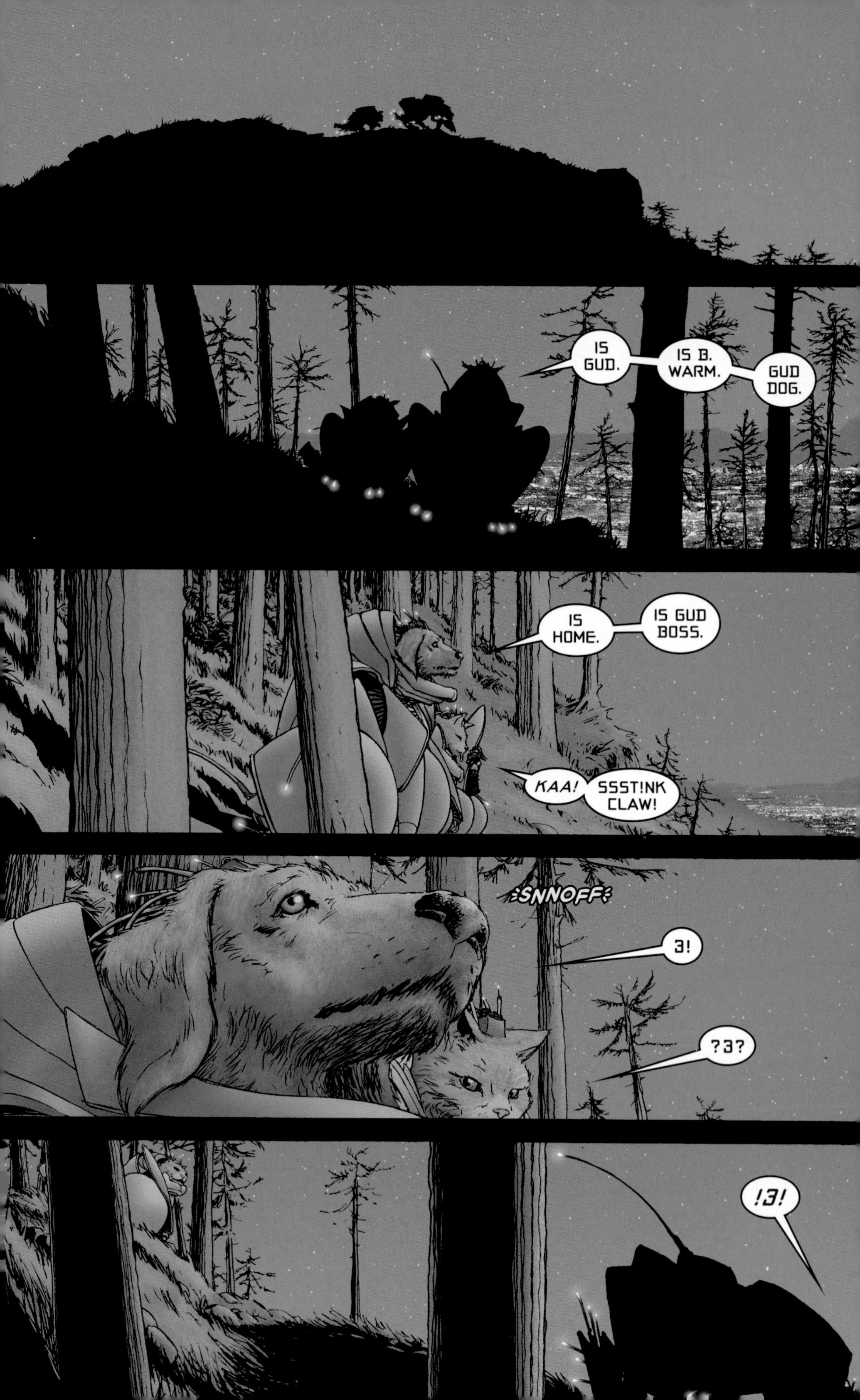
IS GUD.
IS B. WARM.
GUD DOG.
IS HOME.
IS GUD BOSS.
KAA!
SSST!NK CLAW!
SNNOFF
3!
?3?
!3!

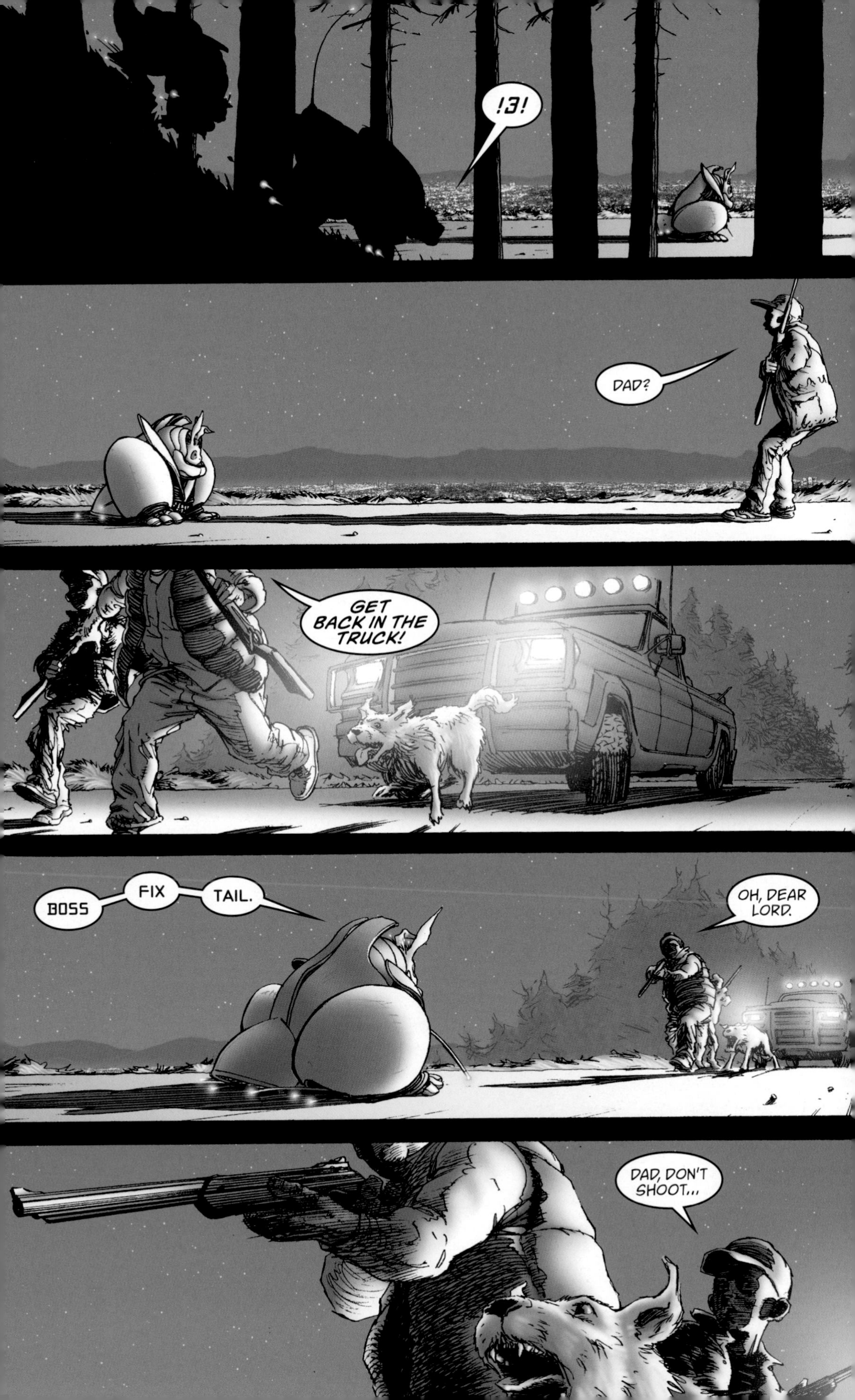
!3!
DAD?
GET BACK IN THE TRUCK!
BOSS
FIX
TAIL.
OH, DEAR LORD.
DAD, DON'T SHOOT...

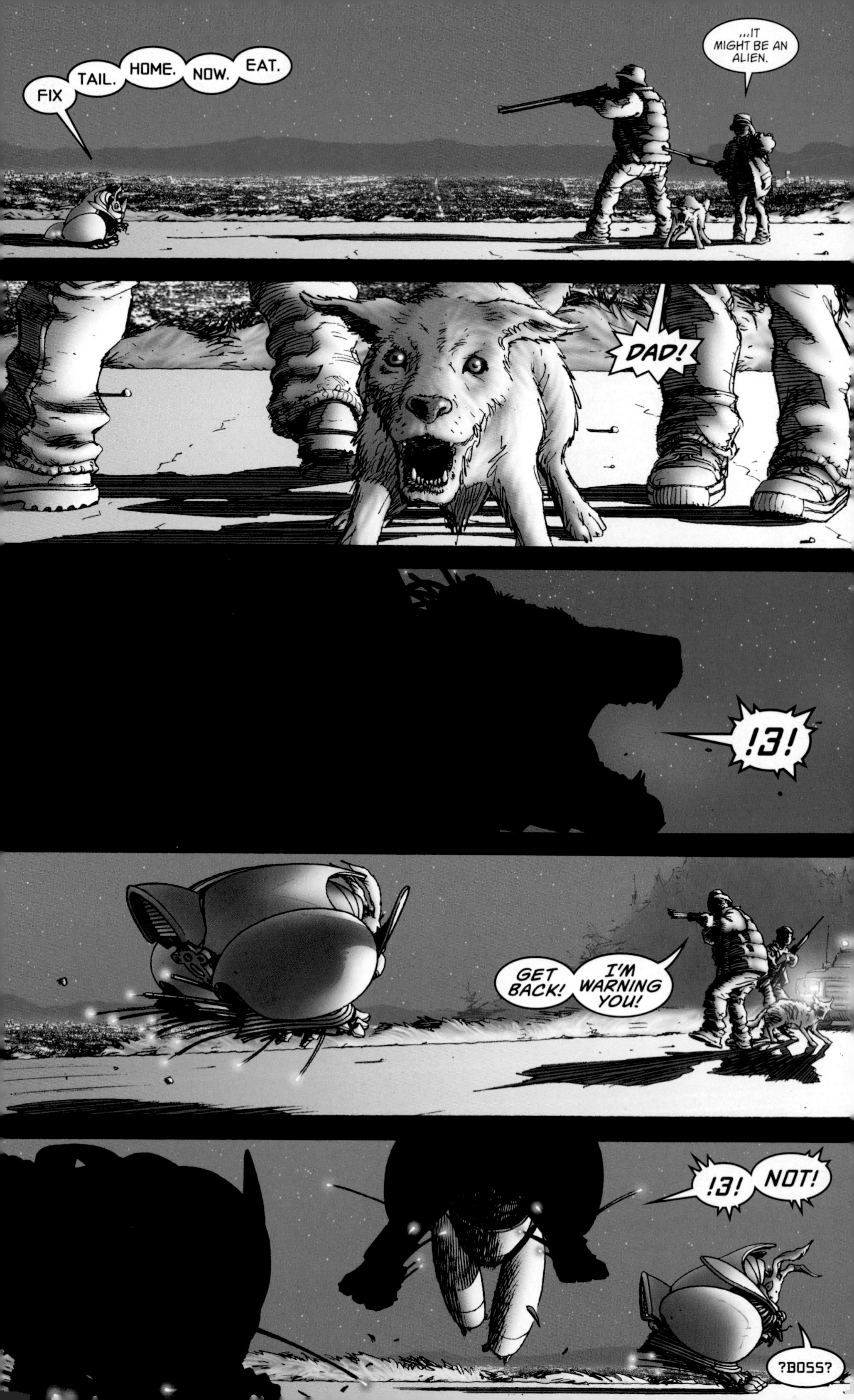
FIX
TAIL.
HOME.
NOW.
EAT.
...IT MIGHT BE AN ALIEN.
DAD!
!3!
GET BACK!
I'M WARNING YOU!
!3!
NOT!
?BOSS?

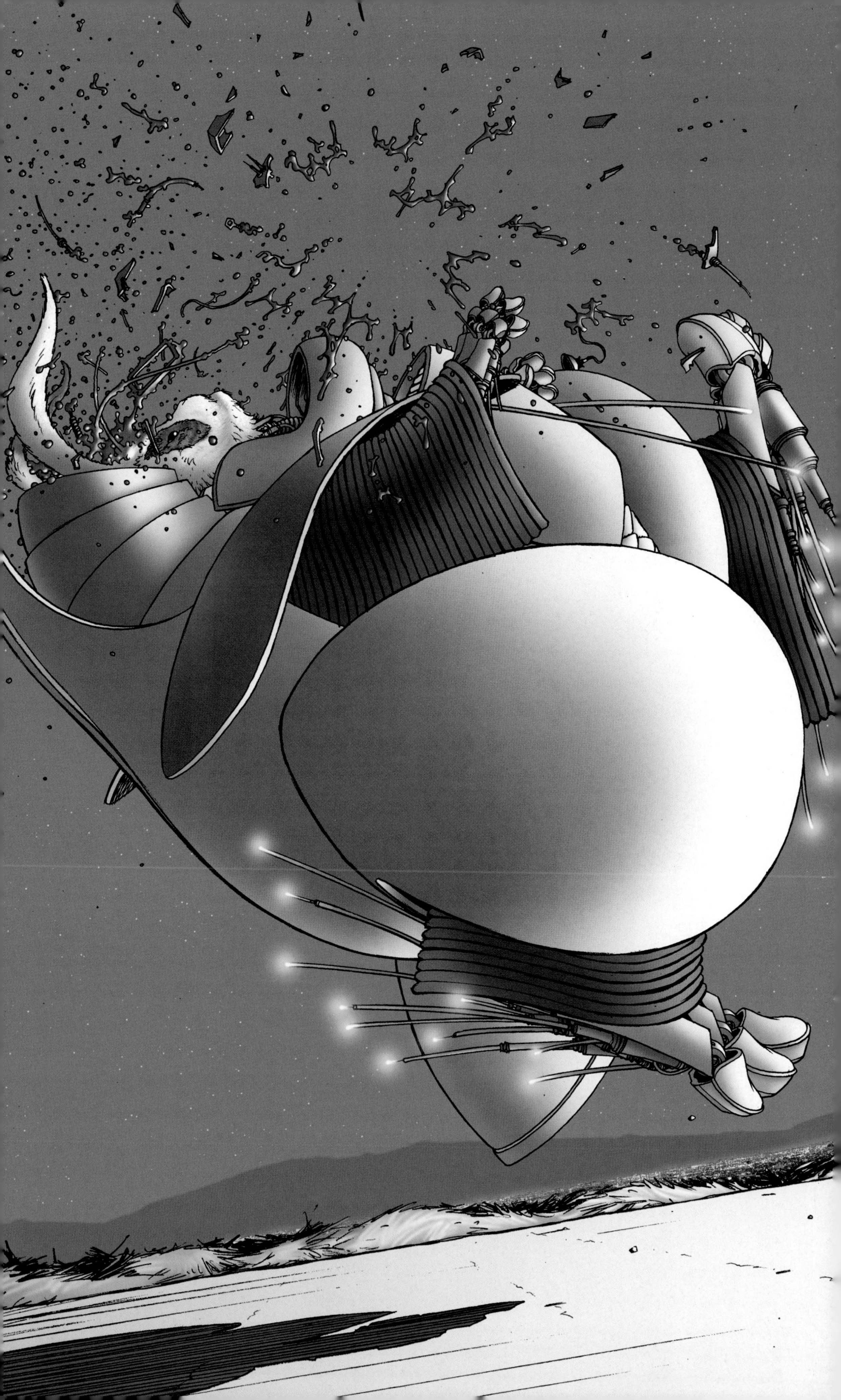

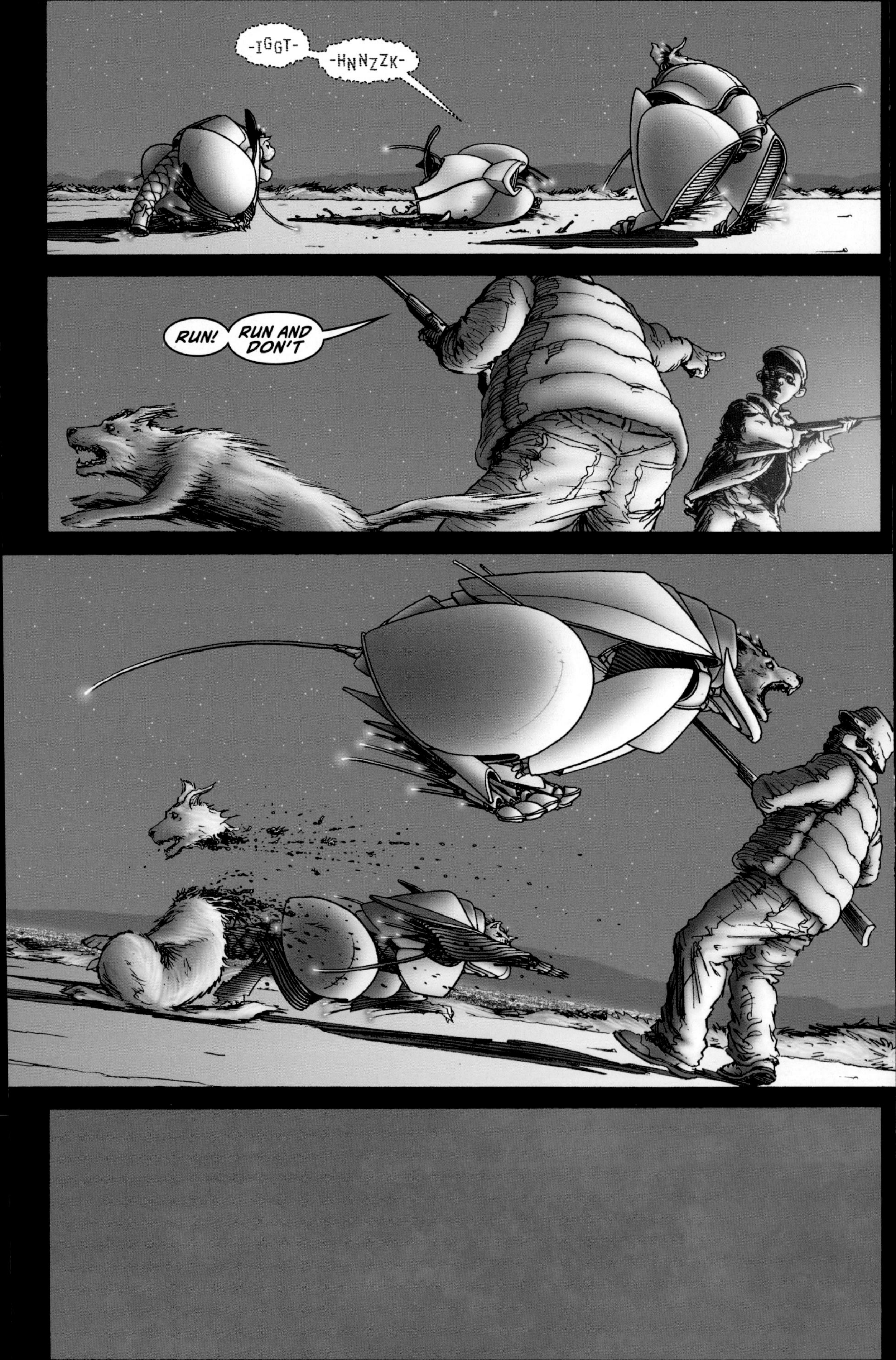
-IGGT-
-HNNZZK-
RUN!
RUN AND DON'T

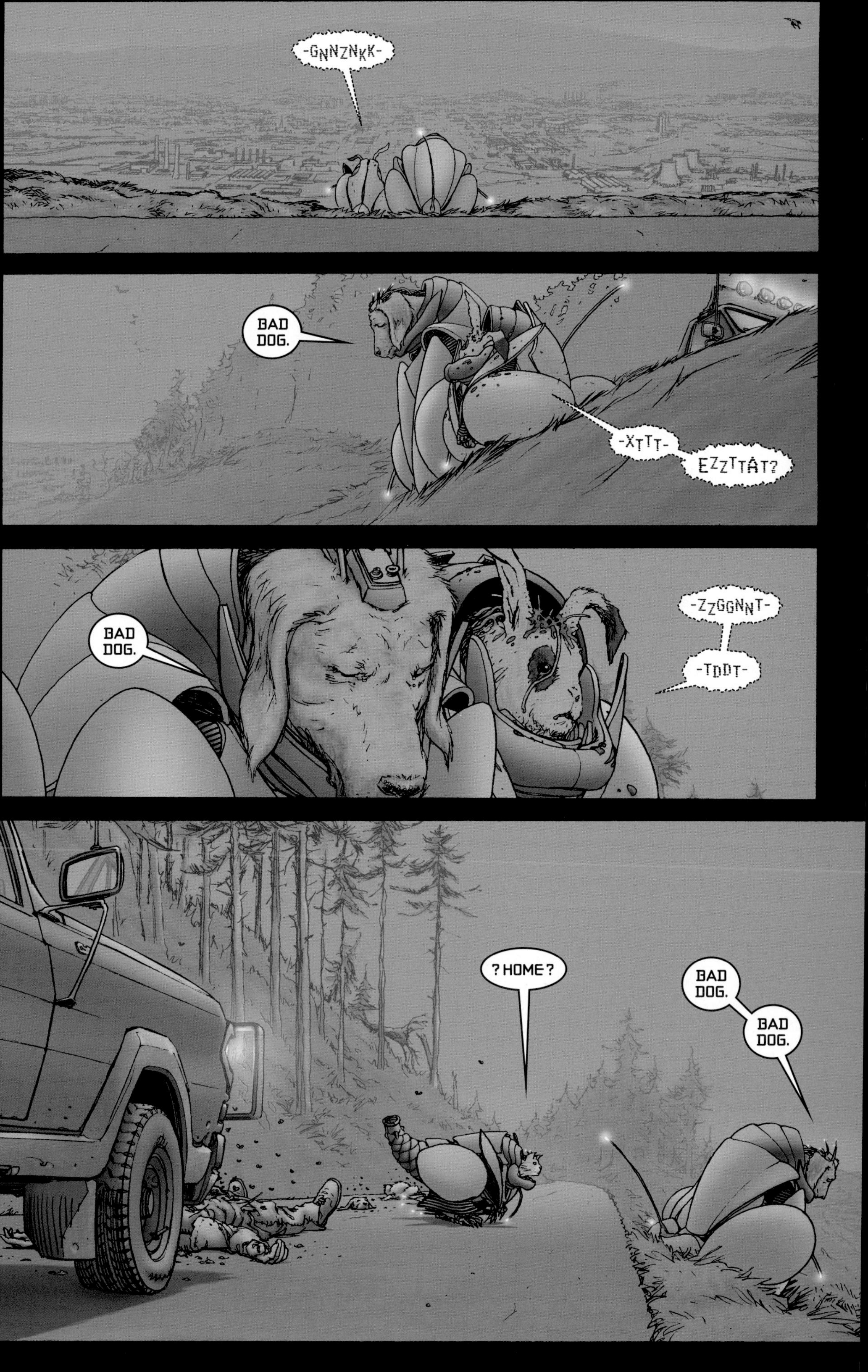
-GNNZNKK-
BAD DOG.
-XTTT-
EZZTTÅT?
BAD DOG.
-ZZGGNNT-
-TDDT-
? HOME ?
BAD DOG.
BAD DOG.

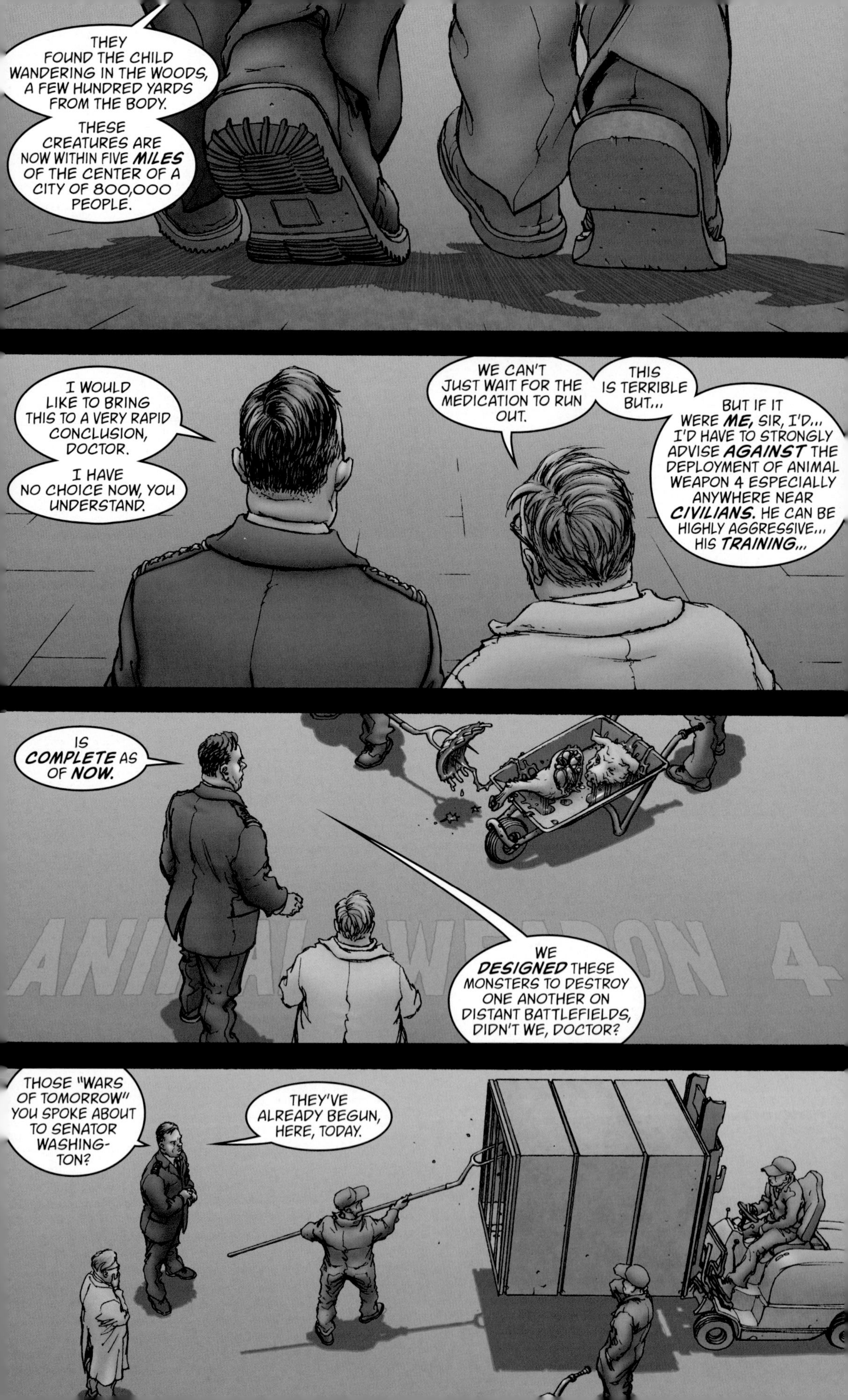
THEY FOUND THE CHILD WANDERING IN THE WOODS, A FEW HUNDRED YARDS FROM THE BODY.
THESE CREATURES ARE NOW WITHIN FIVE MILES OF THE CENTER OF A CITY OF 800,000 PEOPLE.
I WOULD LIKE TO BRING THIS TO A VERY RAPID CONCLUSION, DOCTOR.
I HAVE NO CHOICE NOW, YOU UNDERSTAND.
WE CAN'T JUST WAIT FOR THE MEDICATION TO RUN OUT.
THIS IS TERRIBLE BUT...
BUT IF IT WERE ME, SIR, I'D... I'D HAVE TO STRONGLY ADVISE AGAINST THE DEPLOYMENT OF ANIMAL WEAPON 4 ESPECIALLY ANYWHERE NEAR CIVILIANS. HE CAN BE HIGHLY AGGRESSIVE... HIS TRAINING...
IS COMPLETE AS OF NOW.
WE DESIGNED THESE MONSTERS TO DESTROY ONE ANOTHER ON DISTANT BATTLEFIELDS, DIDN'T WE, DOCTOR?
THOSE "WARS OF TOMORROW" YOU SPOKE ABOUT TO SENATOR WASHING-TON?
THEY'VE ALREADY BEGUN, HERE, TODAY.

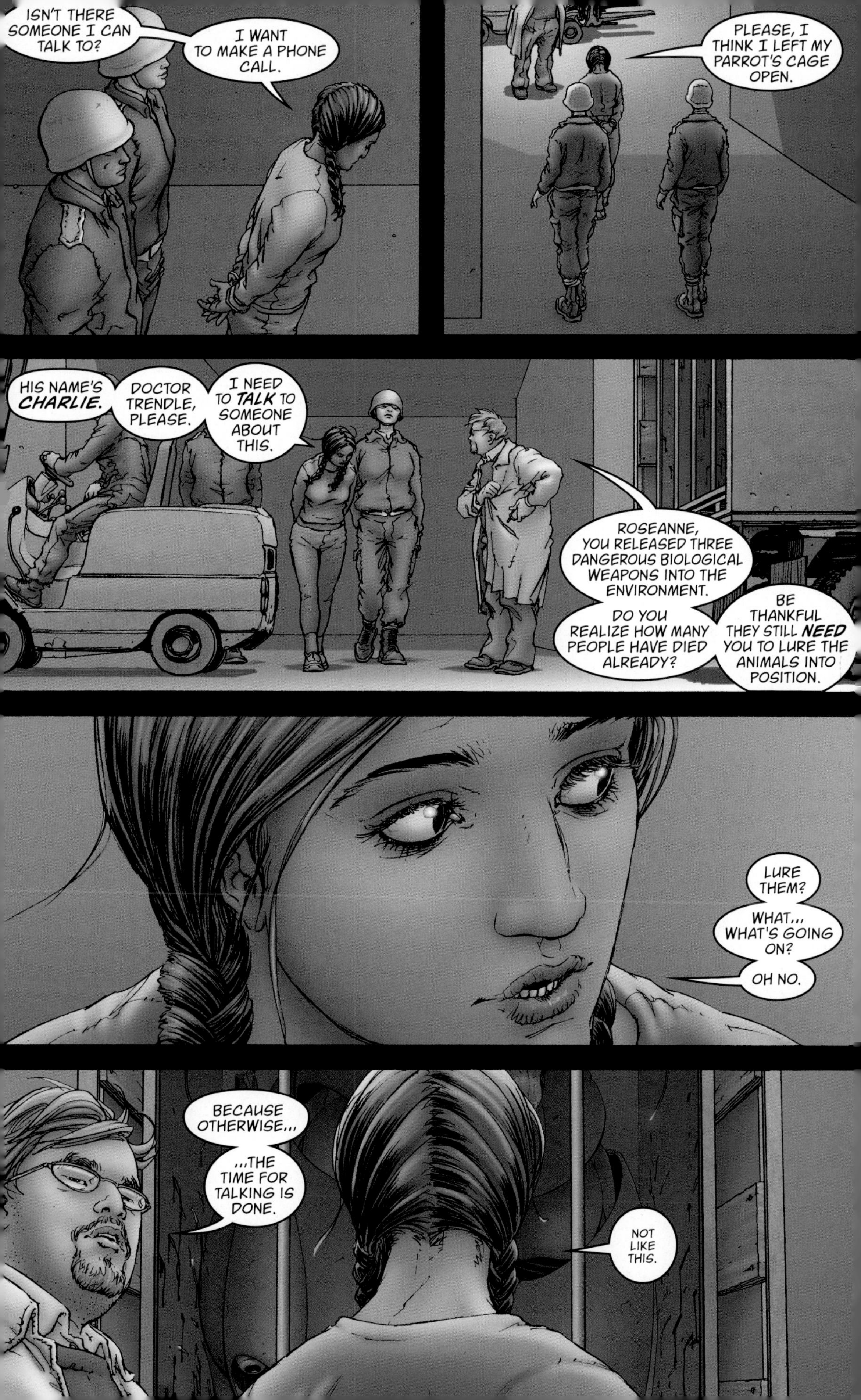
ISN'T THERE SOMEONE I CAN TALK TO?
I WANT TO MAKE A PHONE CALL.
PLEASE, I THINK I LEFT MY PARROT'S CAGE OPEN.
HIS NAME'S **CHARLIE.**
DOCTOR TRENDLE, PLEASE.
I NEED TO **TALK** TO SOMEONE ABOUT THIS.
ROSEANNE, YOU RELEASED THREE DANGEROUS BIOLOGICAL WEAPONS INTO THE ENVIRONMENT.
DO YOU REALIZE HOW MANY PEOPLE HAVE DIED ALREADY?
BE THANKFUL THEY STILL **NEED** YOU TO LURE THE ANIMALS INTO POSITION.
LURE THEM?
WHAT... WHAT'S GOING ON?
OH NO.
BECAUSE OTHERWISE...
...THE TIME FOR TALKING IS DONE.
NOT LIKE THIS.

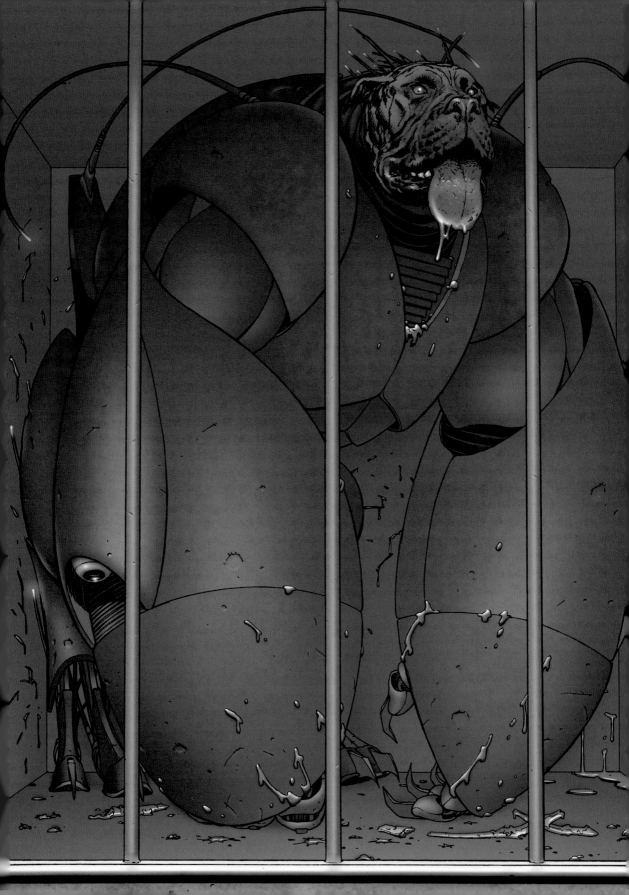

Lost Rabbit

Can you help us find Pirate? He is white with a brown patch over his eye. He likes lettuce and carrots.
Thank you Johnny and Claire

(PLS PHONE - MRS MORTIMER : 555 6783)

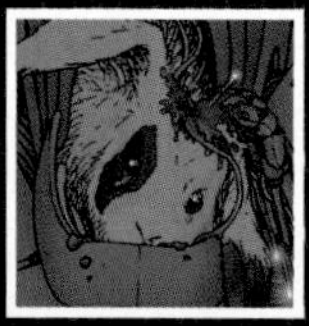

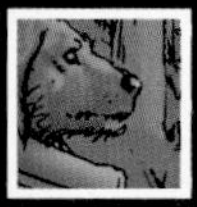

CHAPTER 3

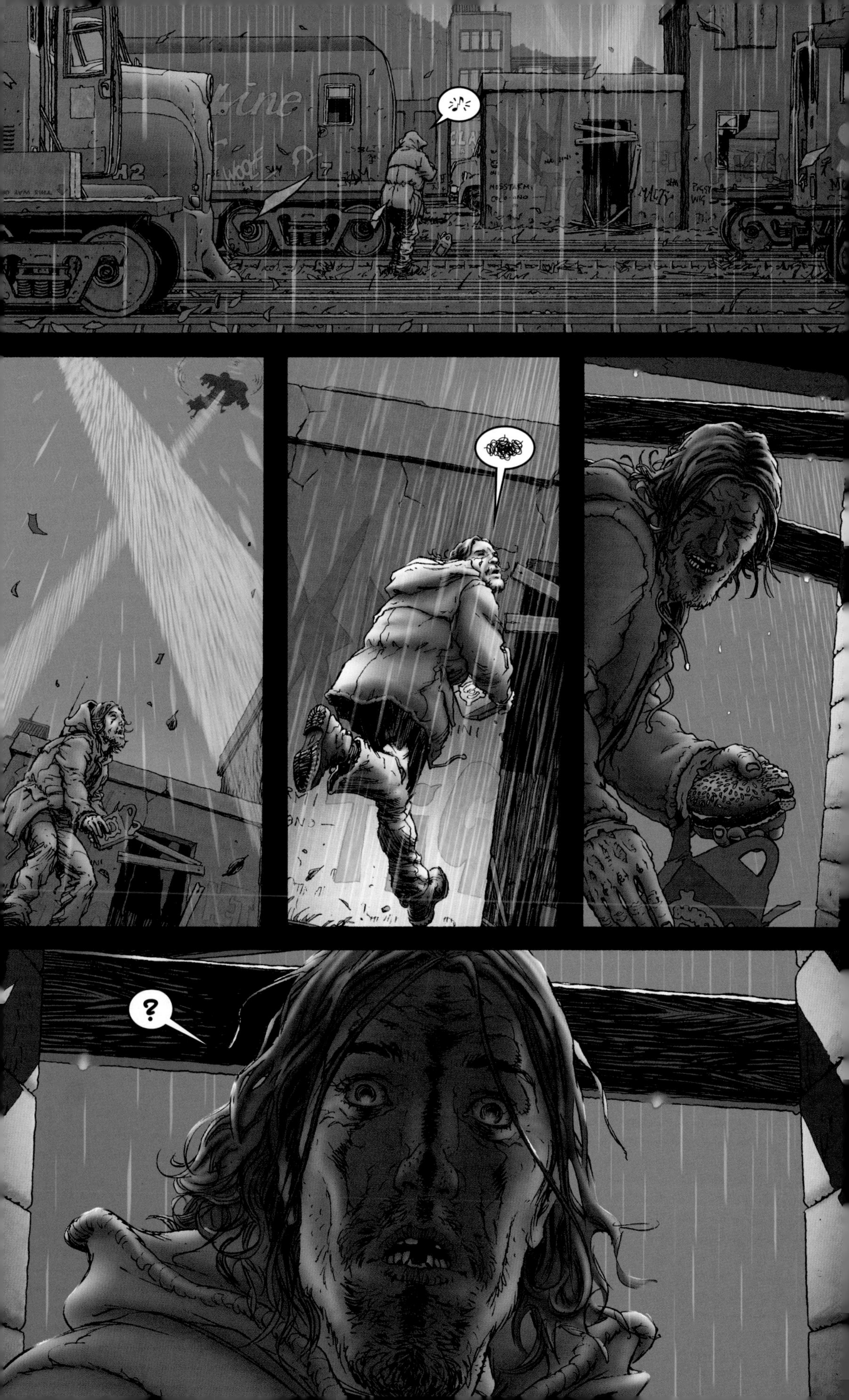
?

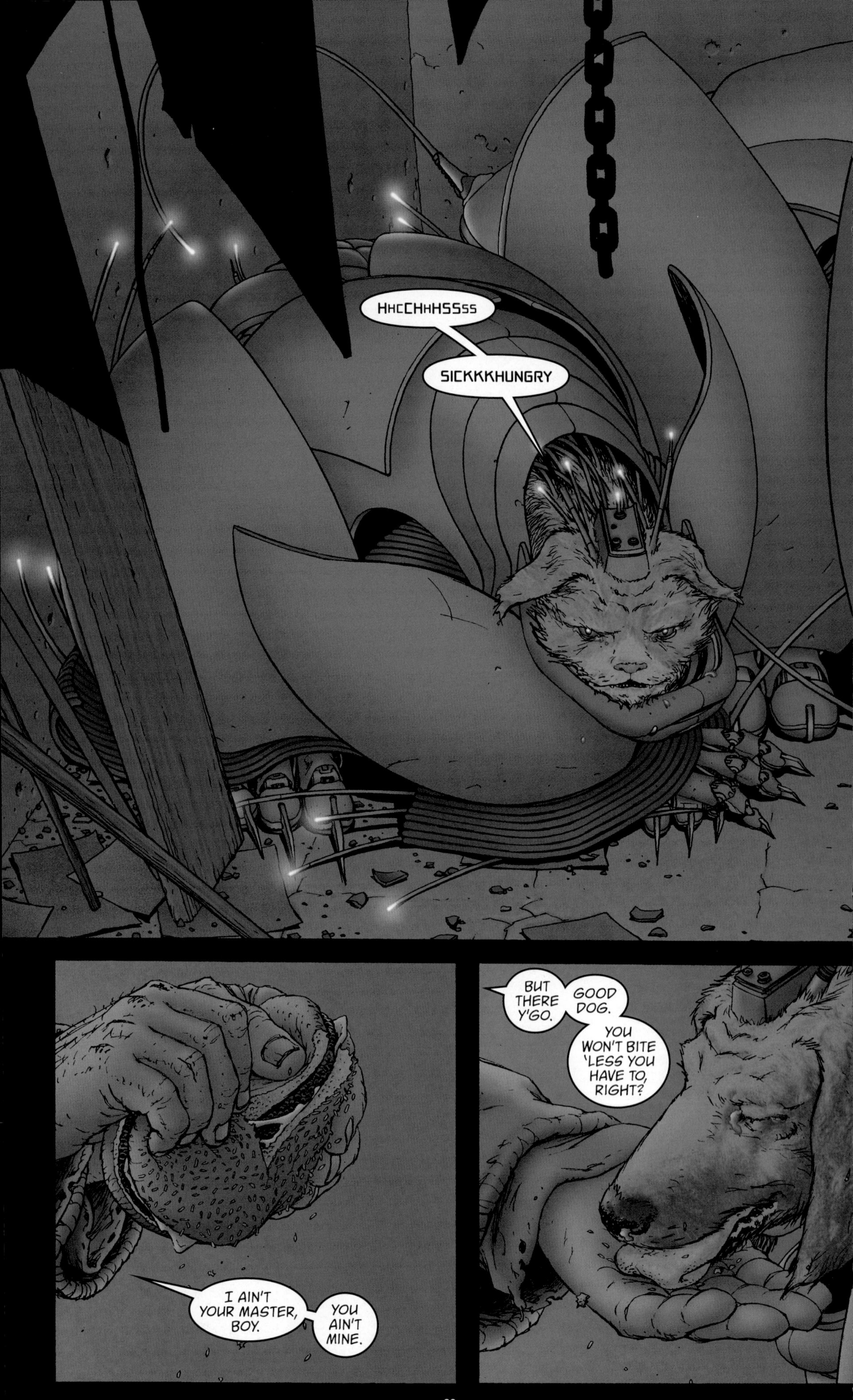
HhcCHhHSSss
SICKKKHUNGRY
I AIN'T YOUR MASTER, BOY.
YOU AIN'T MINE.
BUT THERE Y'GO.
GOOD DOG.
YOU WON'T BITE 'LESS YOU HAVE TO, RIGHT?

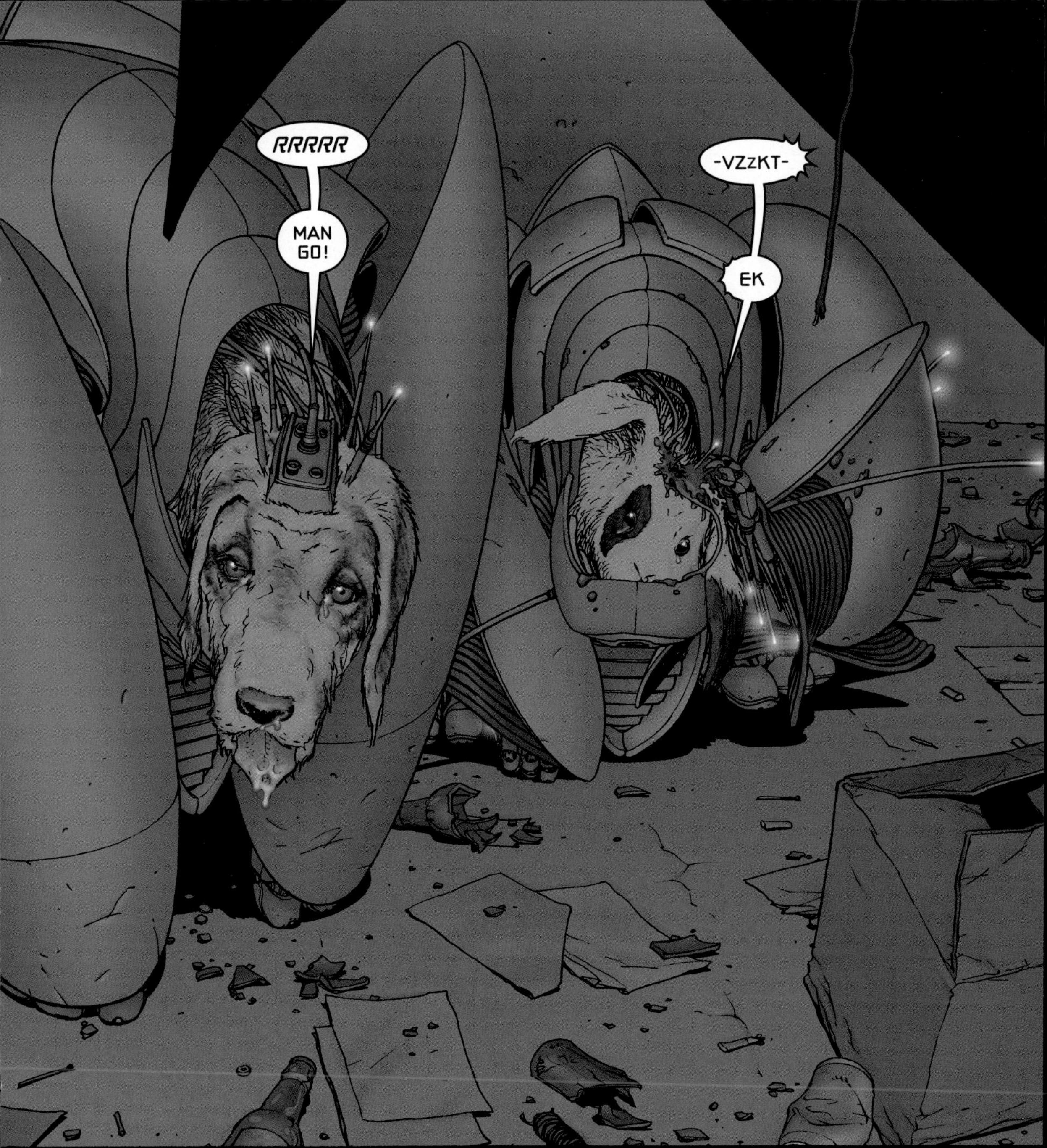
RRRRR
MAN GO!
-VZzKT-
EK

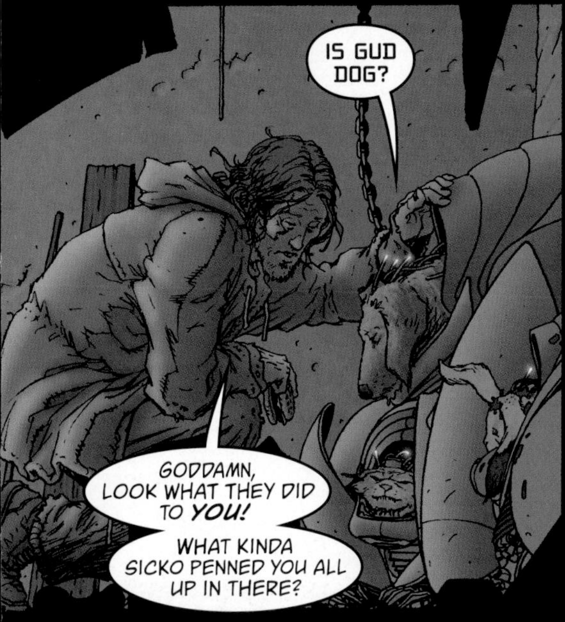
IS GUD DOG?
GODDAMN, LOOK WHAT THEY DID TO YOU!
WHAT KINDA SICKO PENNED YOU ALL UP IN THERE?

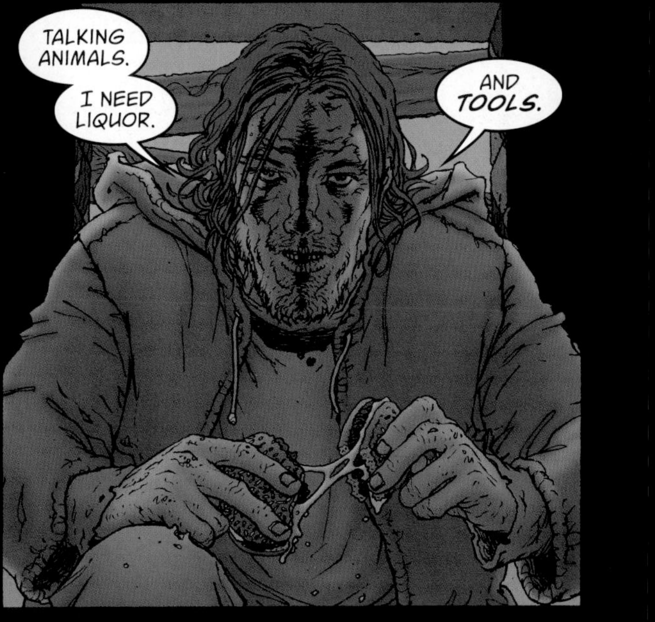
TALKING ANIMALS.
I NEED LIQUOR.
AND TOOLS.

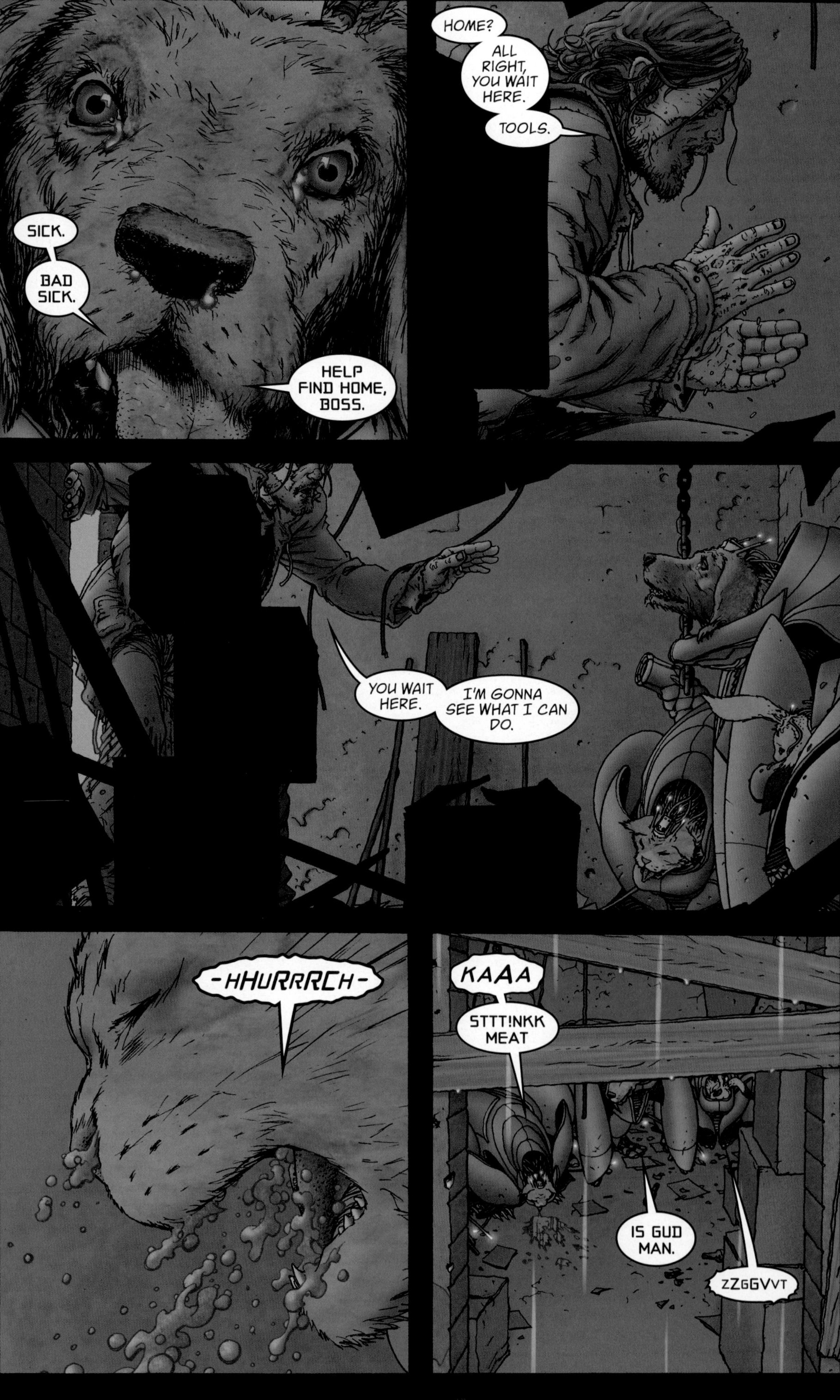
SICK.
BAD SICK.
HELP FIND HOME, BOSS.
HOME?
ALL RIGHT, YOU WAIT HERE.
TOOLS.
YOU WAIT HERE.
I'M GONNA SEE WHAT I CAN DO.
-HHURRRCH-
KAAA
STTT!NKK MEAT
IS GUD MAN.
zZGGVVT

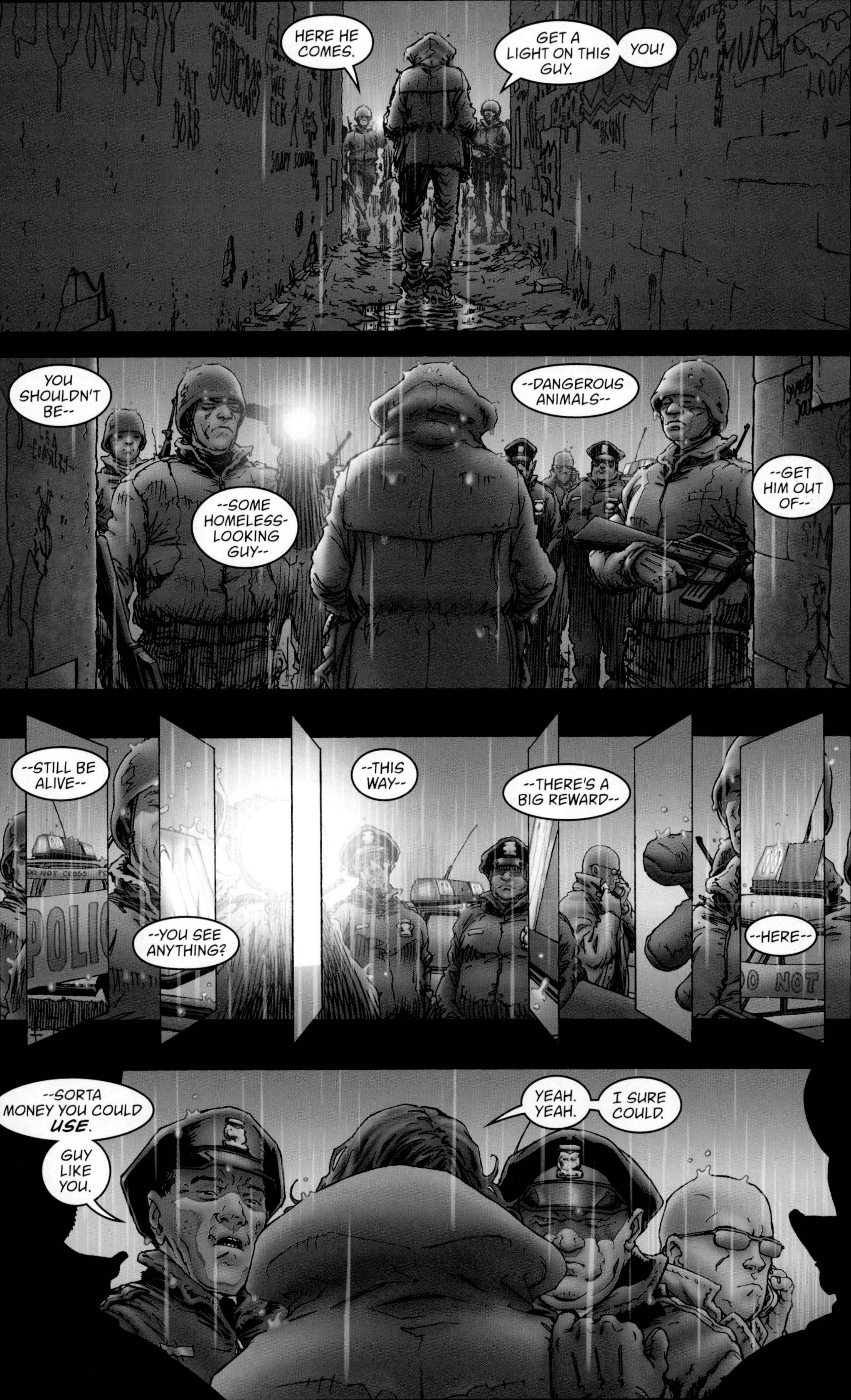
HERE HE COMES.
GET A LIGHT ON THIS GUY.
YOU!
YOU SHOULDN'T BE--
--DANGEROUS ANIMALS--
--SOME HOMELESS-LOOKING GUY--
--GET HIM OUT OF--
--STILL BE ALIVE--
--THIS WAY--
--THERE'S A BIG REWARD--
--YOU SEE ANYTHING?
--HERE--
--SORTA MONEY YOU COULD **USE**.
GUY LIKE YOU.
YEAH. YEAH.
I SURE COULD.

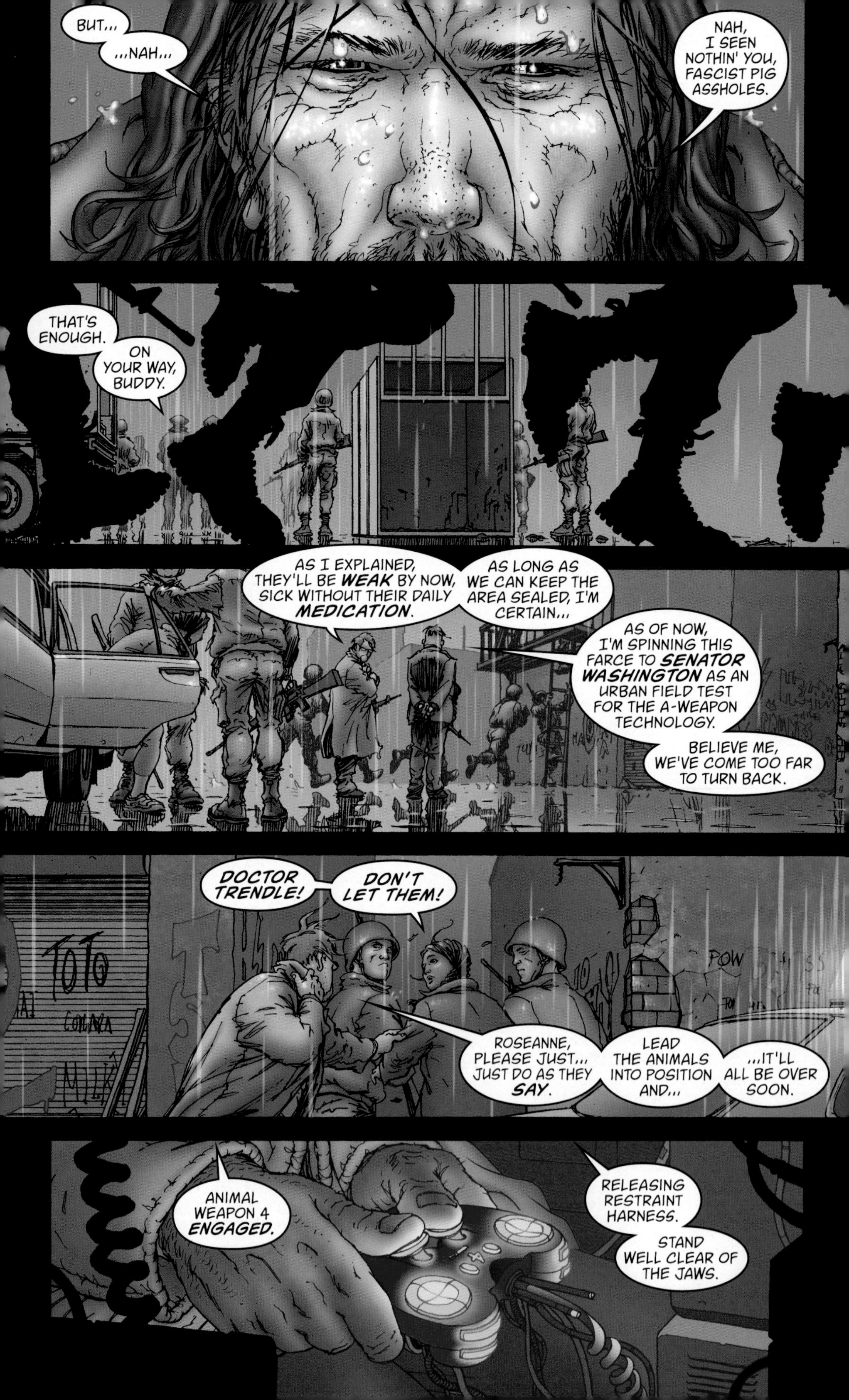
BUT...
...NAH...
NAH, I SEEN NOTHIN' YOU, FASCIST PIG ASSHOLES.
THAT'S ENOUGH.
ON YOUR WAY, BUDDY.
AS I EXPLAINED, THEY'LL BE WEAK BY NOW, SICK WITHOUT THEIR DAILY MEDICATION.
AS LONG AS WE CAN KEEP THE AREA SEALED, I'M CERTAIN...
AS OF NOW, I'M SPINNING THIS FARCE TO SENATOR WASHINGTON AS AN URBAN FIELD TEST FOR THE A-WEAPON TECHNOLOGY.
BELIEVE ME, WE'VE COME TOO FAR TO TURN BACK.
DOCTOR TRENDLE!
DON'T LET THEM!
ROSEANNE, PLEASE JUST... JUST DO AS THEY SAY.
LEAD THE ANIMALS INTO POSITION AND...
...IT'LL ALL BE OVER SOON.
ANIMAL WEAPON 4 ENGAGED.
RELEASING RESTRAINT HARNESS.
STAND WELL CLEAR OF THE JAWS.

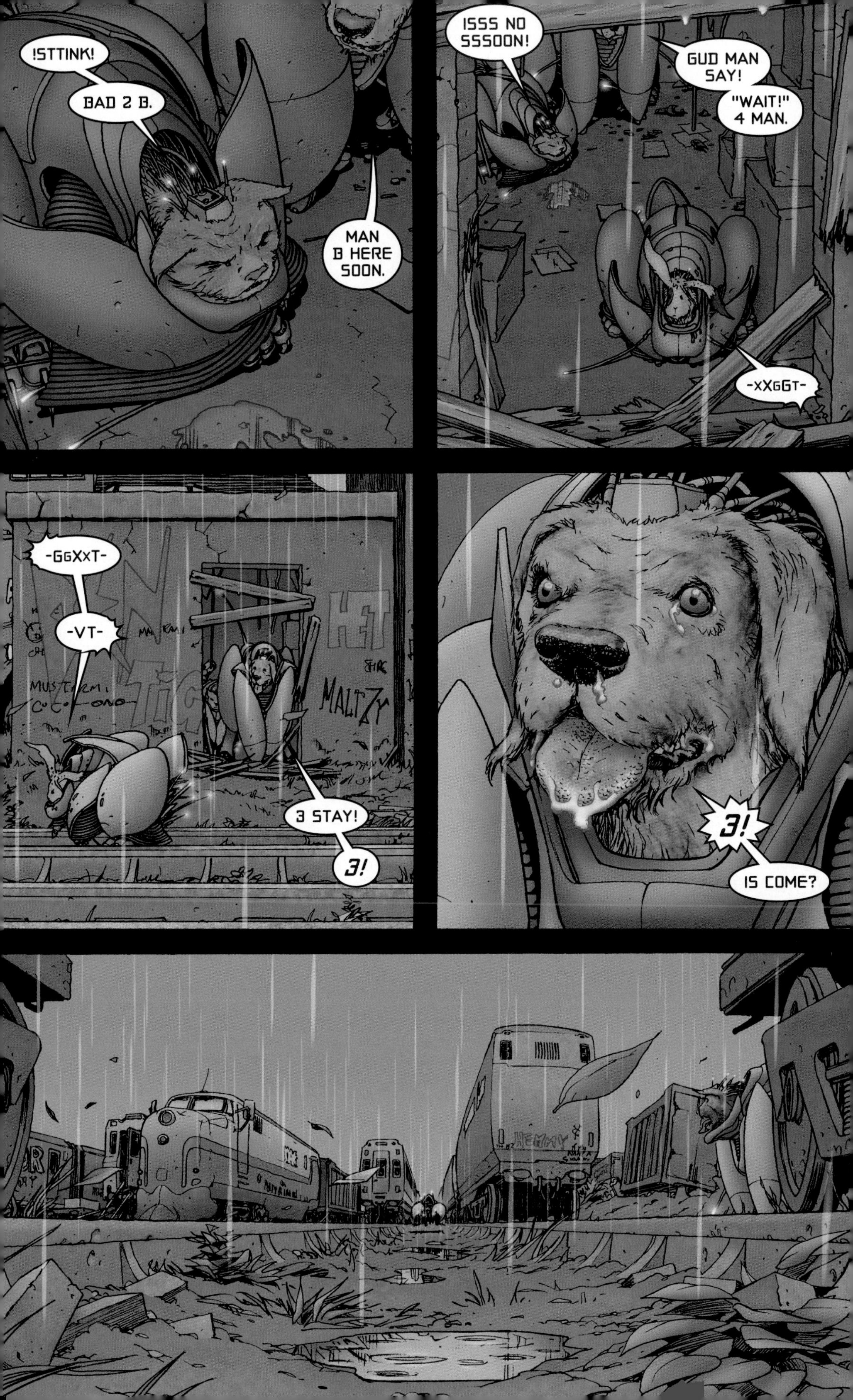
!STTINK!
BAD 2 B.
MAN B HERE SOON.
ISSS NO SSSOON!
GUD MAN SAY!
"WAIT!" 4 MAN.
-XXGGT-
-GGXXT-
-VT-
3 STAY!
3!
3!
IS COME?

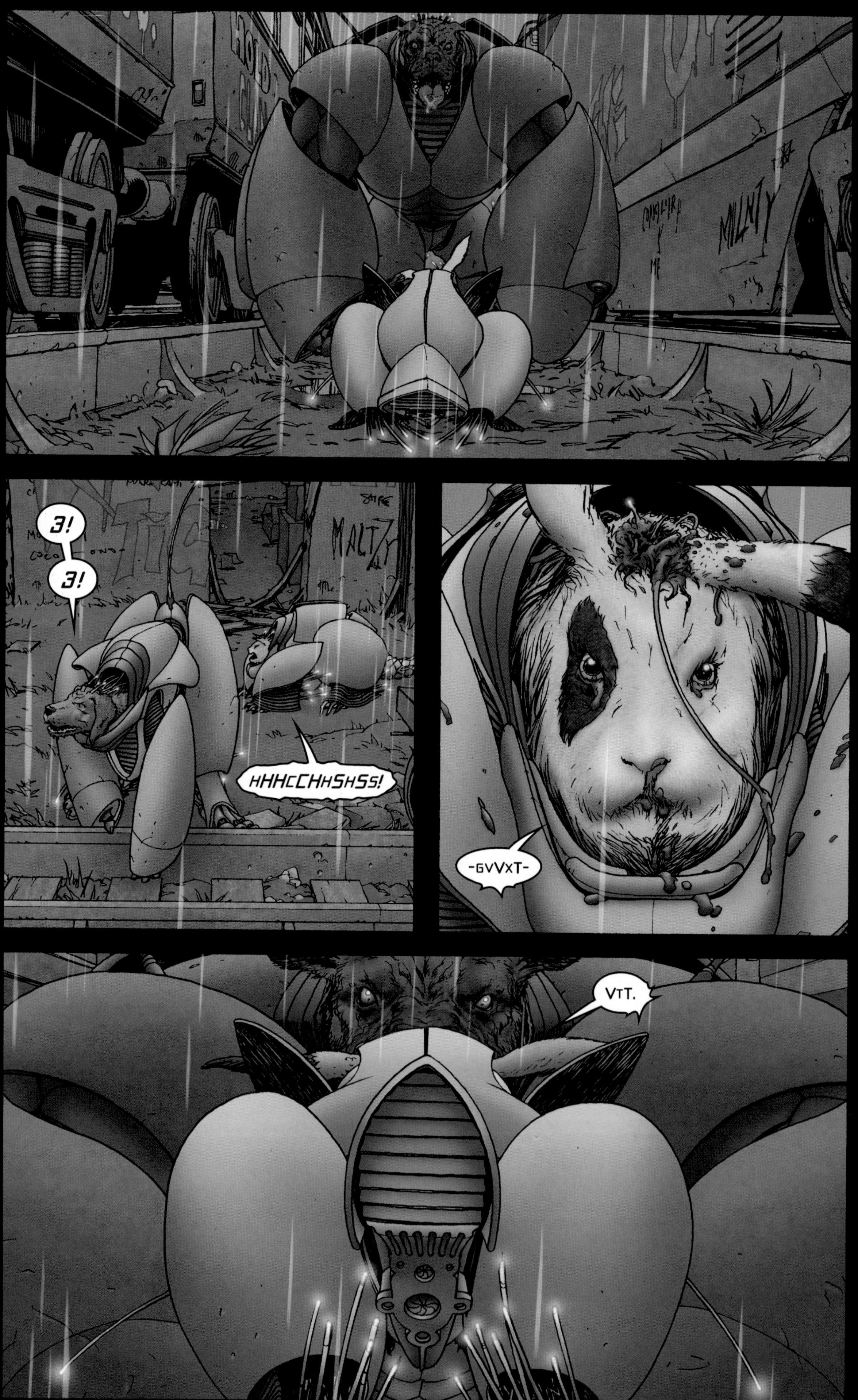
3!
3!
HHHCCHHSHSS!
-GVVXT-
VTT.

SNNNUURFF
AFRAID SMELL!
BIG AFRAID BIG
3!
RUN!
3!

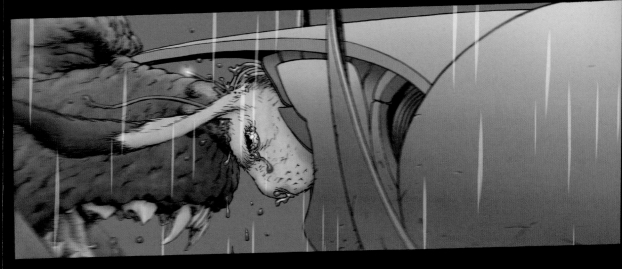

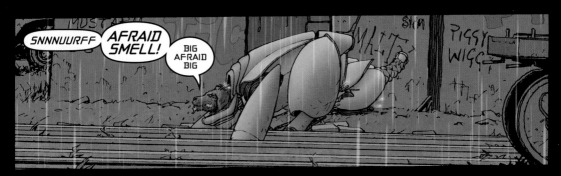

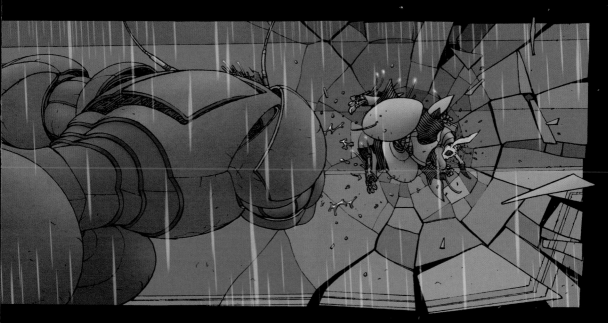

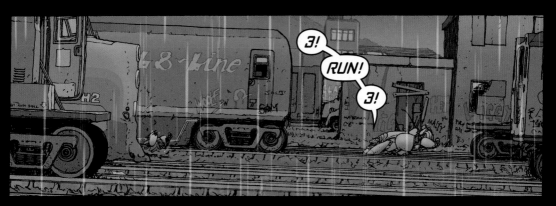

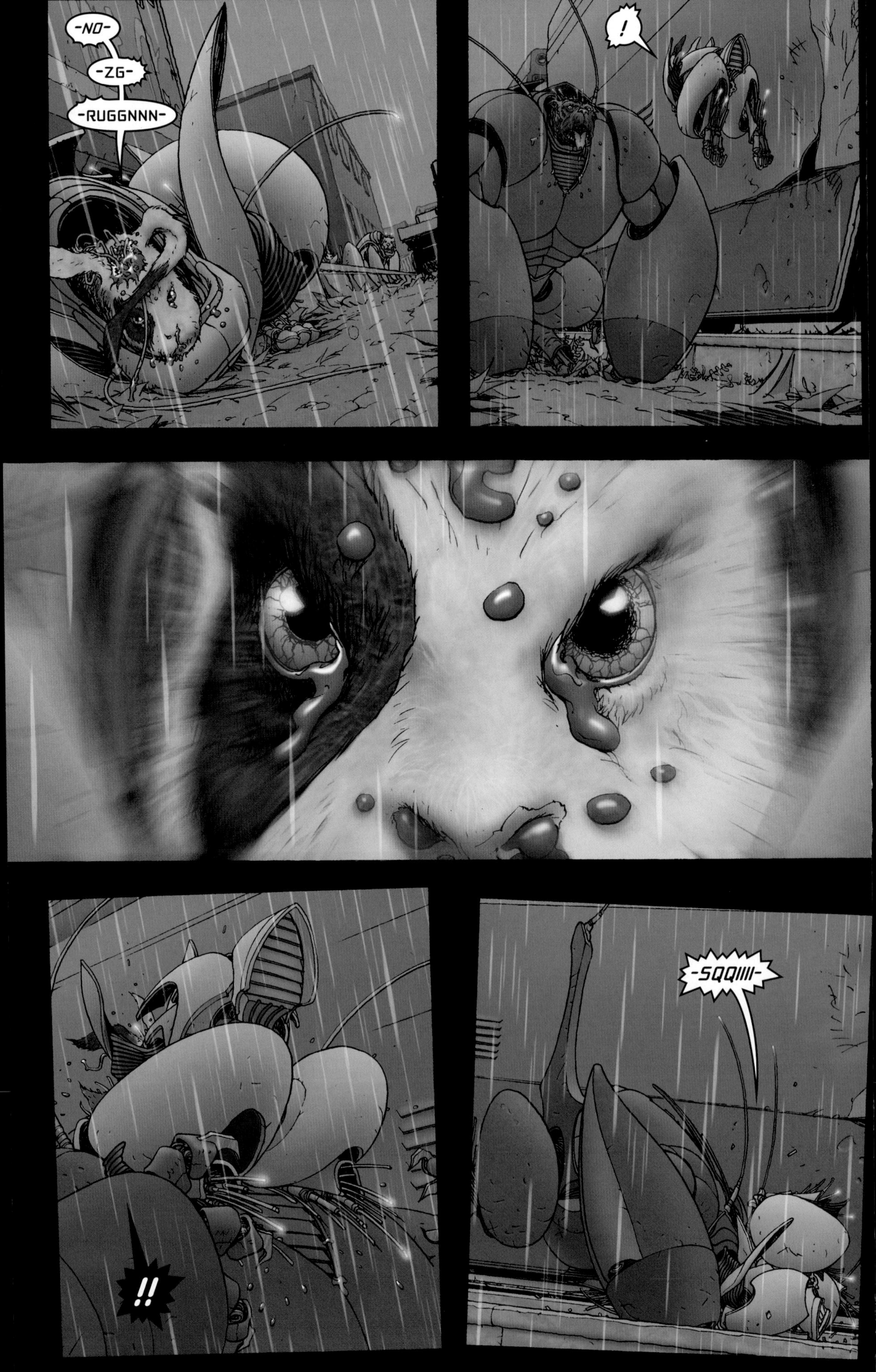
-NO-
-ZG-
-RUGGNNN-
!
!!
-SQQIIII-

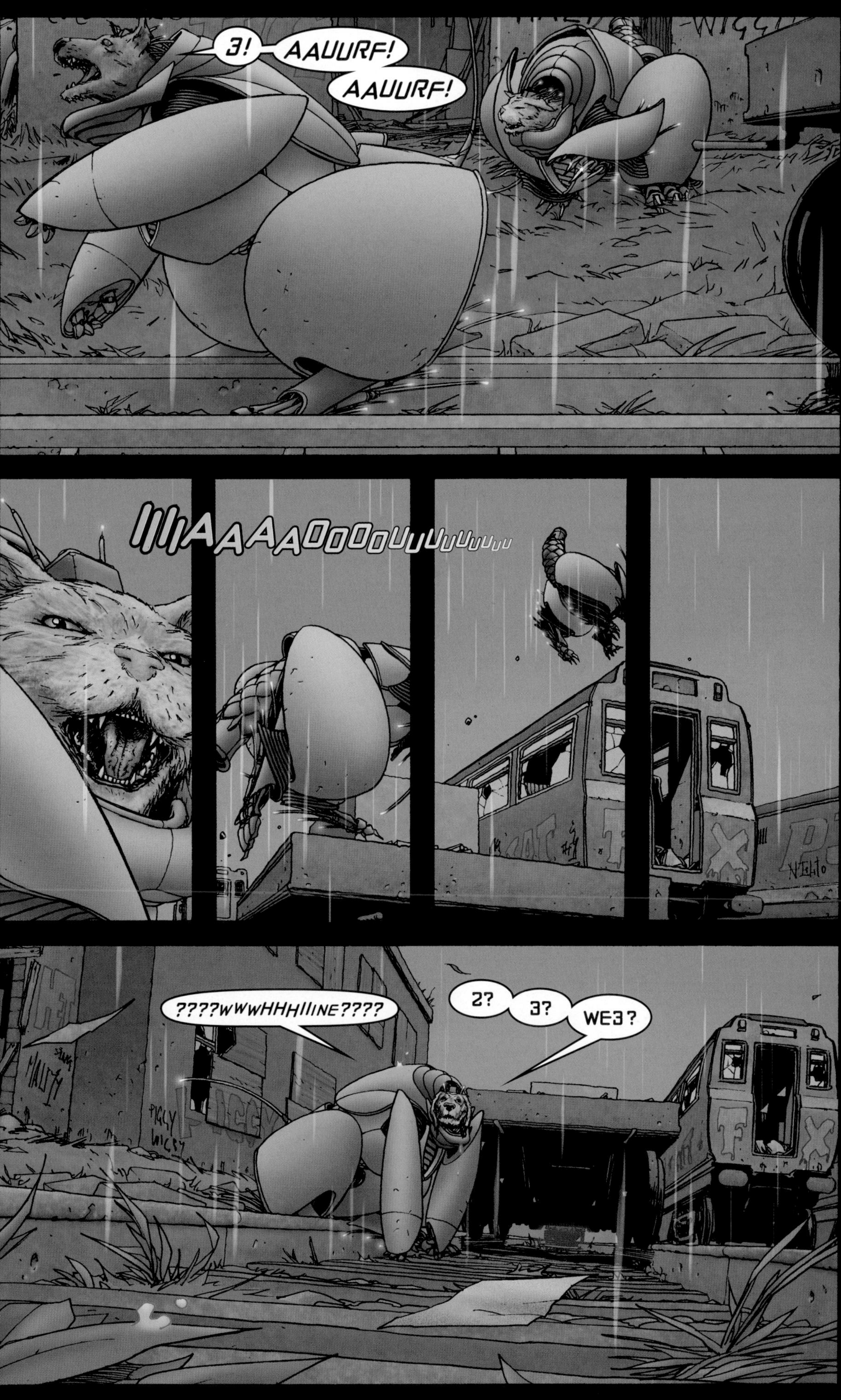
3! AAUURF!
AAUURF!
IIIIAAAAOOOOOUUUUUUUU
????WWWHHHIIINE????
2?
3?
WE3?

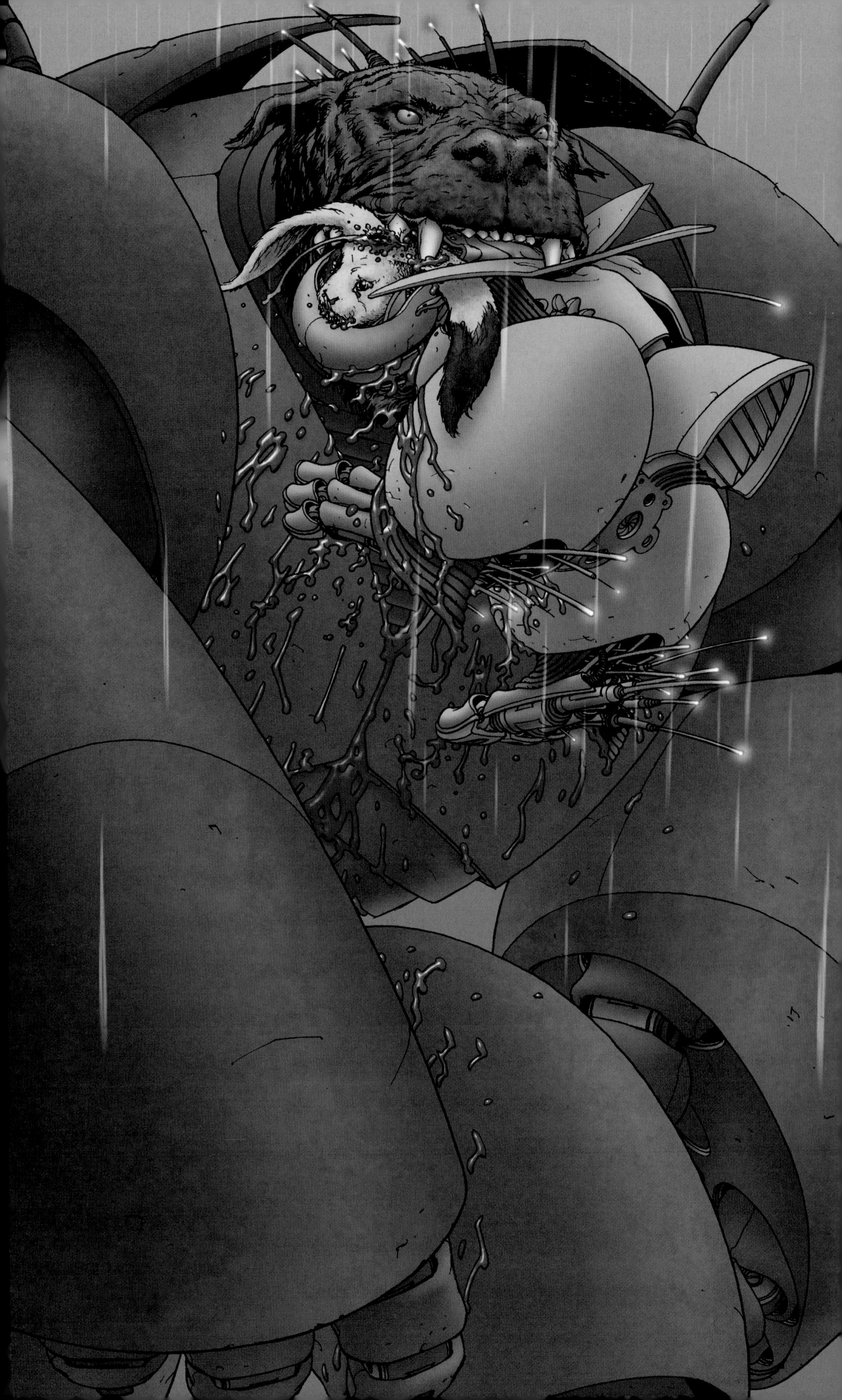

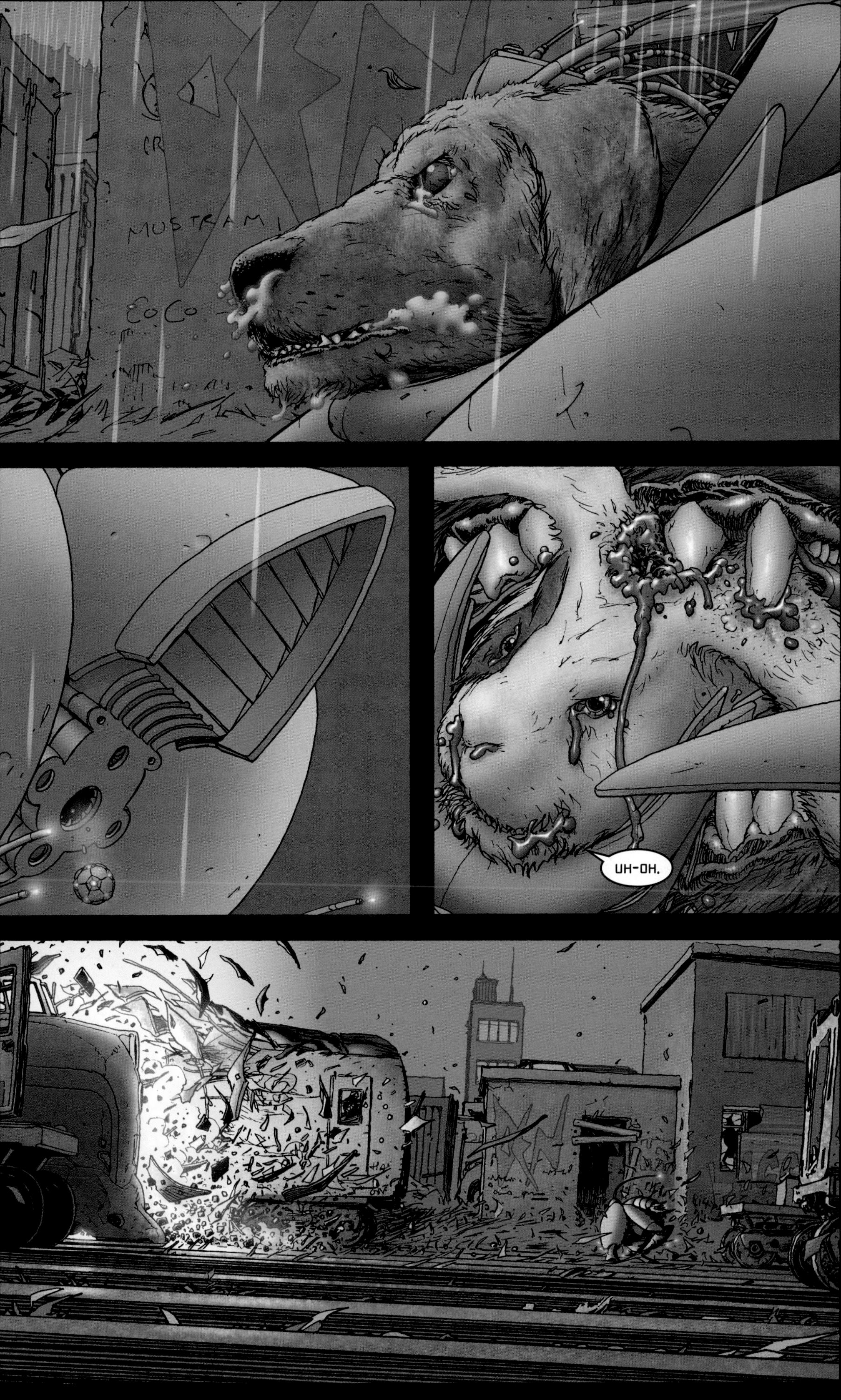
MUSTRAM
COCO
UH-OH.

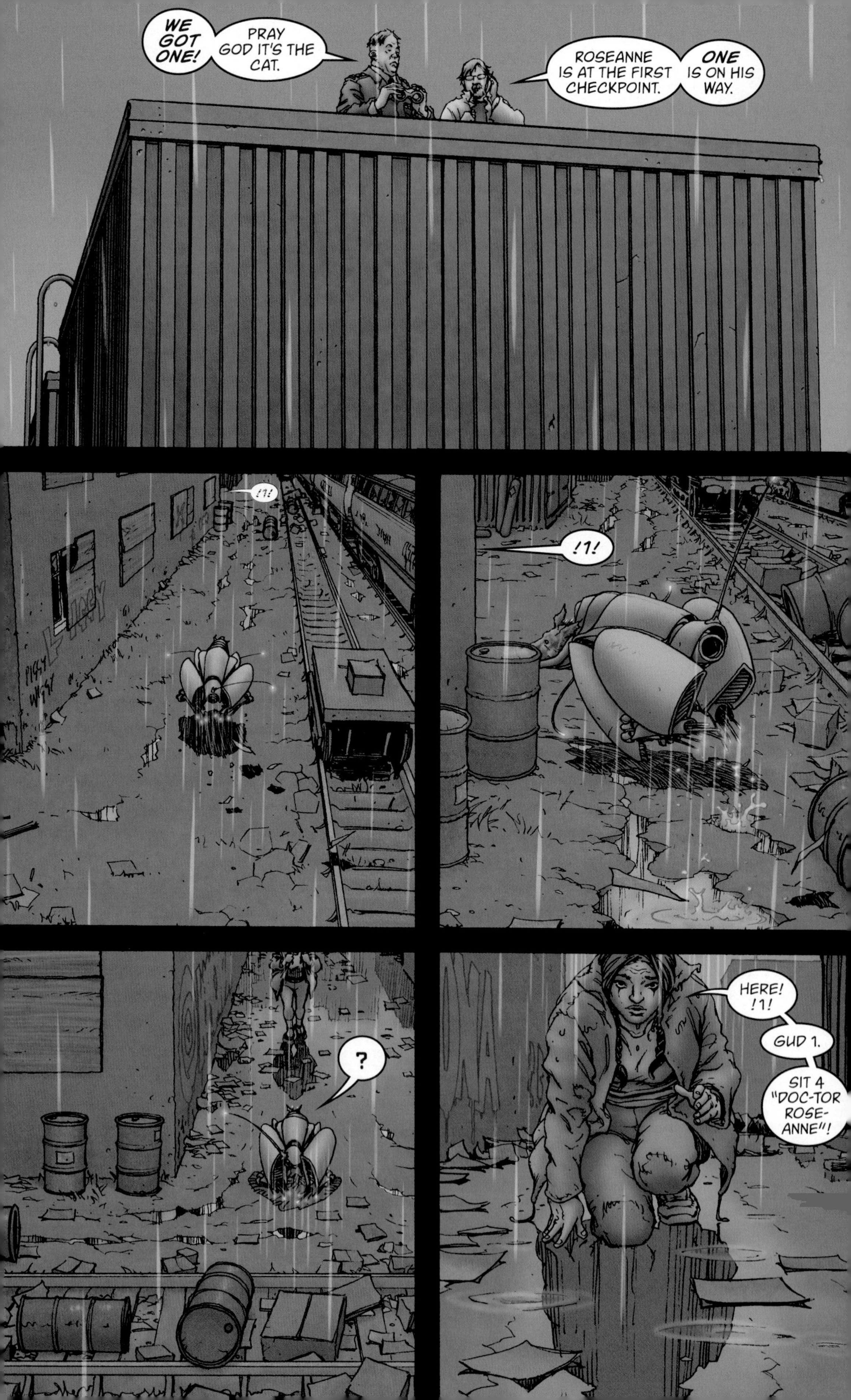
WE GOT ONE!
PRAY GOD IT'S THE CAT.
ROSEANNE IS AT THE FIRST CHECKPOINT.
ONE IS ON HIS WAY.
!1!
!1!
?
HERE! !1!
GUD 1.
SIT 4 "DOC-TOR ROSE-ANNE"!

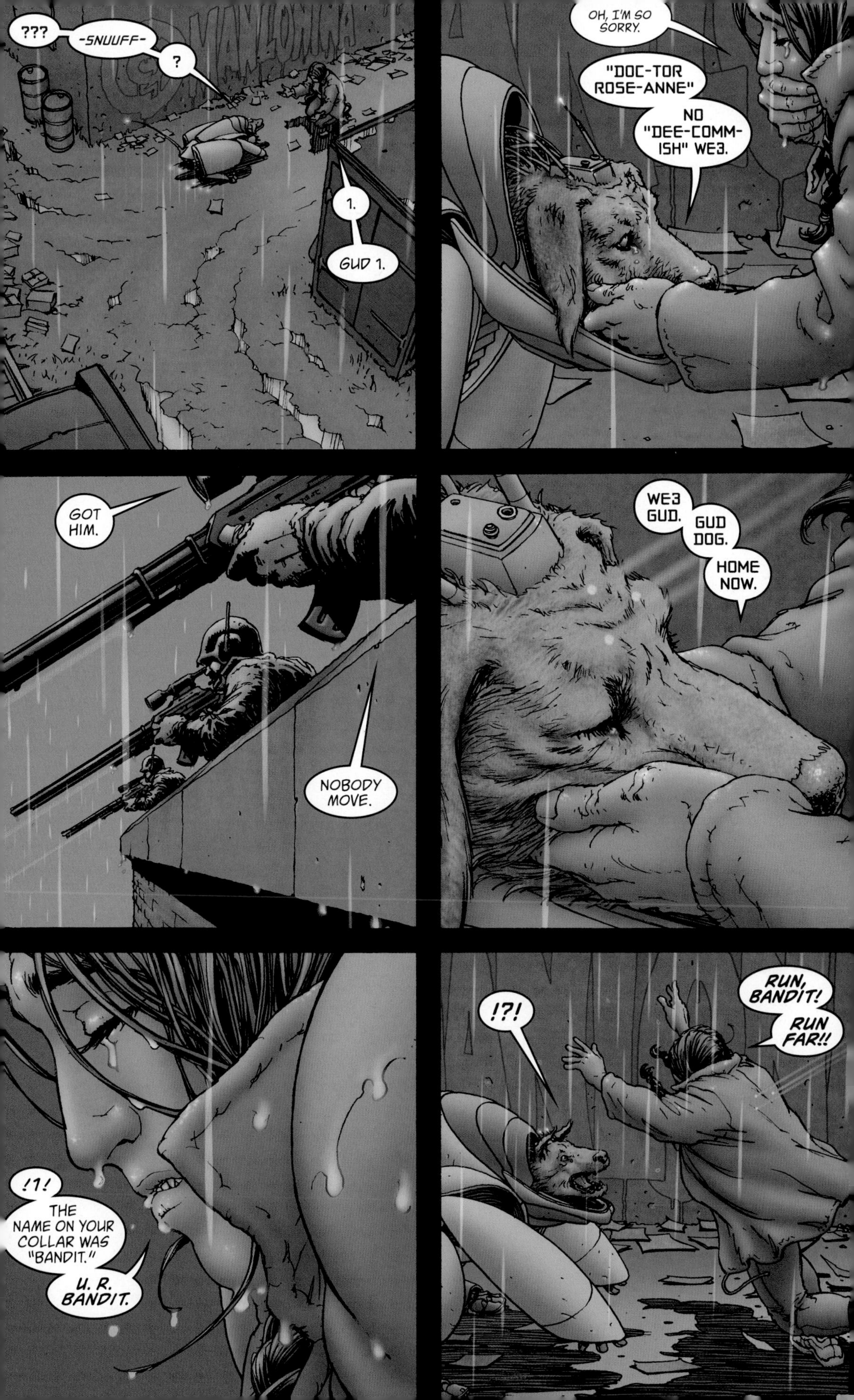
???
-SNUUFF-
?
1.
GUD 1.
OH, I'M SO SORRY.
"DOC-TOR ROSE-ANNE"
NO "DEE-COMM-ISH" WE3.
GOT HIM.
NOBODY MOVE.
WE3 GUD.
GUD DOG.
HOME NOW.
!1!
THE NAME ON YOUR COLLAR WAS "BANDIT."
U. R. BANDIT.
!?!
RUN, BANDIT!
RUN FAR!!

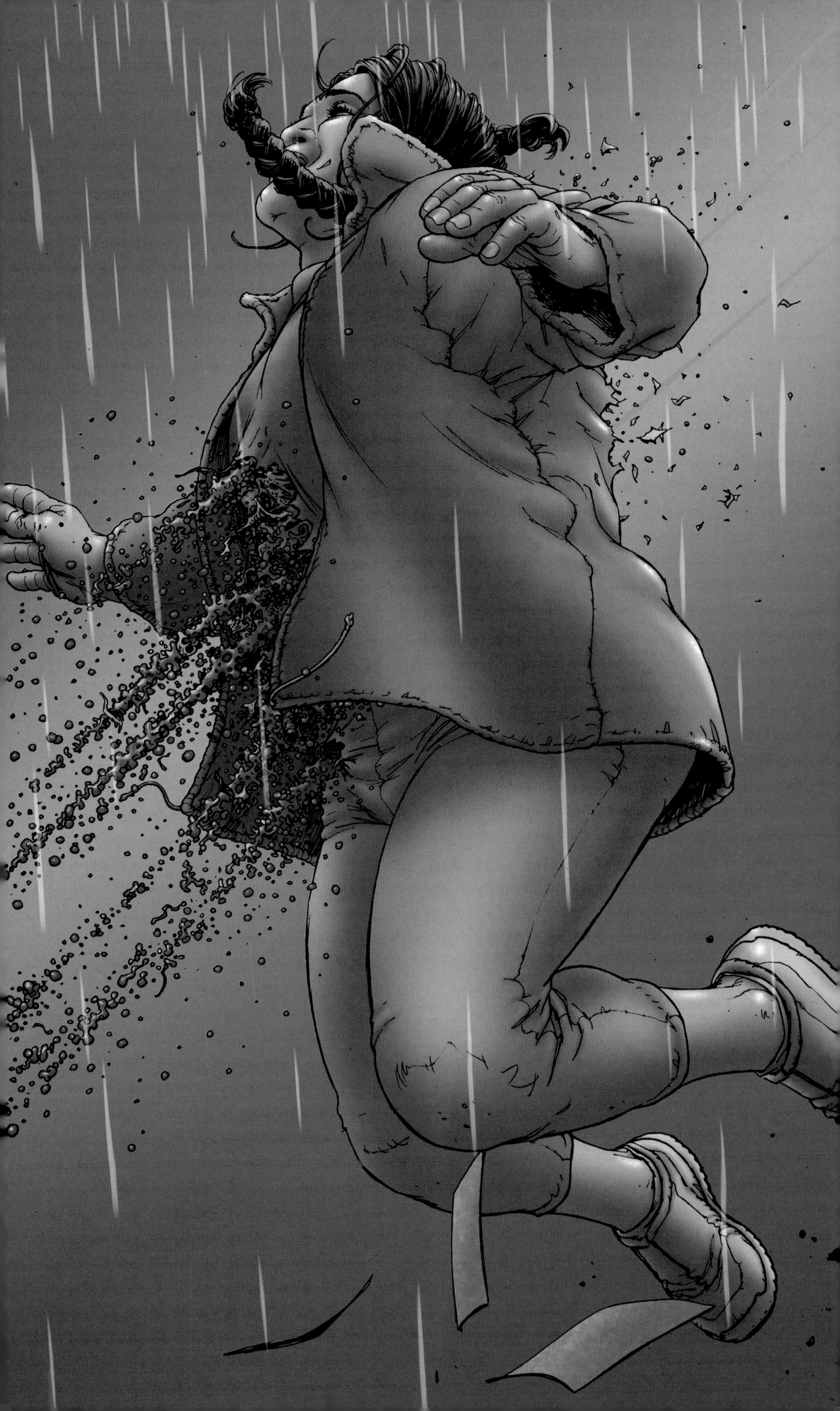

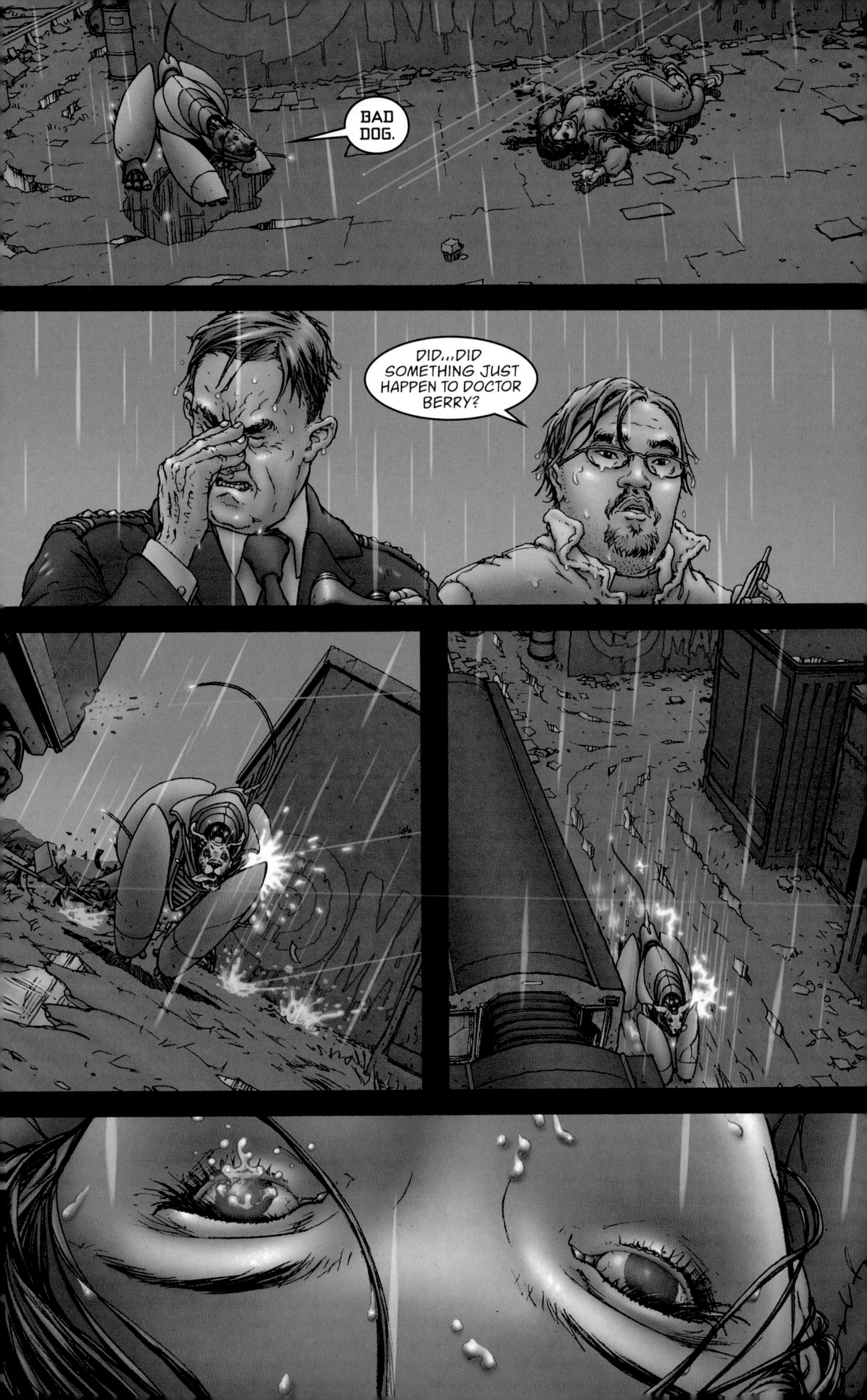
BAD DOG.
DID...DID SOMETHING JUST HAPPEN TO DOCTOR BERRY?

BAD DOG.

BAD DOG.

BAD DOG.

BAD!

DOG!

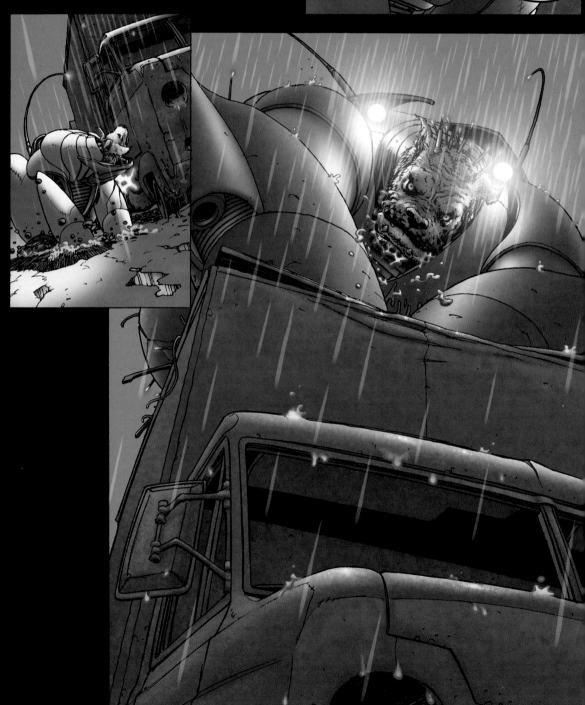

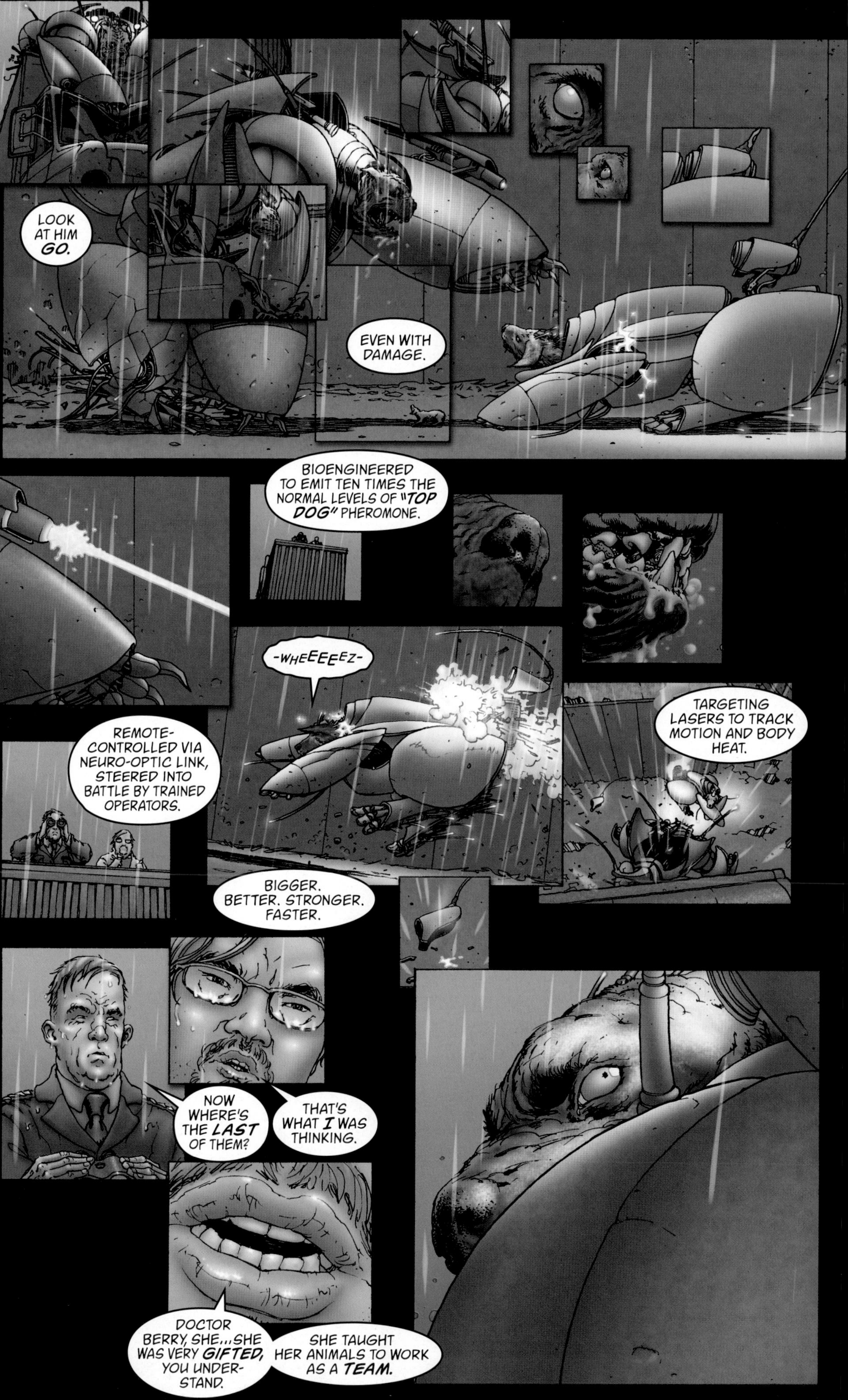
LOOK AT HIM GO.
EVEN WITH DAMAGE.
BIOENGINEERED TO EMIT TEN TIMES THE NORMAL LEVELS OF "TOP DOG" PHEROMONE.
-WHEEEEEZ-
REMOTE-CONTROLLED VIA NEURO-OPTIC LINK, STEERED INTO BATTLE BY TRAINED OPERATORS.
TARGETING LASERS TO TRACK MOTION AND BODY HEAT.
BIGGER. BETTER. STRONGER. FASTER.
NOW WHERE'S THE LAST OF THEM?
THAT'S WHAT I WAS THINKING.
DOCTOR BERRY, SHE...SHE WAS VERY GIFTED, YOU UNDER-STAND.
SHE TAUGHT HER ANIMALS TO WORK AS A TEAM.

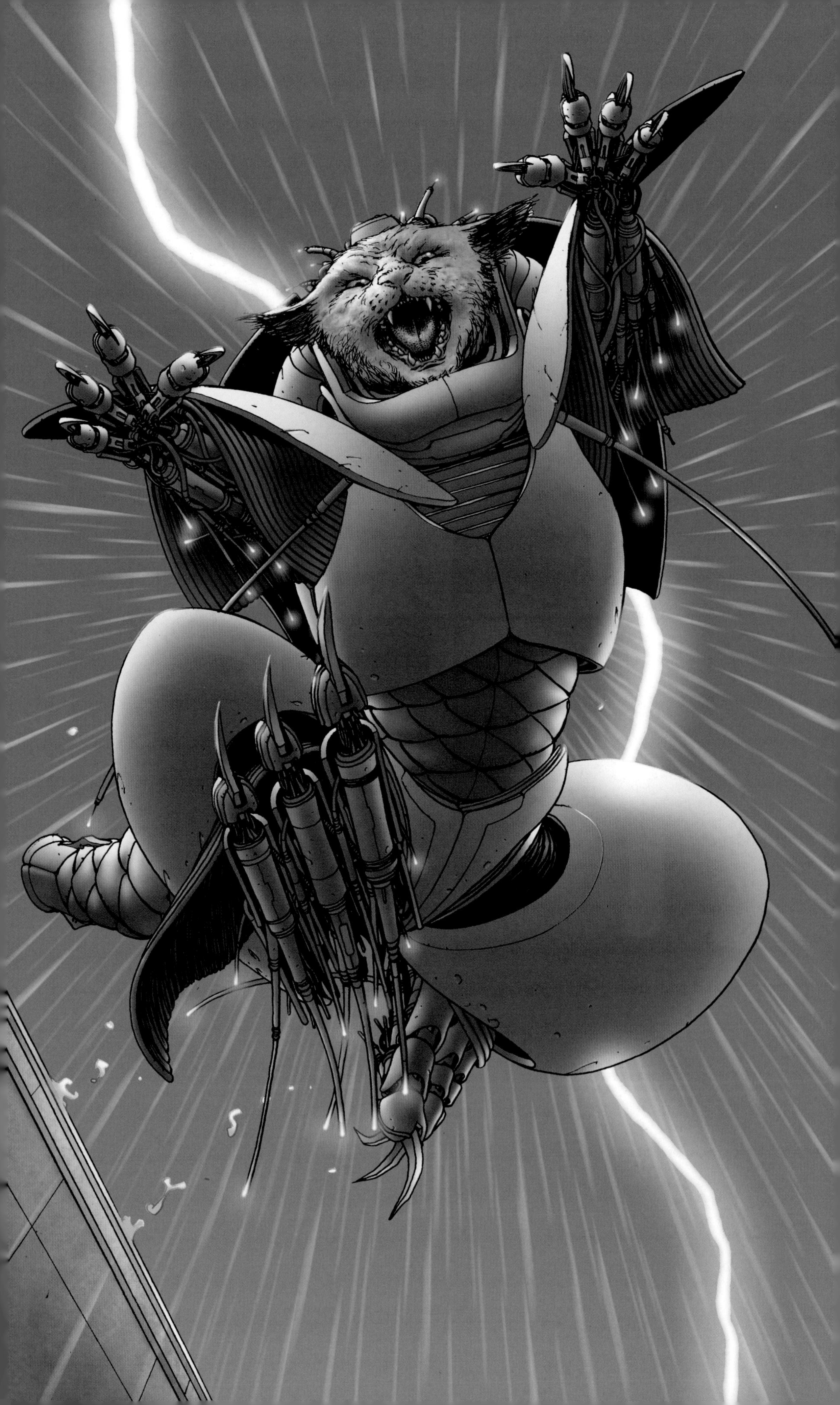

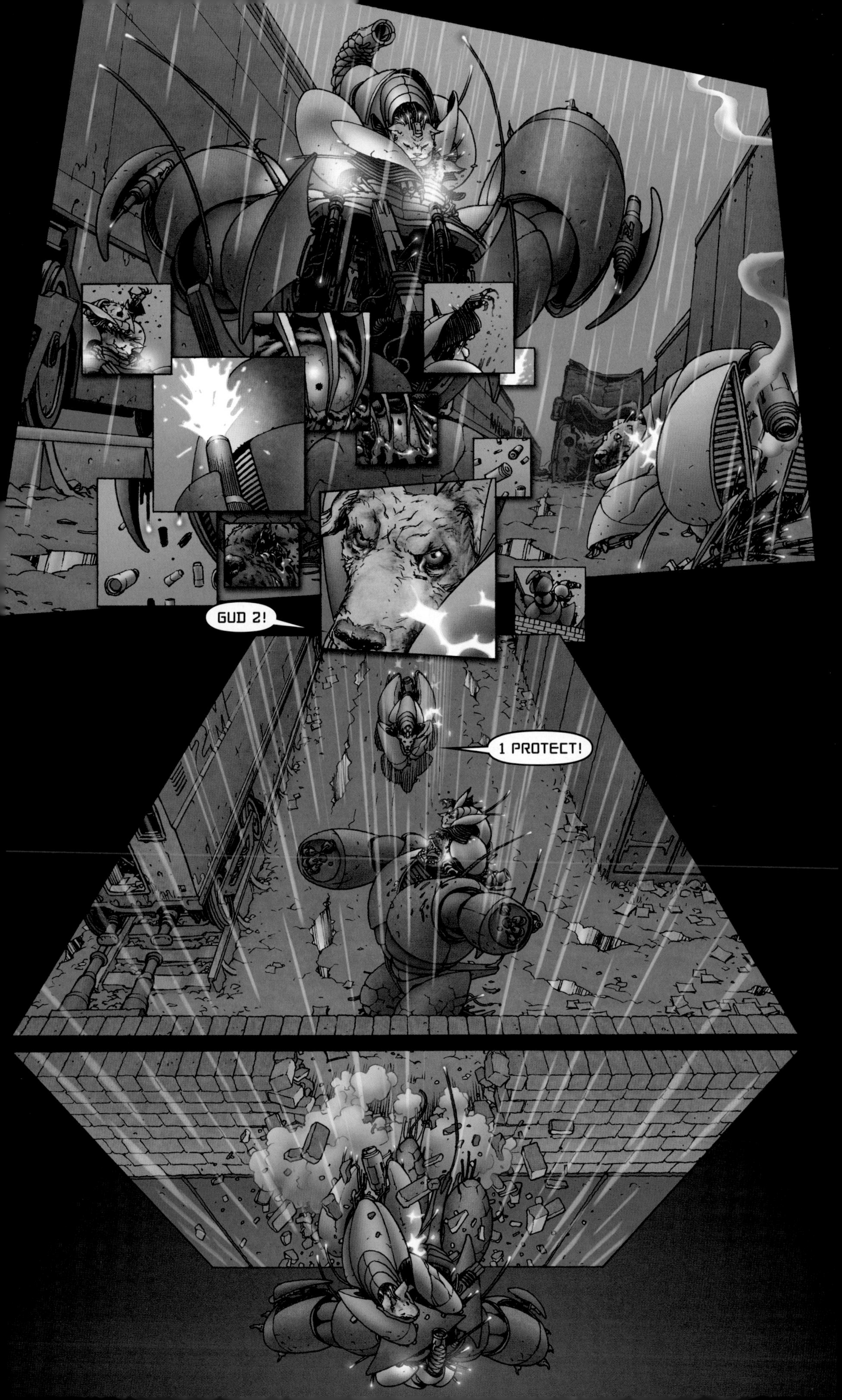
GUD 2!
1 PROTECT!

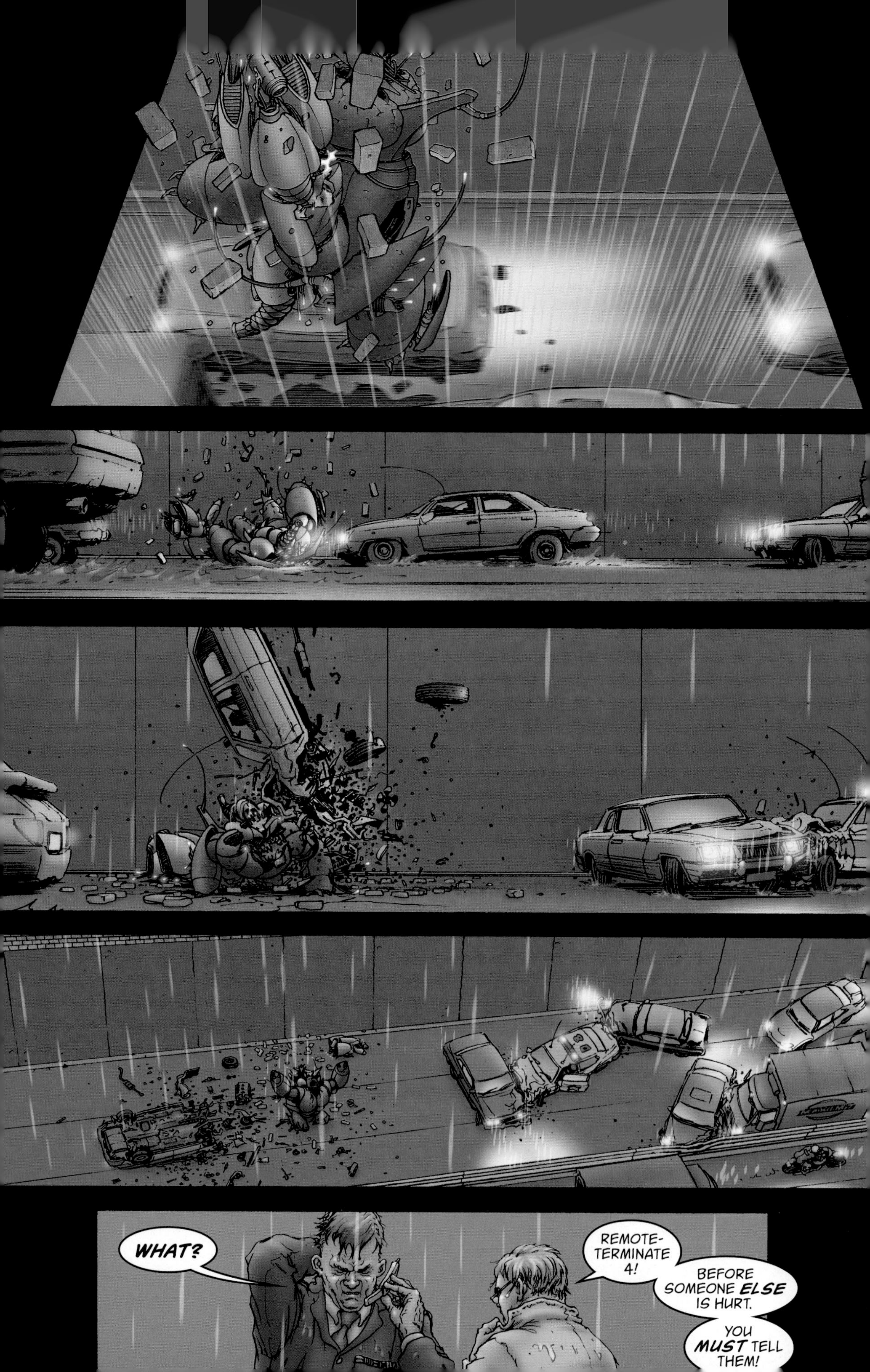

WHAT?
REMOTE-TERMINATE 4!
BEFORE SOMEONE ELSE IS HURT.
YOU MUST TELL THEM!

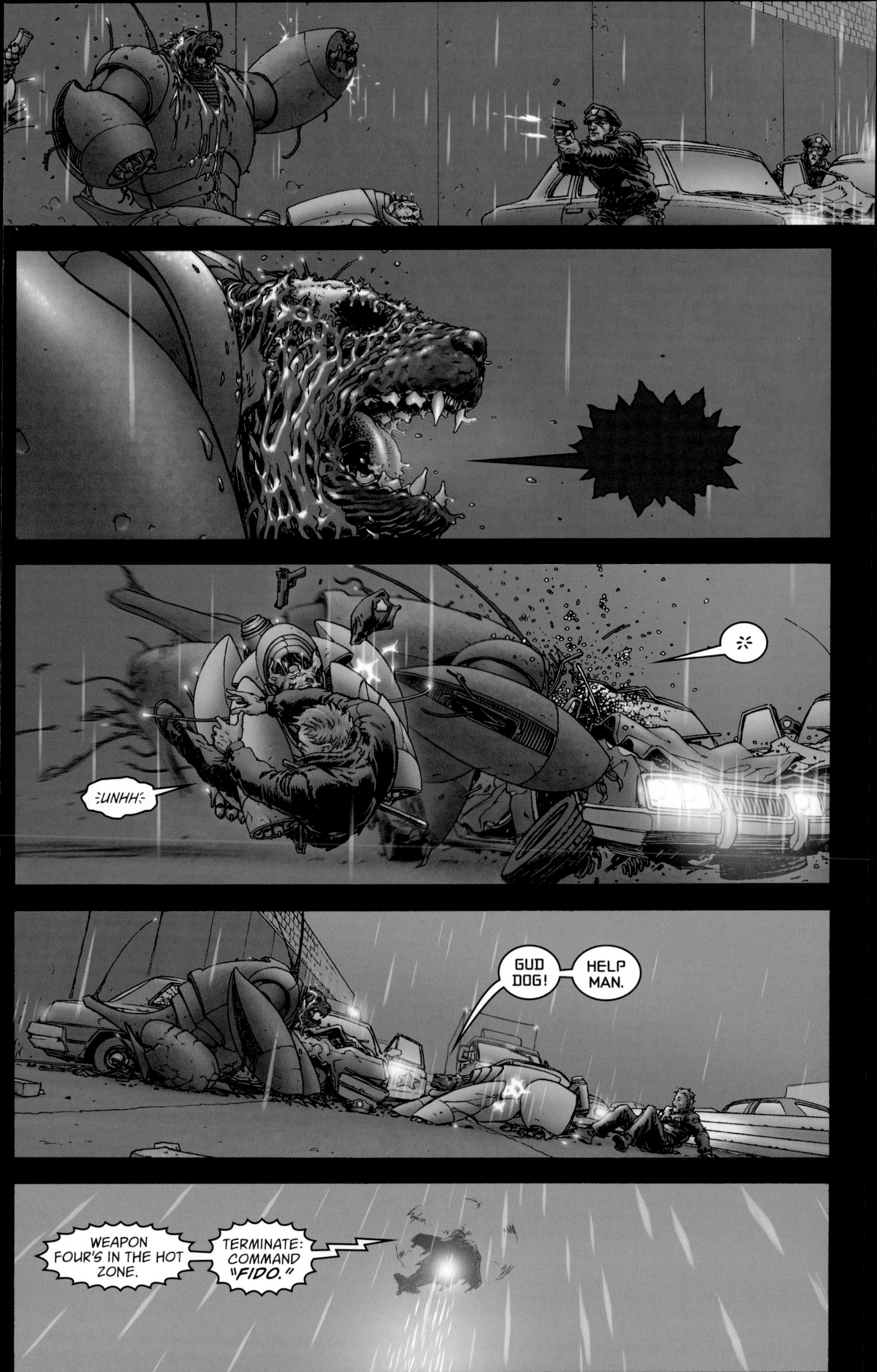
UNHH
GUD DOG!
HELP MAN.
WEAPON FOUR'S IN THE HOT ZONE.
TERMINATE: COMMAND "FIDO."

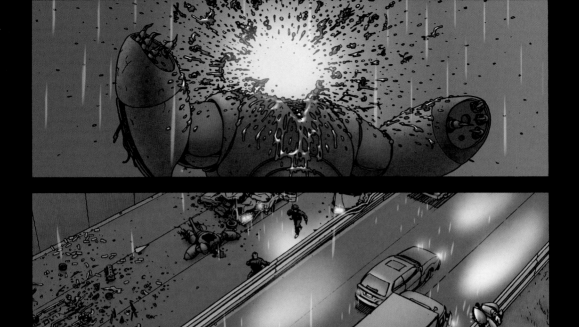

DAMN THING ALMOST ATE A POLICE OFFICER.

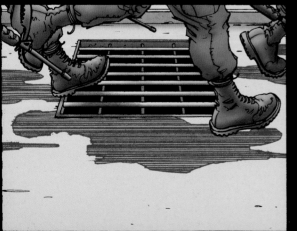

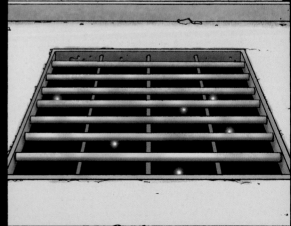

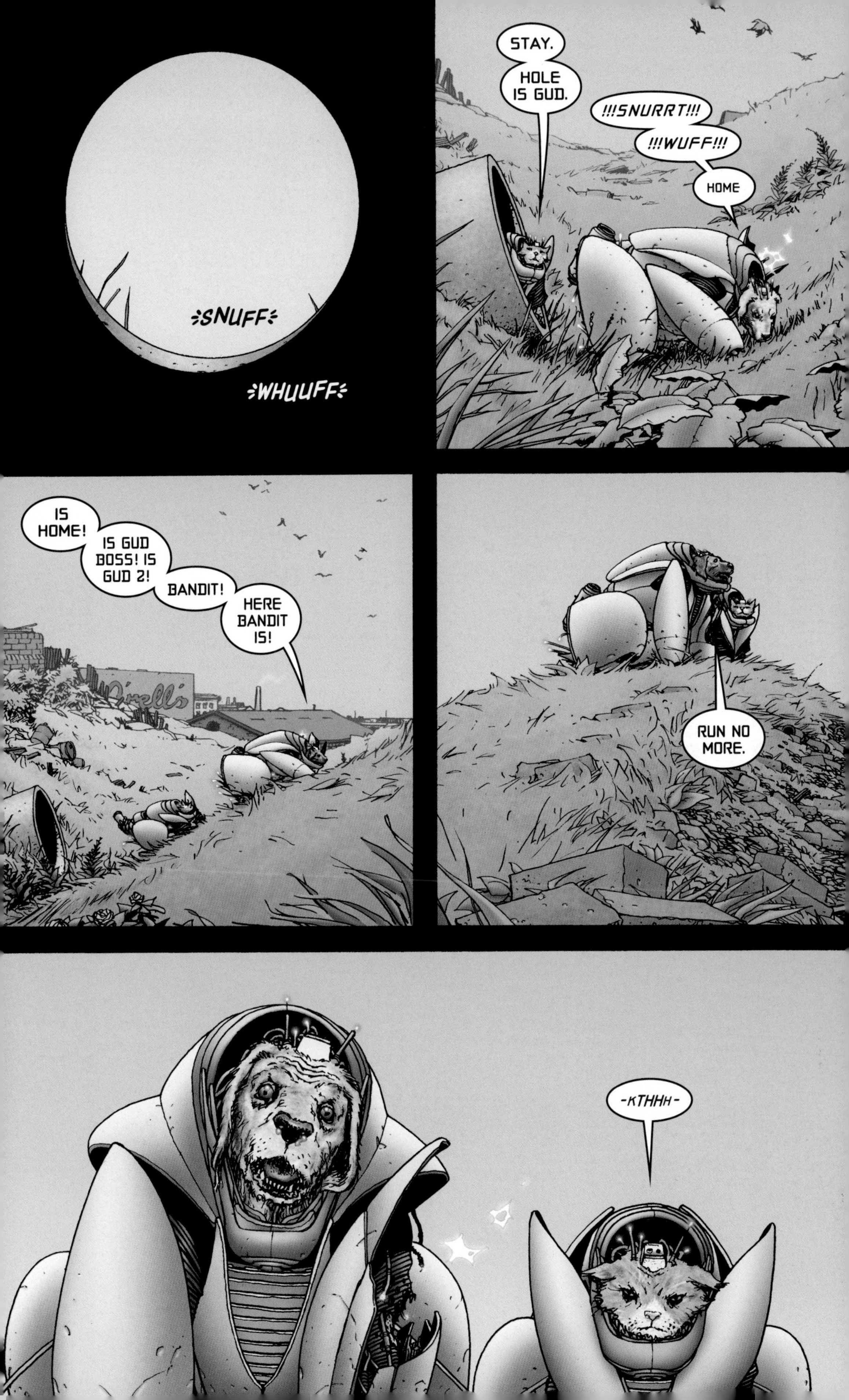
SNUFF
WHUUFF
STAY.
HOLE IS GUD.
!!!SNURRT!!!
!!!WUFF!!!
HOME
IS HOME!
IS GUD BOSS! IS GUD 2!
BANDIT!
HERE BANDIT IS!
RUN NO MORE.
-KTHHH-

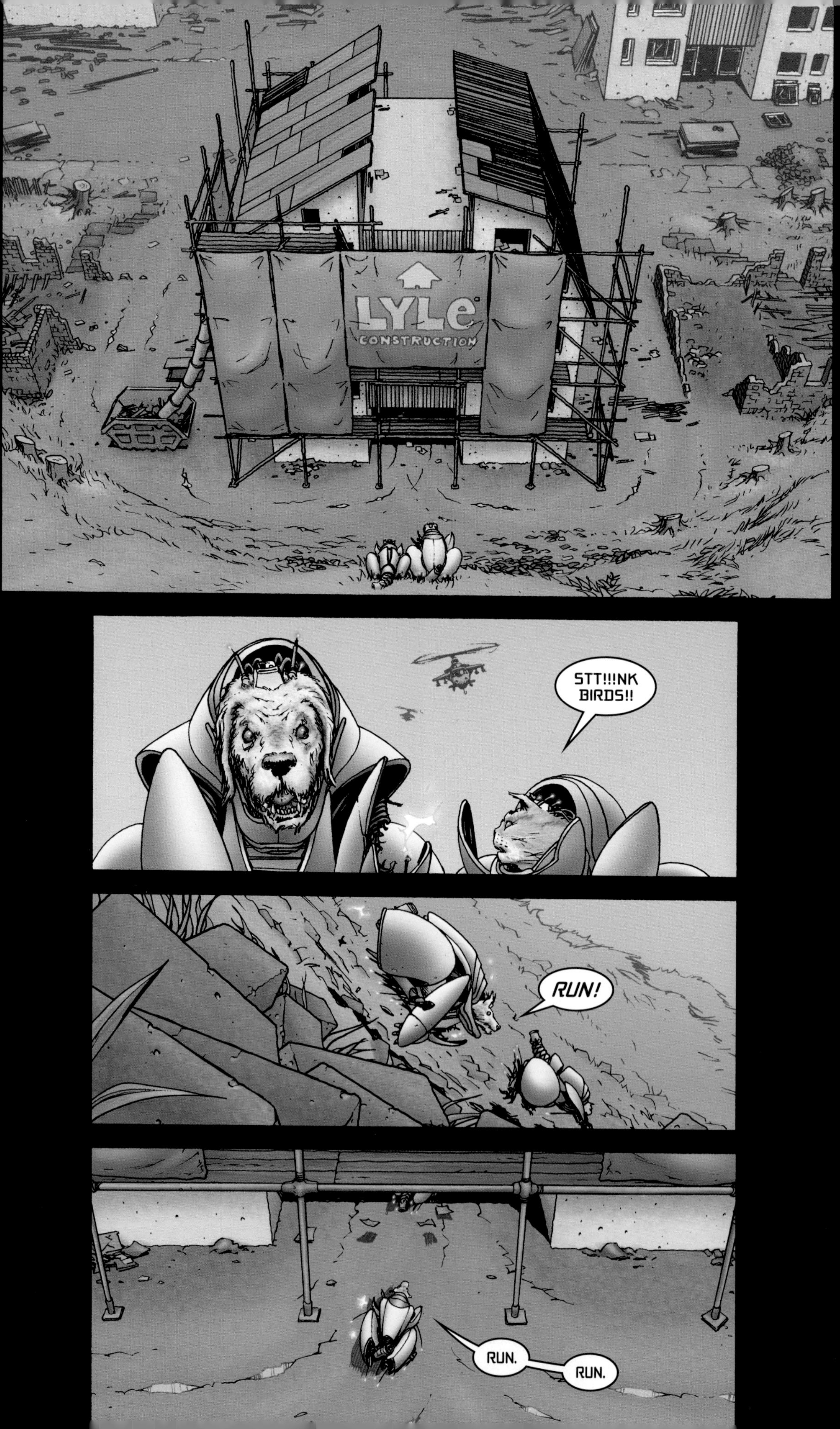
LYLE
CONSTRUCTION
STT!!!NK BIRDS!!
RUN!
RUN.
RUN.

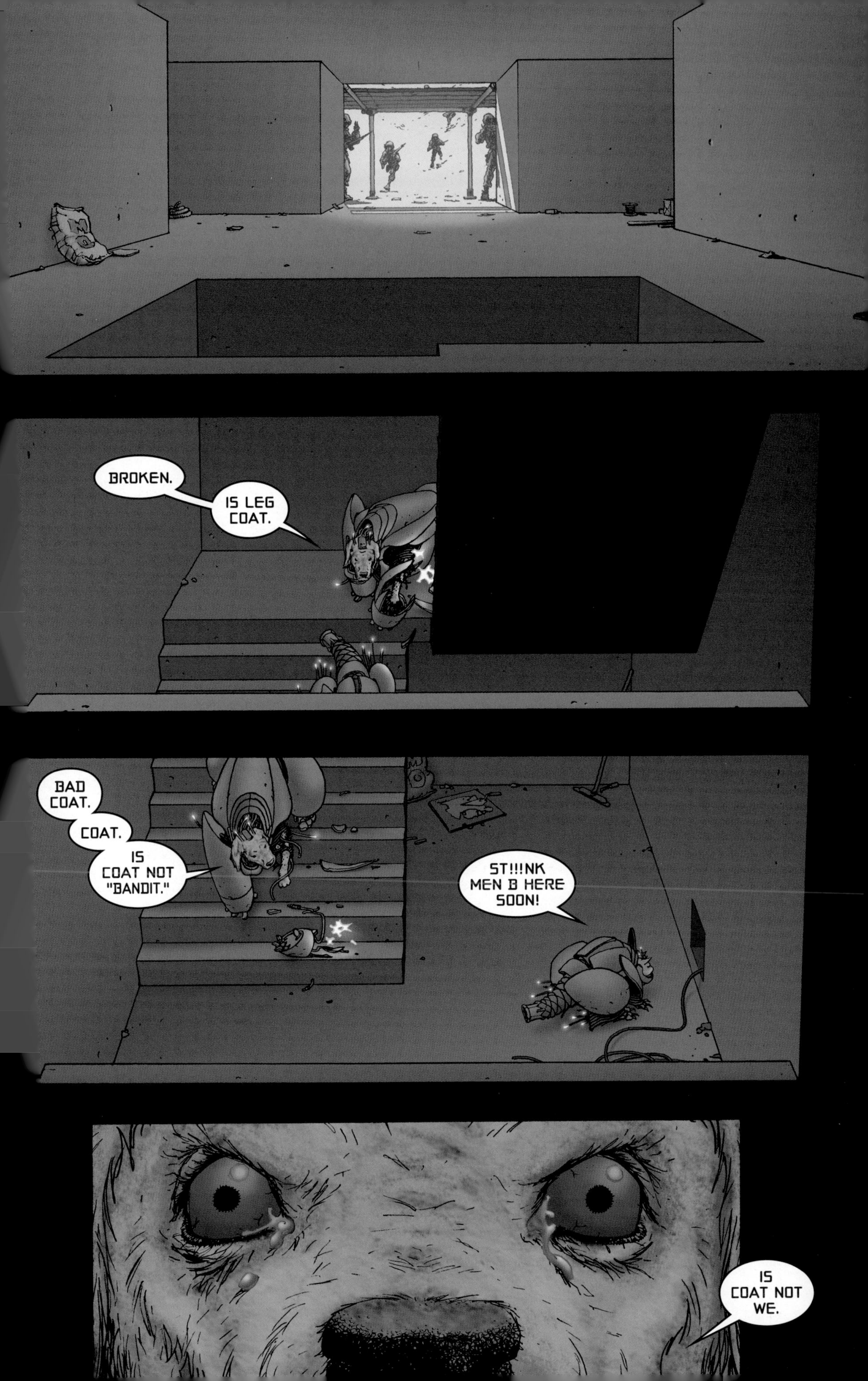
BROKEN.
IS LEG COAT.
BAD COAT.
COAT.
IS COAT NOT "BANDIT."
ST!!!NK MEN B HERE SOON!
IS COAT NOT WE.

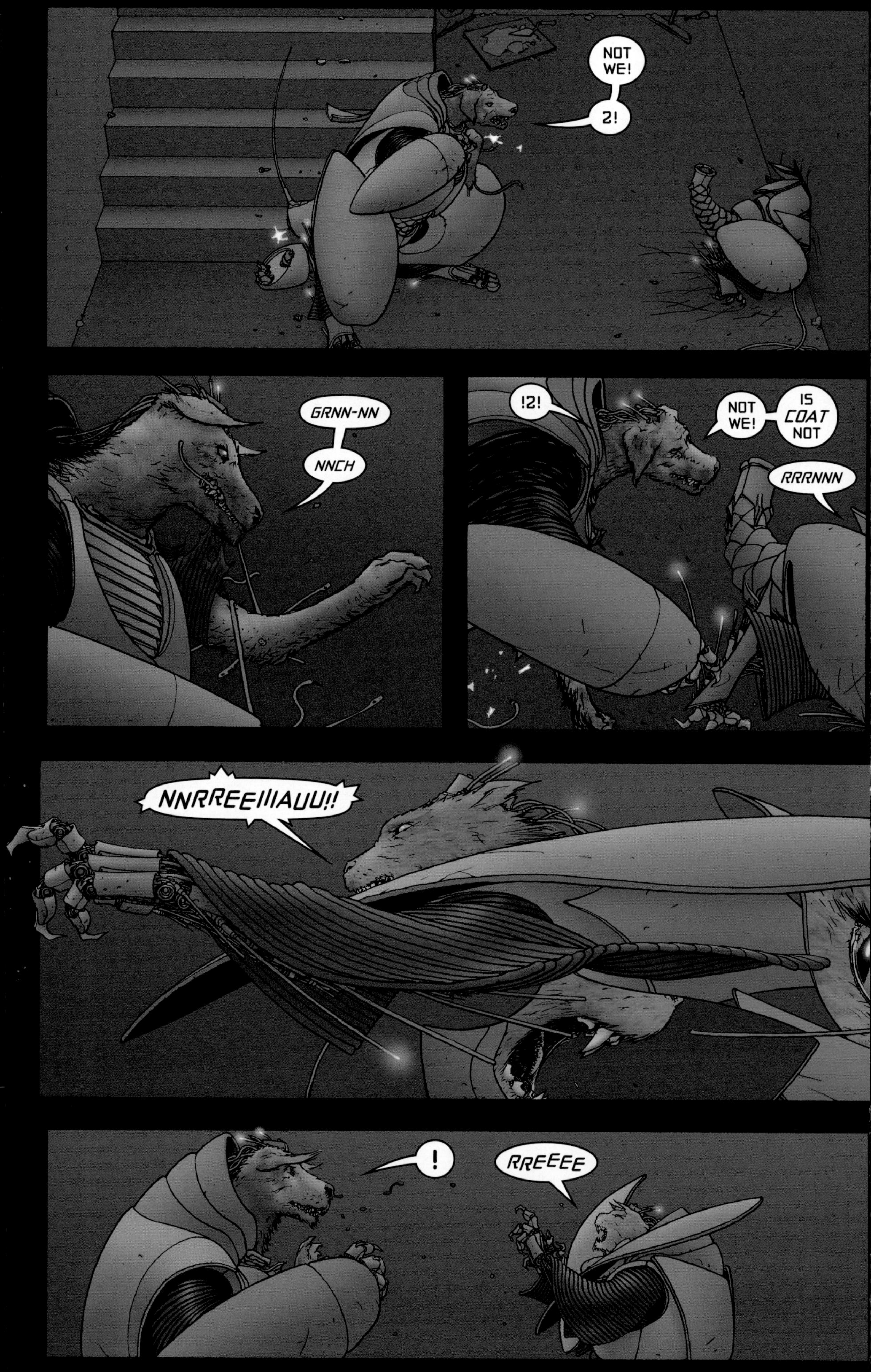
NOT WE!
2!
GRNN-NN
NNCH
!2!
NOT WE!
IS COAT NOT
RRRNNN
NNRREEIIIAUU!!
!
RREEEE

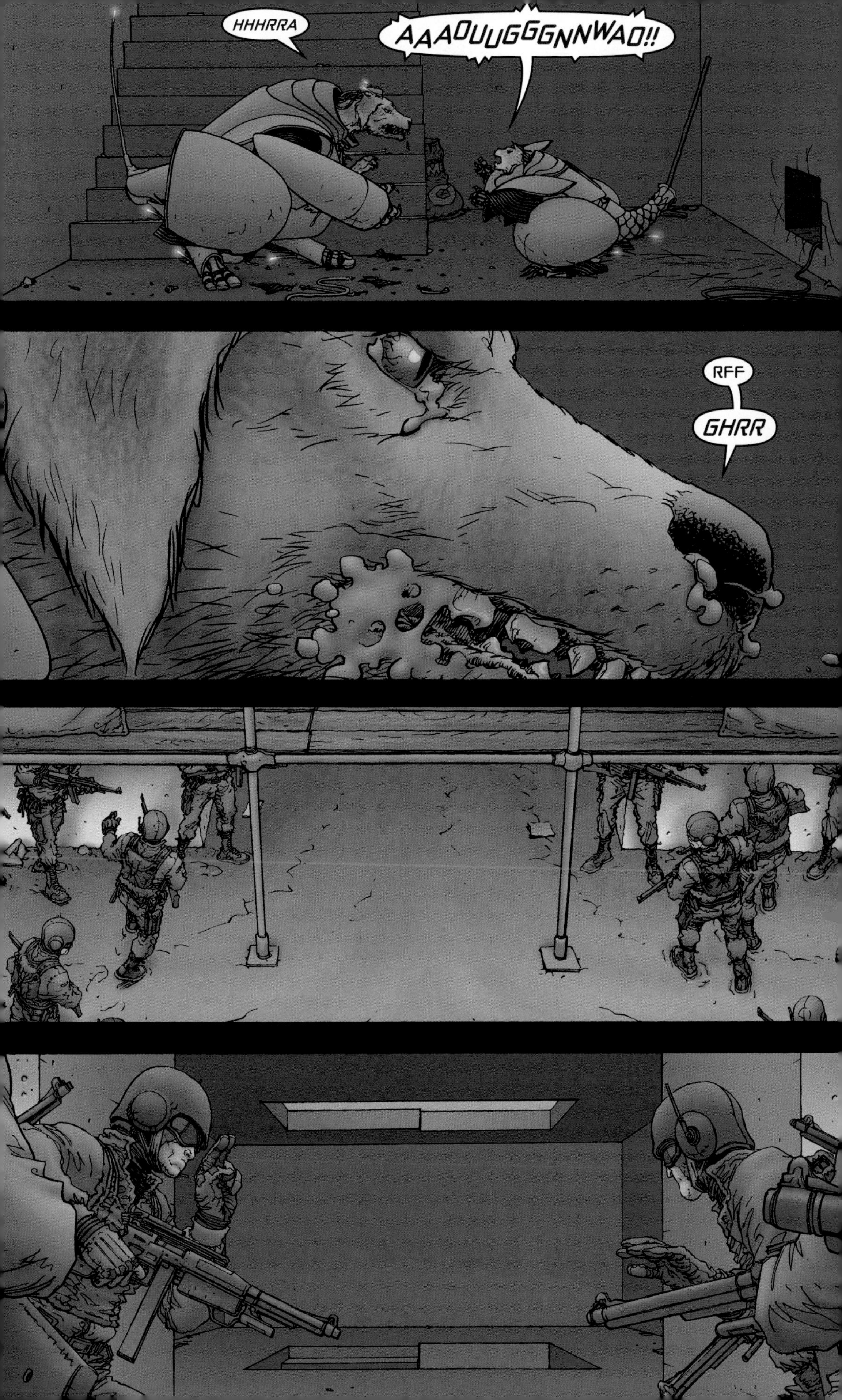
HHHRRA
AAAOUUGGGNNWAO!!
RFF
GHRR

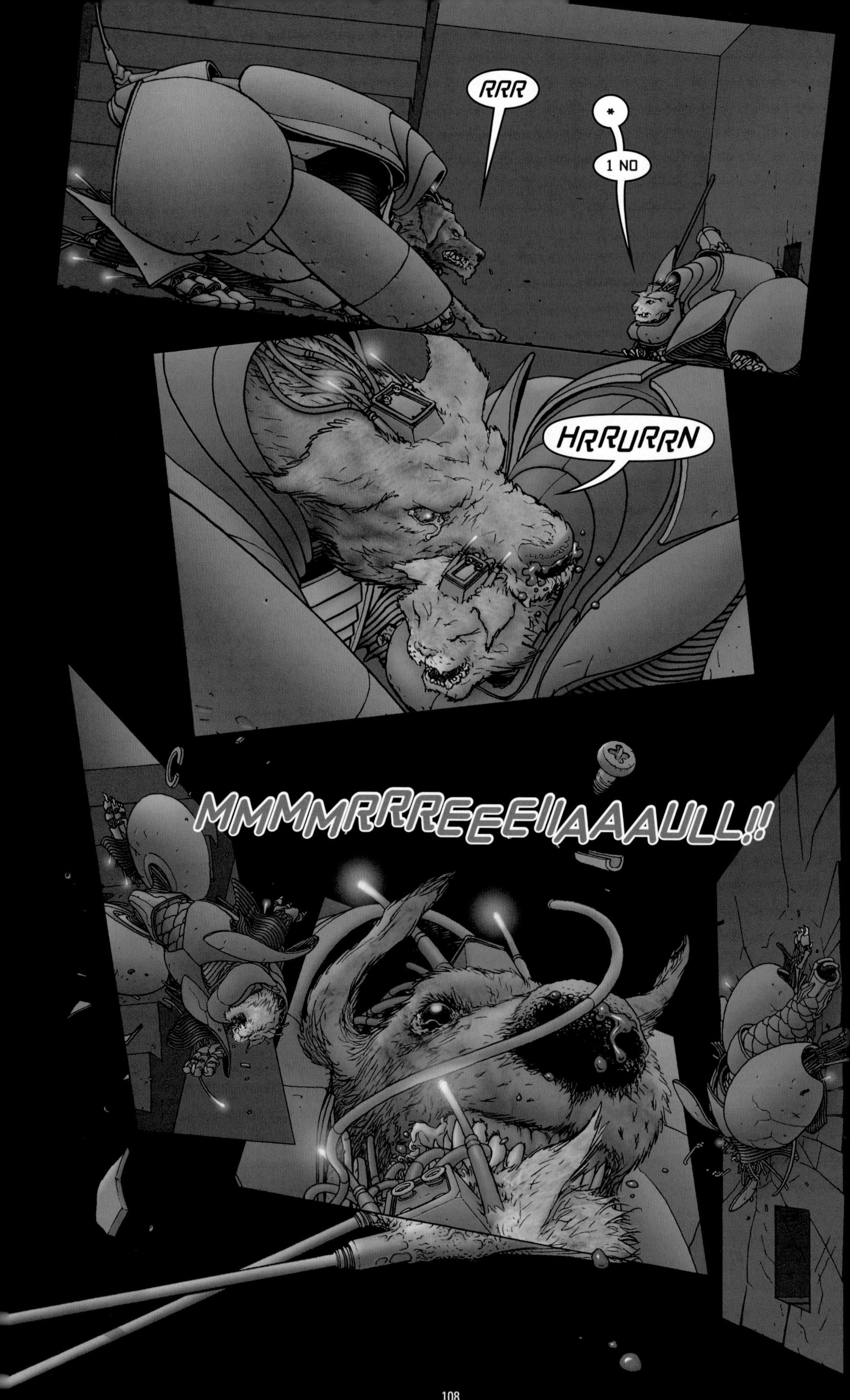
RRR
*
1 NO
HRRURRN
MMMMRRREEEIIAAAULL!!

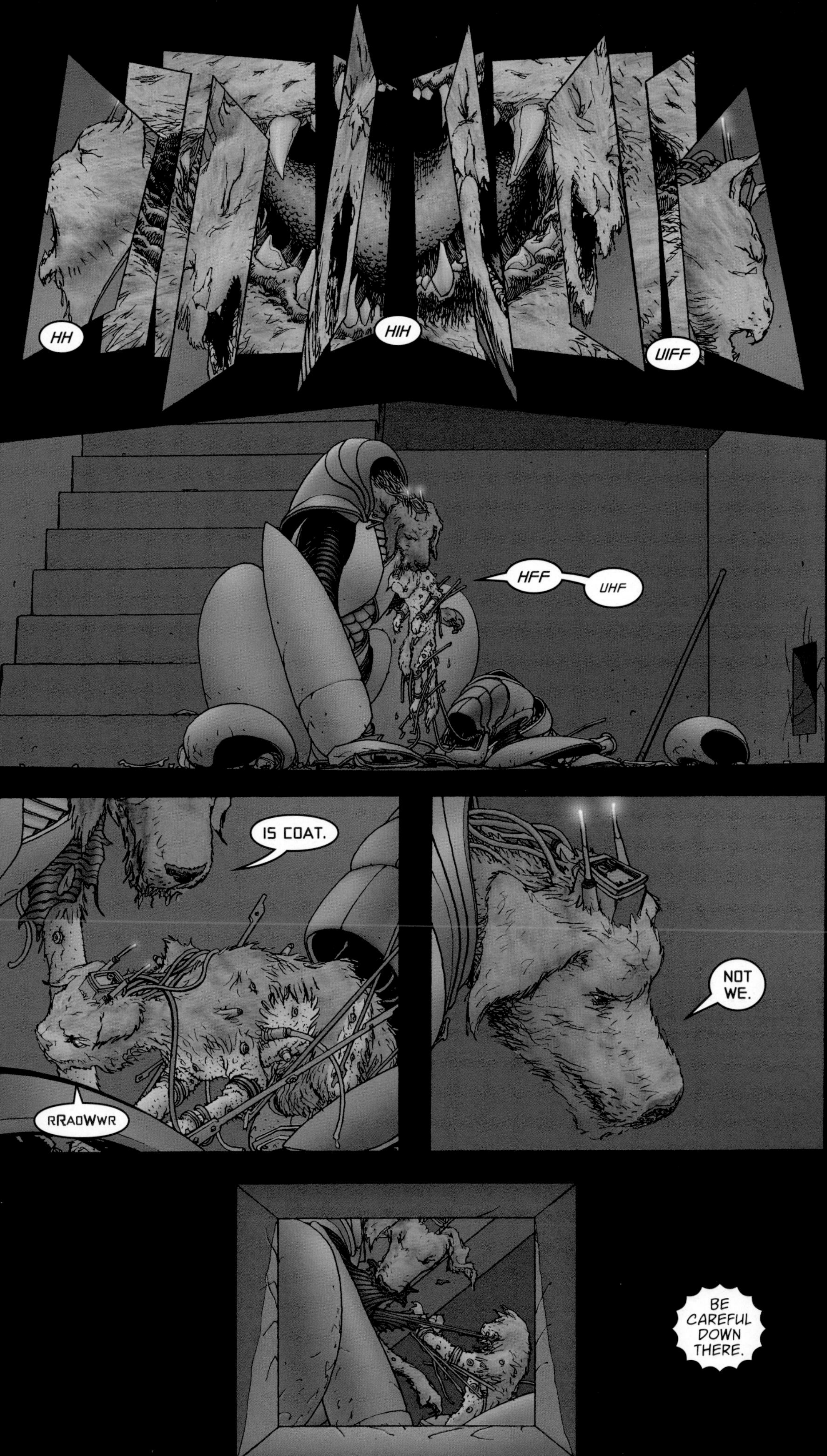
HH
HIH
UIFF
HFF
UHF
IS COAT.
RRAOWWR
NOT WE.
BE CAREFUL DOWN THERE.

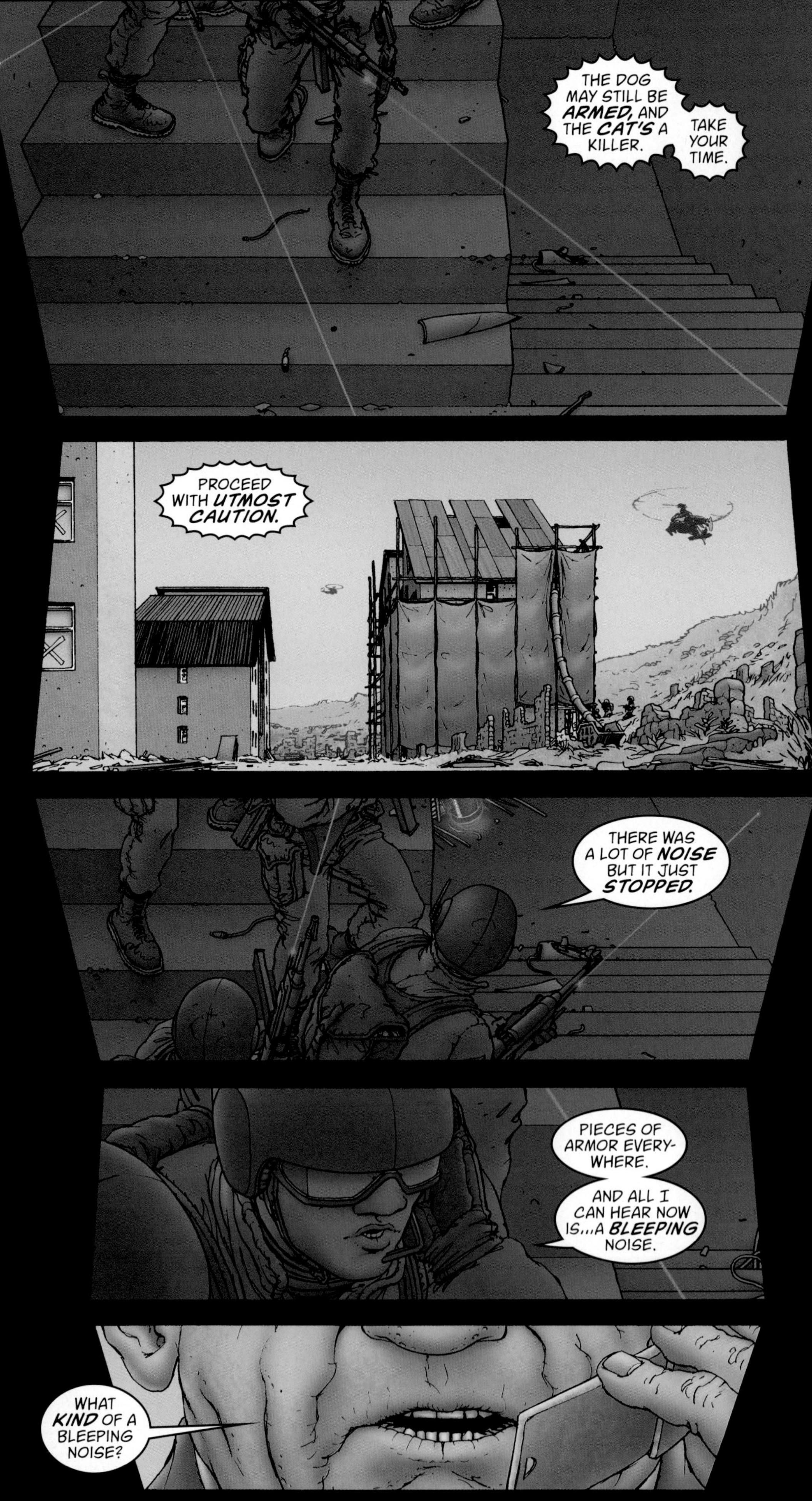
THE DOG MAY STILL BE ARMED, AND THE CAT'S A KILLER.
TAKE YOUR TIME.
PROCEED WITH UTMOST CAUTION.
THERE WAS A LOT OF NOISE BUT IT JUST STOPPED.
PIECES OF ARMOR EVERY-WHERE.
AND ALL I CAN HEAR NOW IS...A BLEEPING NOISE.
WHAT KIND OF A BLEEPING NOISE?

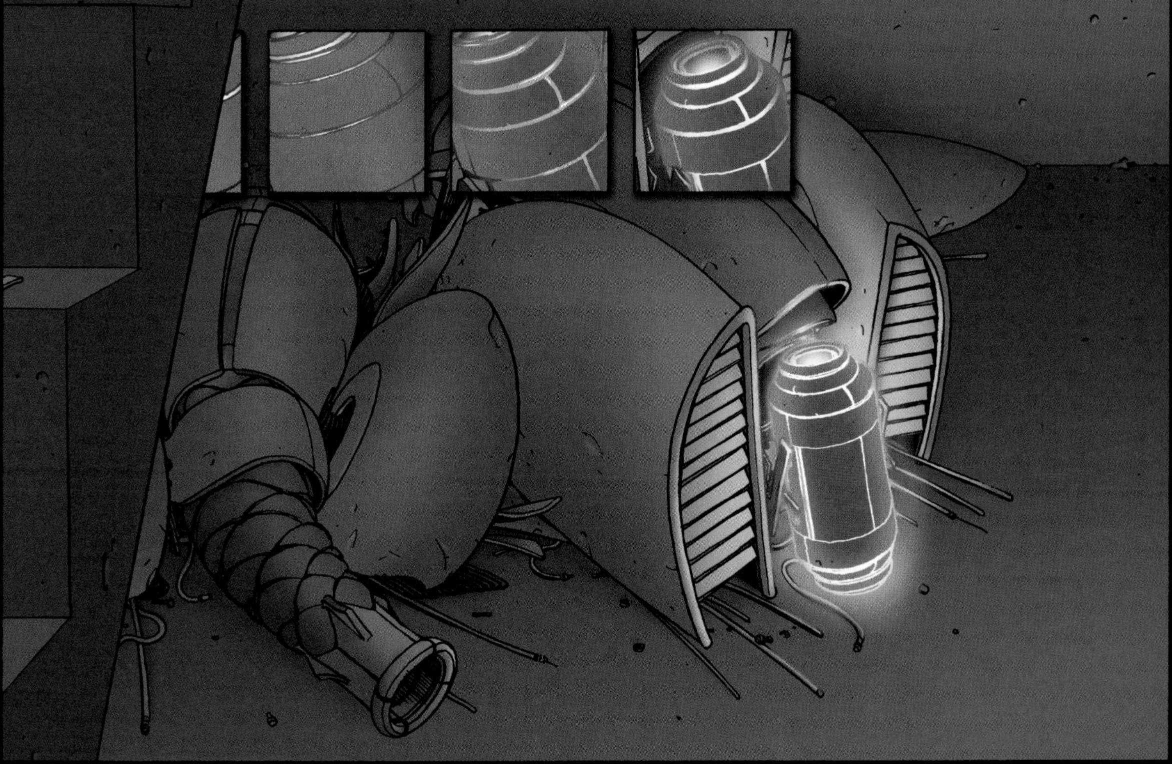

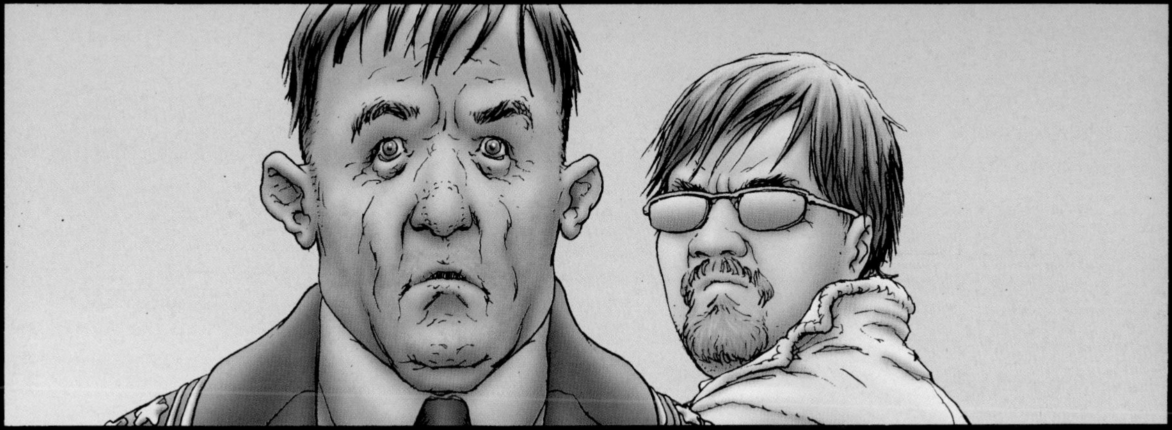

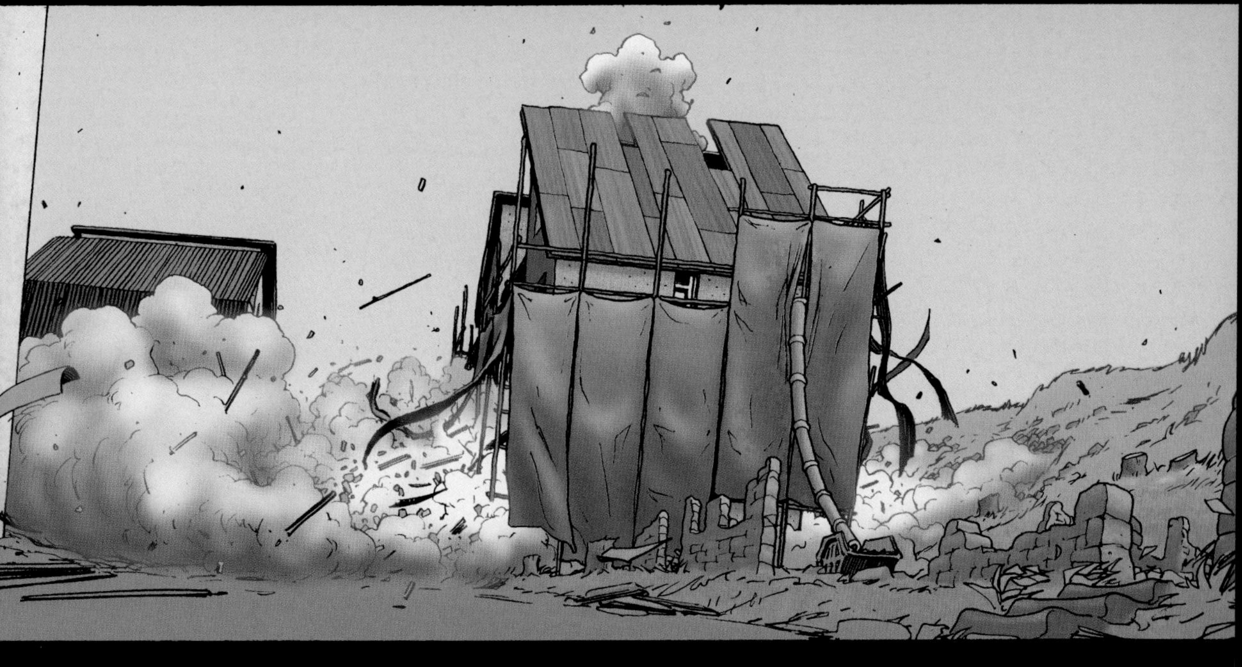

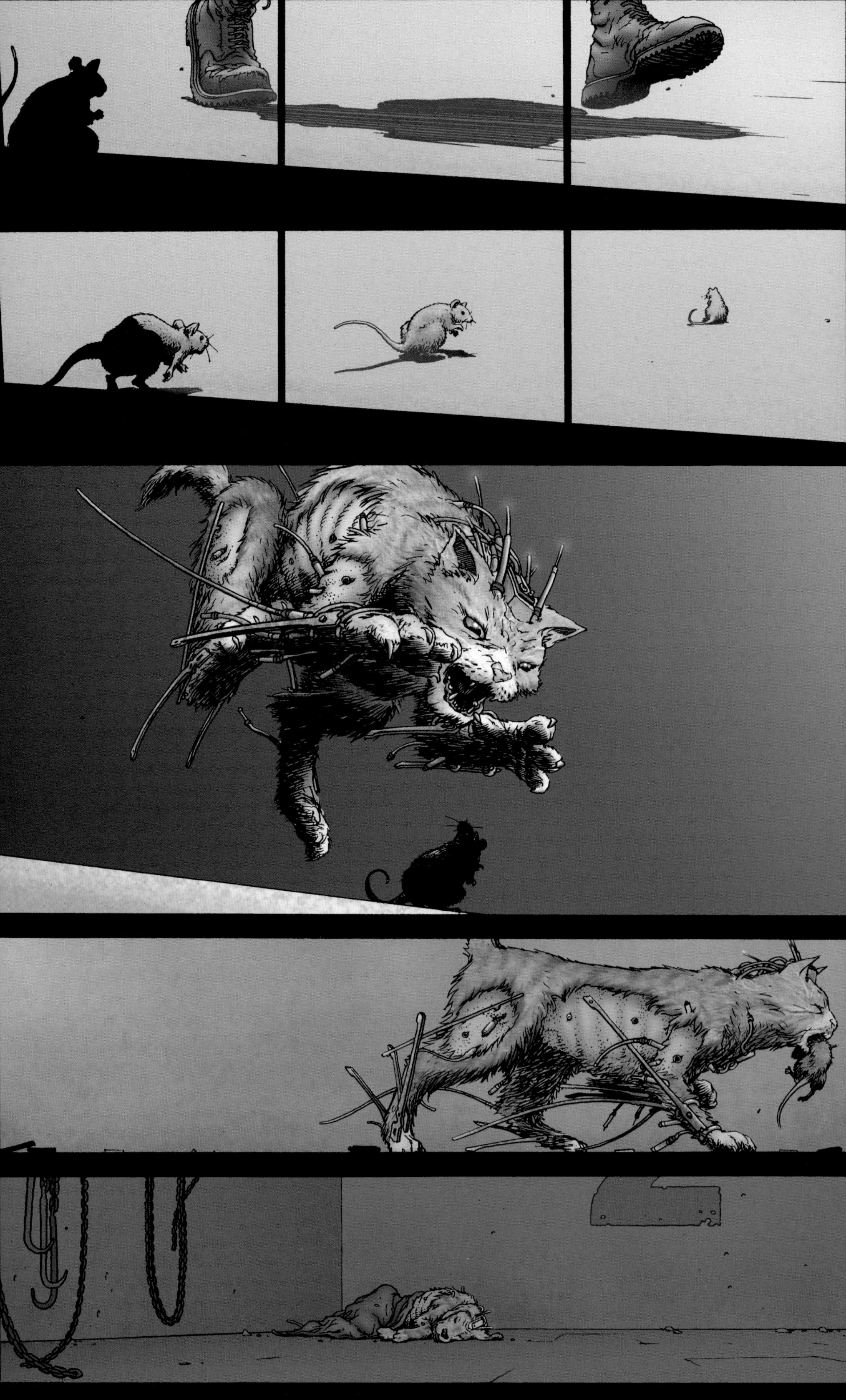

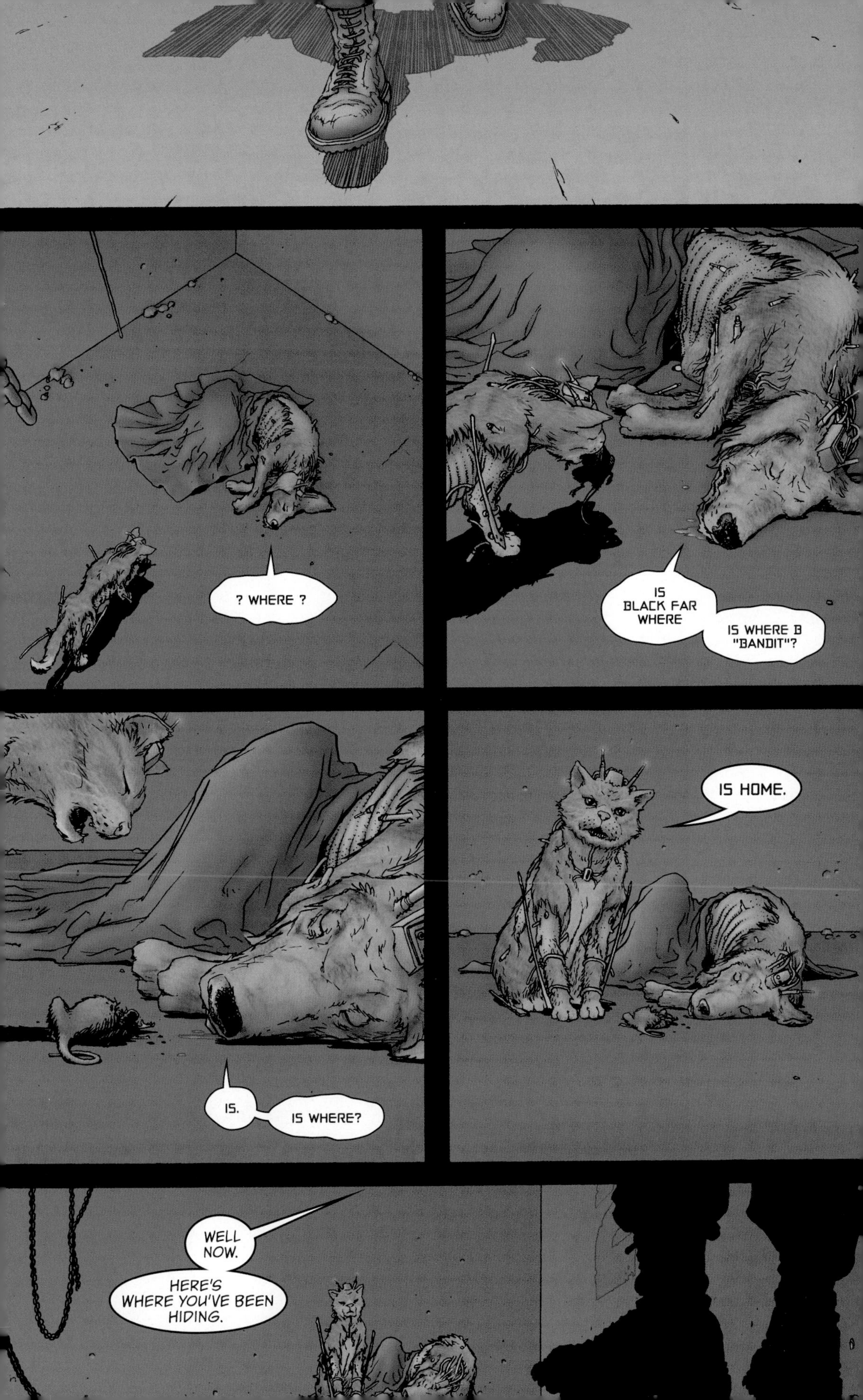
? WHERE ?
IS BLACK FAR WHERE
IS WHERE B "BANDIT"?
IS.
IS WHERE?
IS HOME.
WELL NOW.
HERE'S WHERE YOU'VE BEEN HIDING.

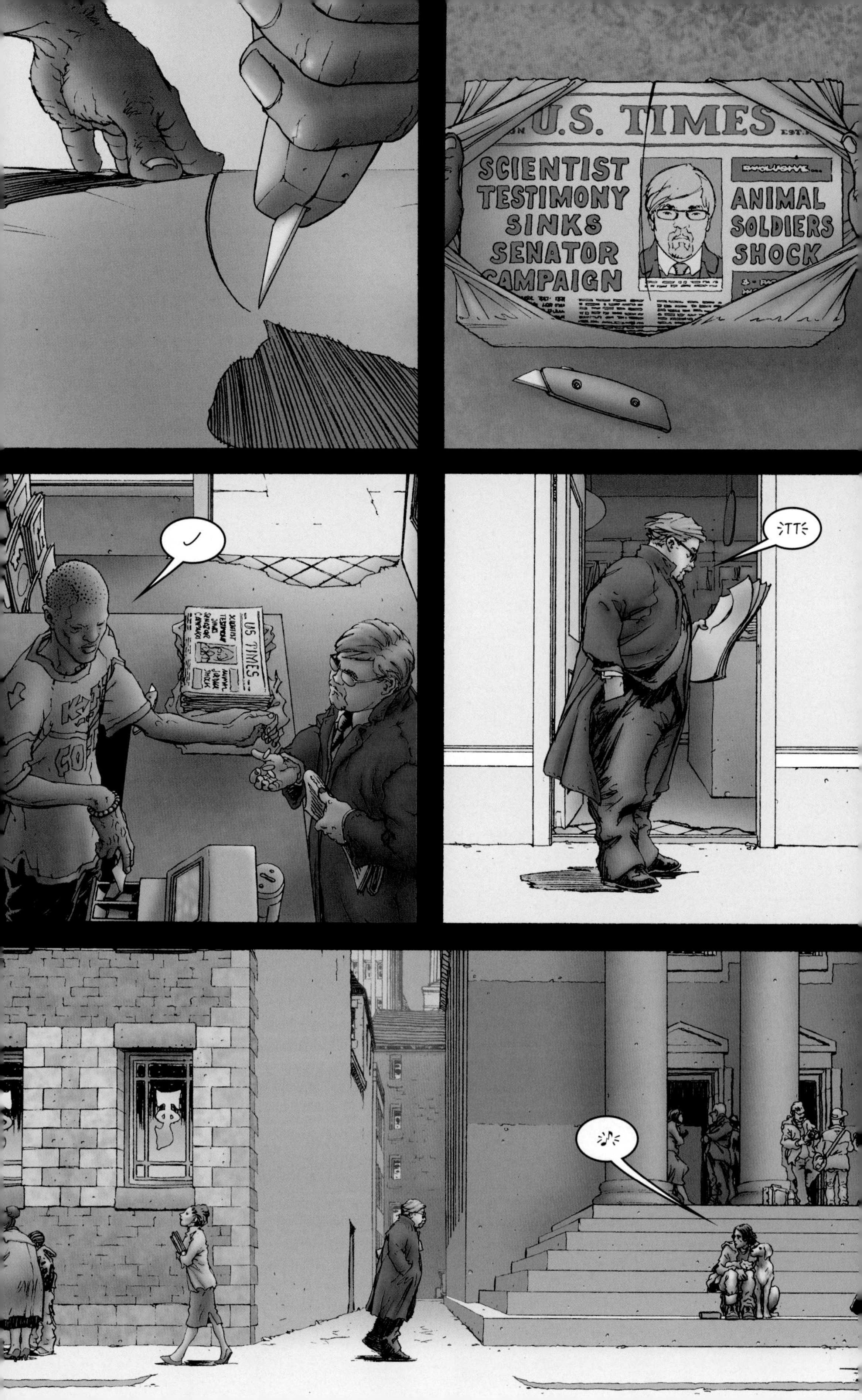
U.S. TIMES
SCIENTIST TESTIMONY SINKS SENATOR CAMPAIGN
ANIMAL SOLDIERS SHOCK
TT

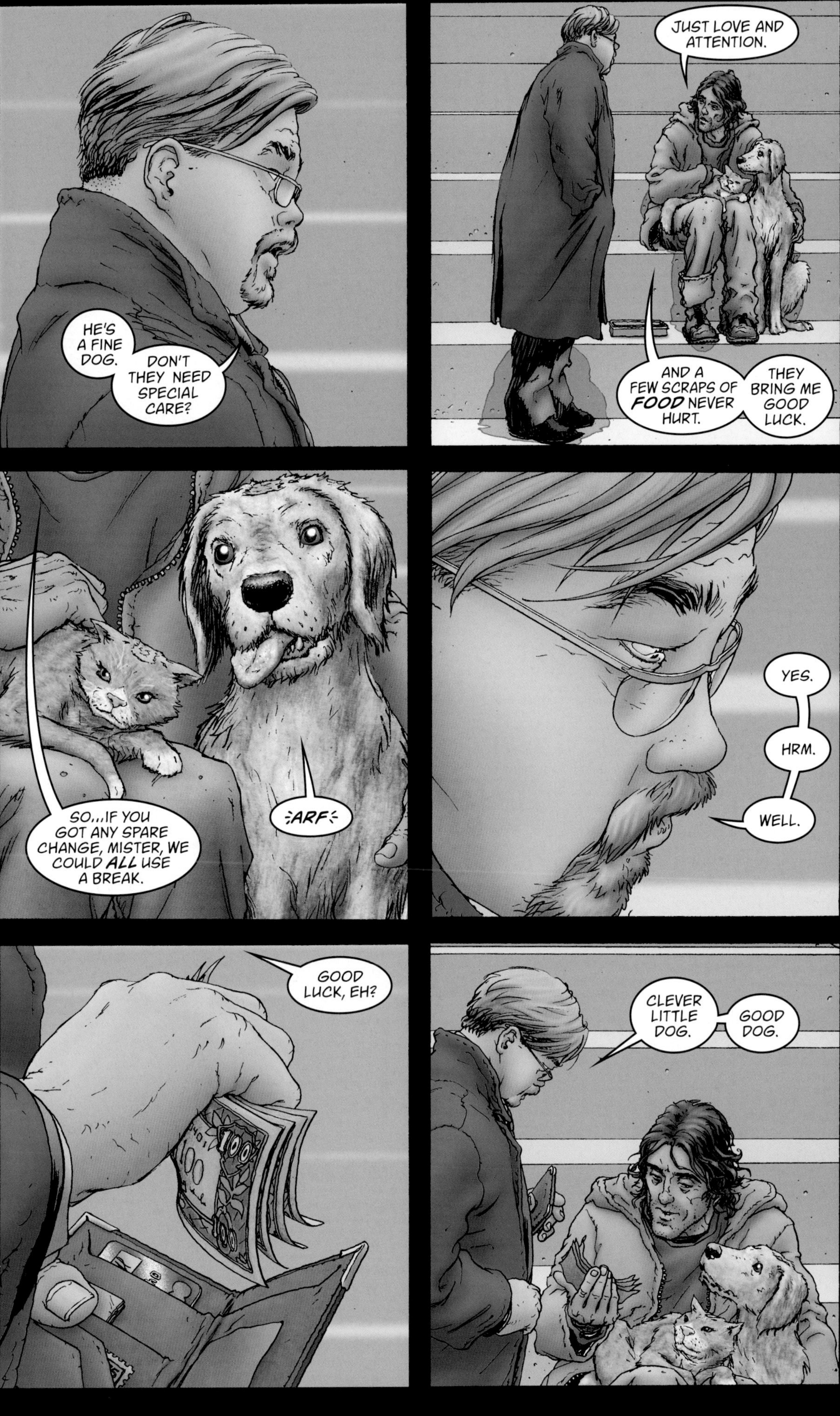
HE'S A FINE DOG.
DON'T THEY NEED SPECIAL CARE?
JUST LOVE AND ATTENTION.
AND A FEW SCRAPS OF FOOD NEVER HURT.
THEY BRING ME GOOD LUCK.
SO...IF YOU GOT ANY SPARE CHANGE, MISTER, WE COULD ALL USE A BREAK.
ARF
YES.
HRM.
WELL.
GOOD LUCK, EH?
CLEVER LITTLE DOG.
GOOD DOG.

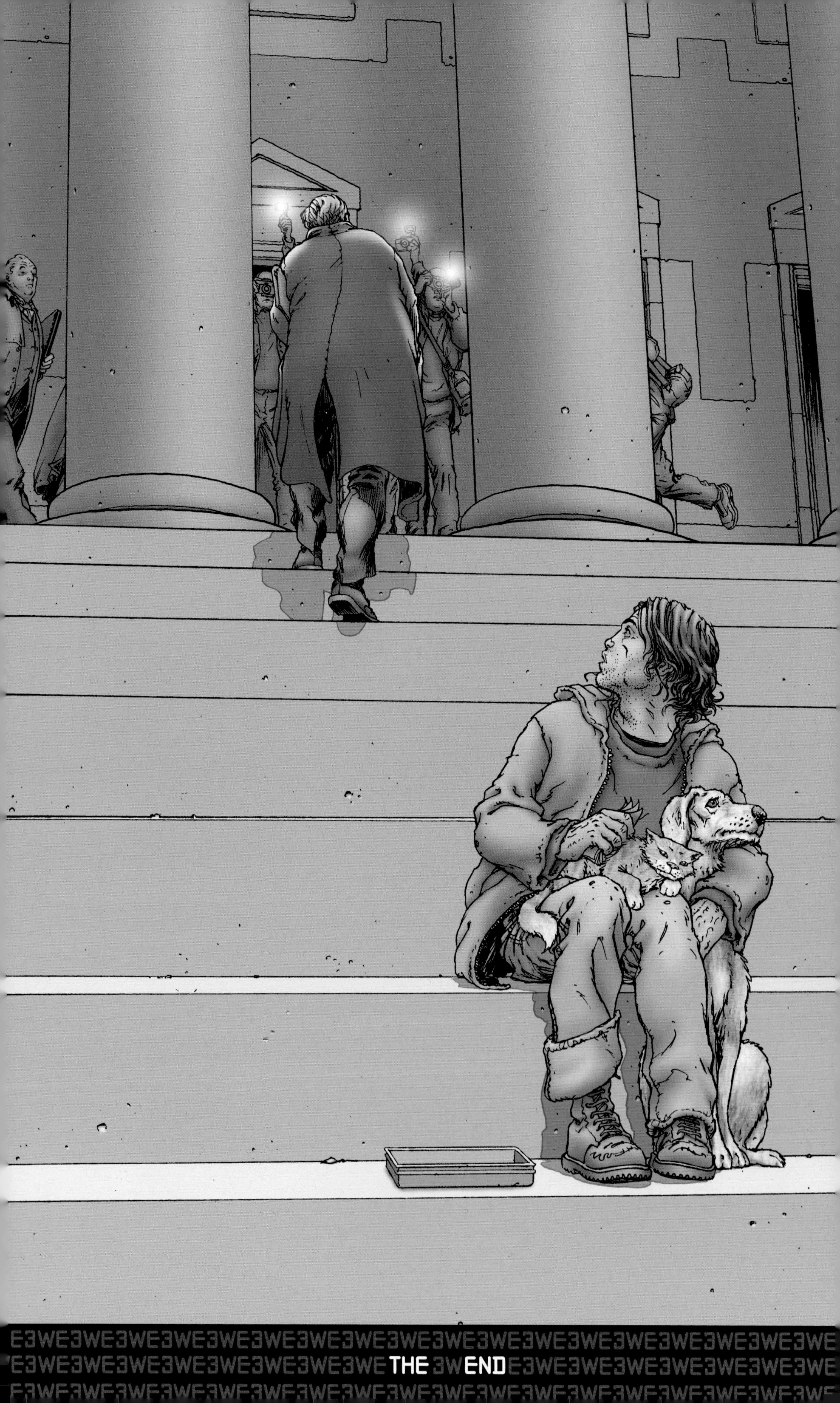
THE END

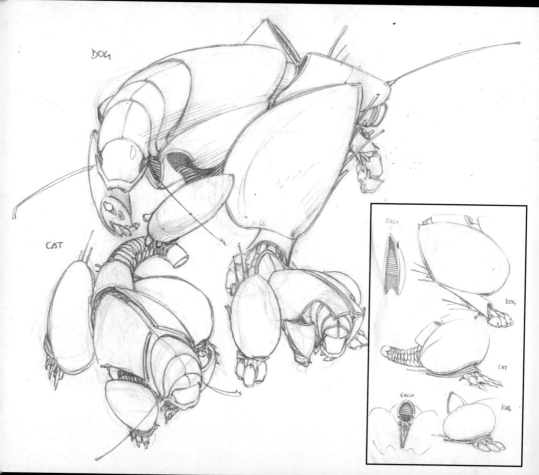

DOG

CAT

BACK

DOG

CAT

BACK

RAB

CHARACTER DESIGNS

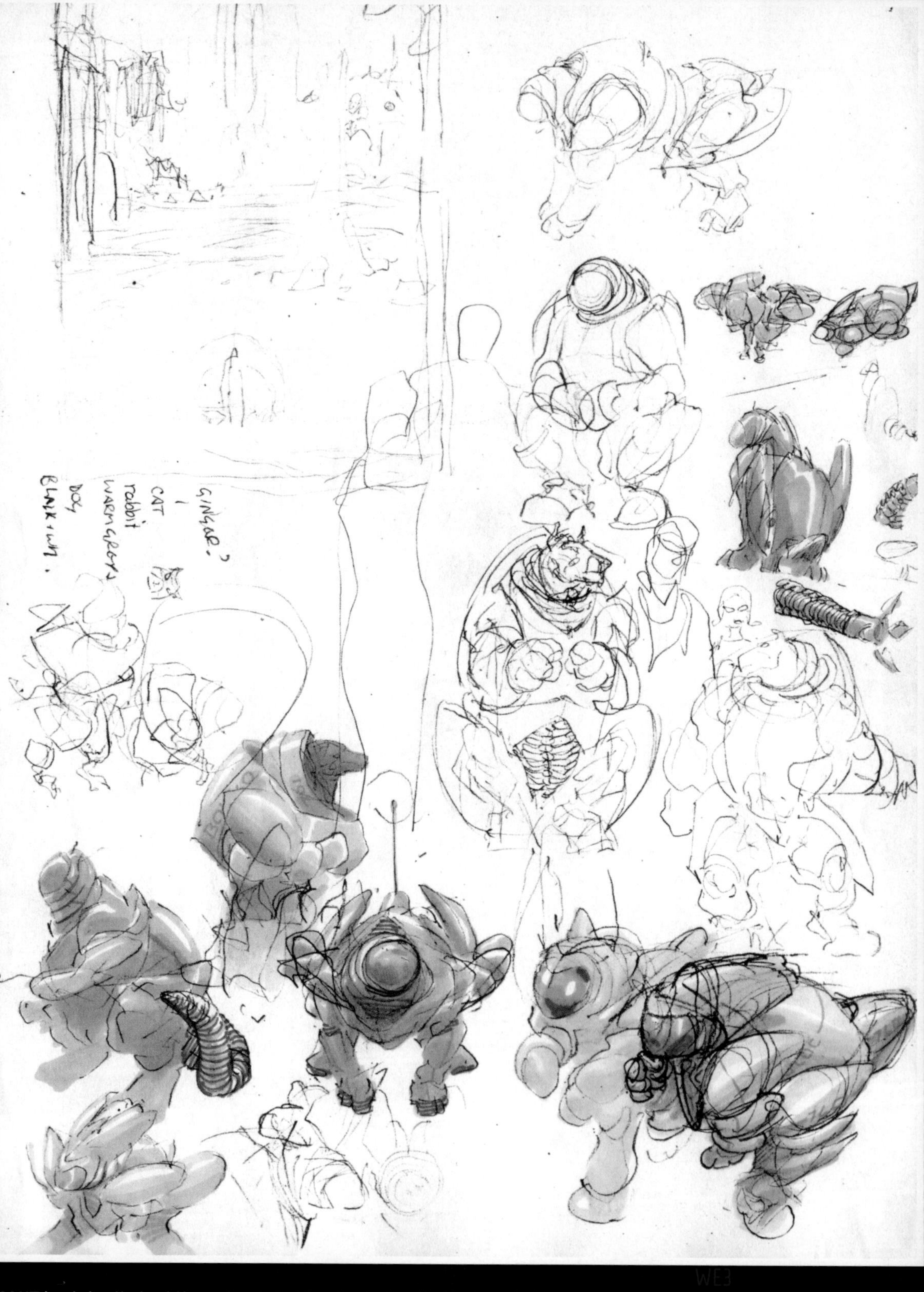
GINGER?
CAT
rabbit
warm greys
DOG
BLACK + WHT.

GRANT I originally had the animals in biped robot suits that made them look more like bulky humans with animal heads, but it just didn't work and we decided instead to make the armor conform more closely to the shape of the animal underneath, which was much more visually appealing and allowed Frank to create some truly

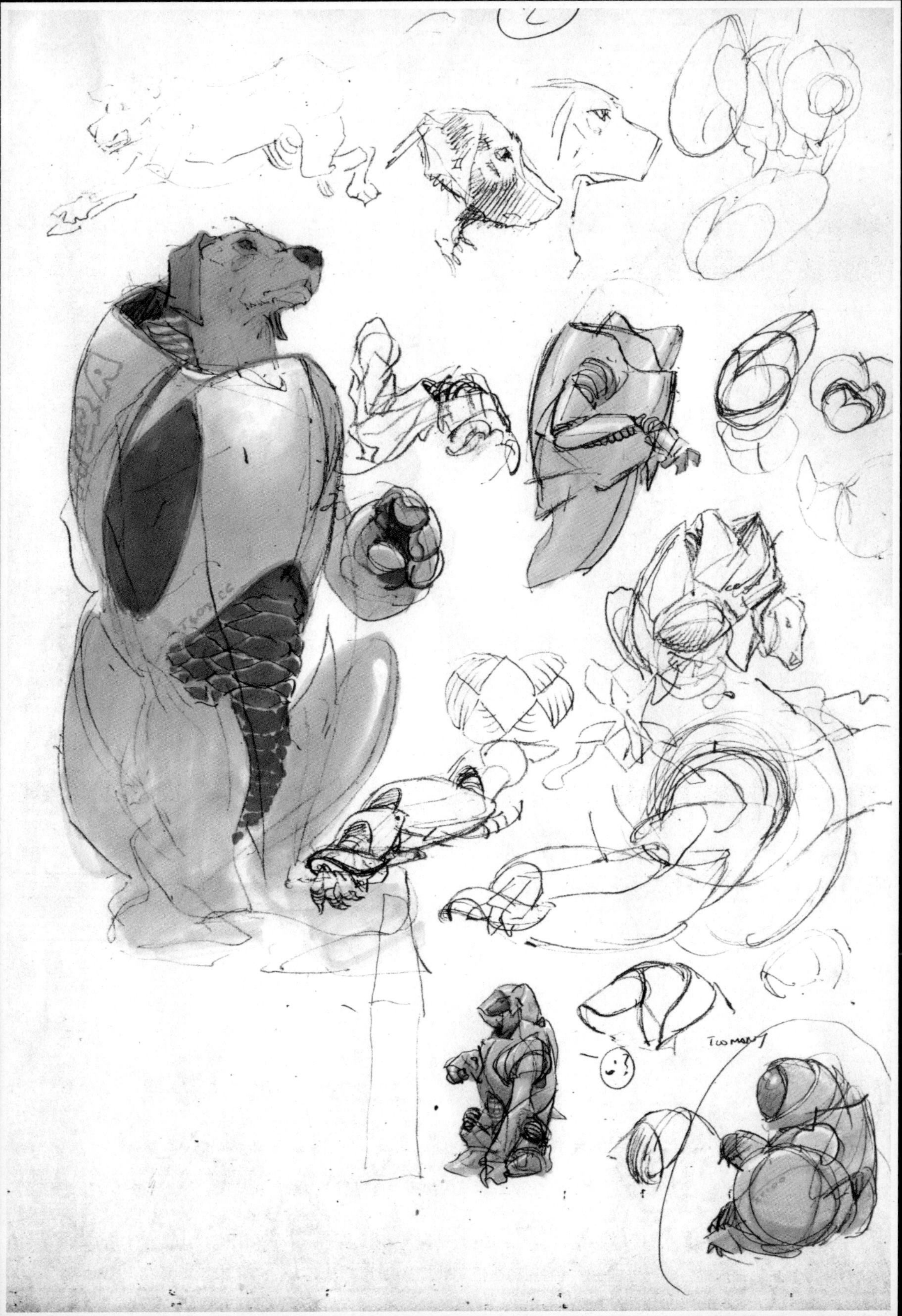
TOO MANY

FRANK: The animals' armor was designed from the ground up and began with practical considerations rather than aesthetic ones, as though I was designing something that could conceivably be made and used. I looked closely at fleas, roaches, pangolins and other naturally armored creatures; robots, sports watches, American cars and Italian and Japanese mopeds also helped to inform the styling. We decided against camouflaged finishes in the interest of clarity, and instead settled on a two-tone scheme using color and grey that is typical of many mammals in the natural world.

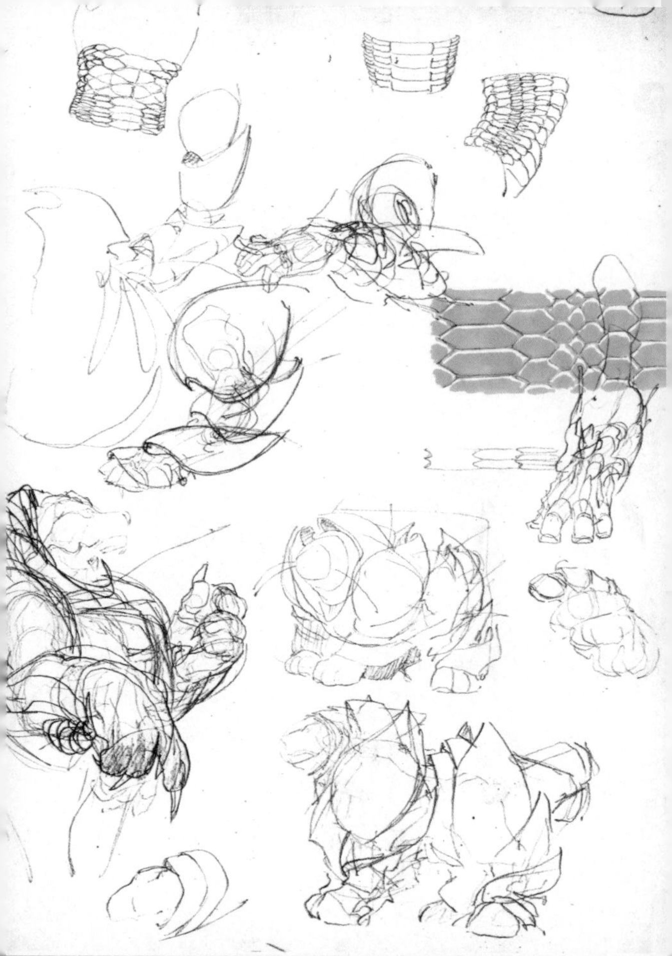

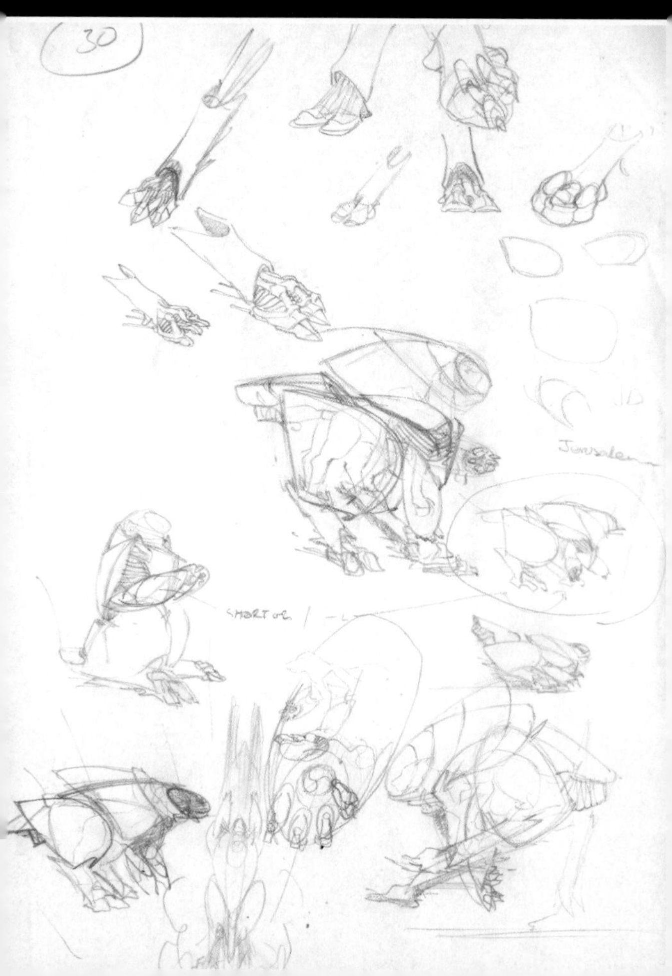
30
Jerusalem
SHORT OR

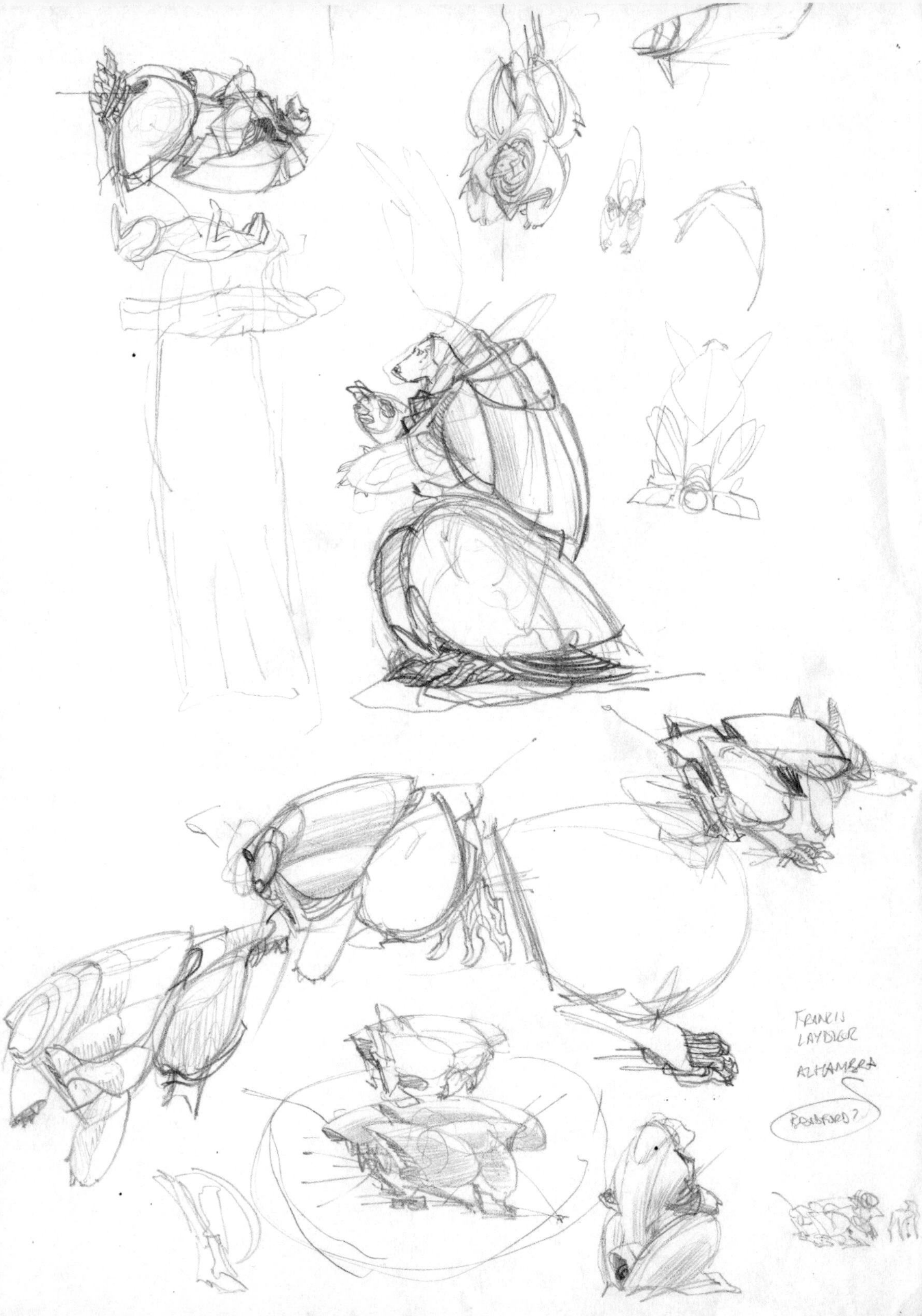
FRANCIS
LAYDIER
ALHAMBRA

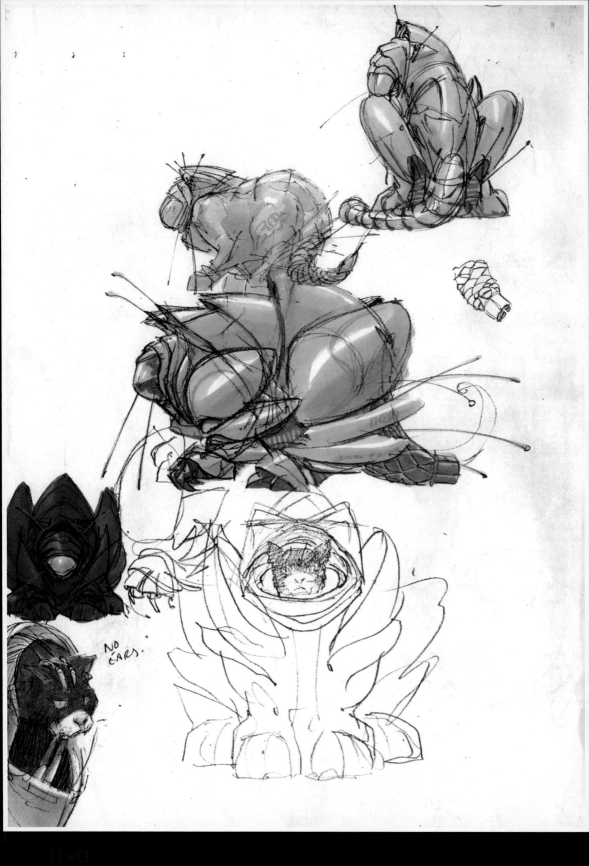

NO
EARS.

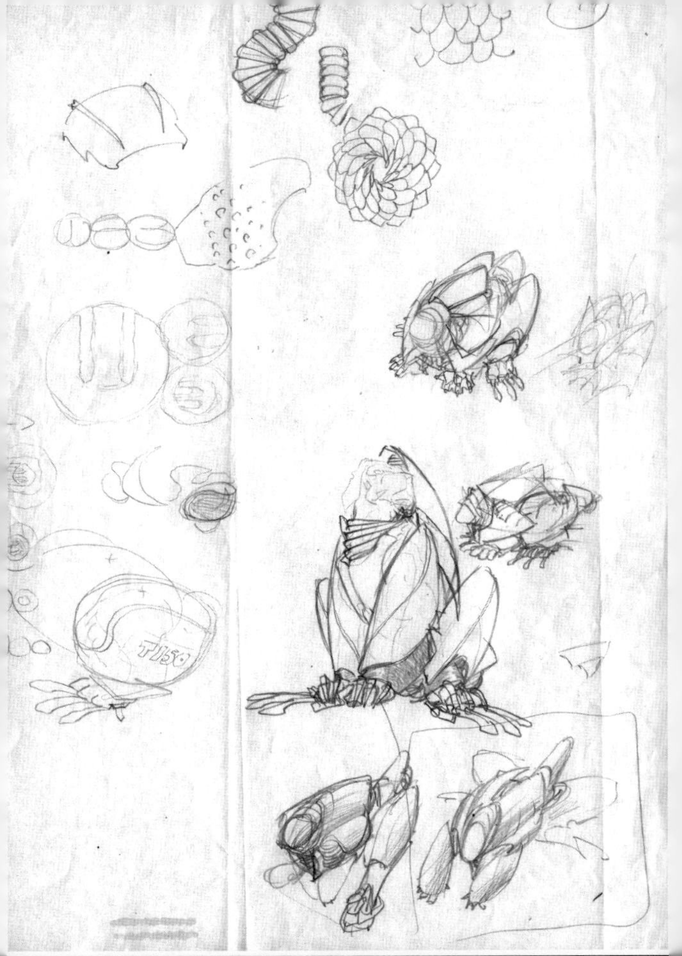

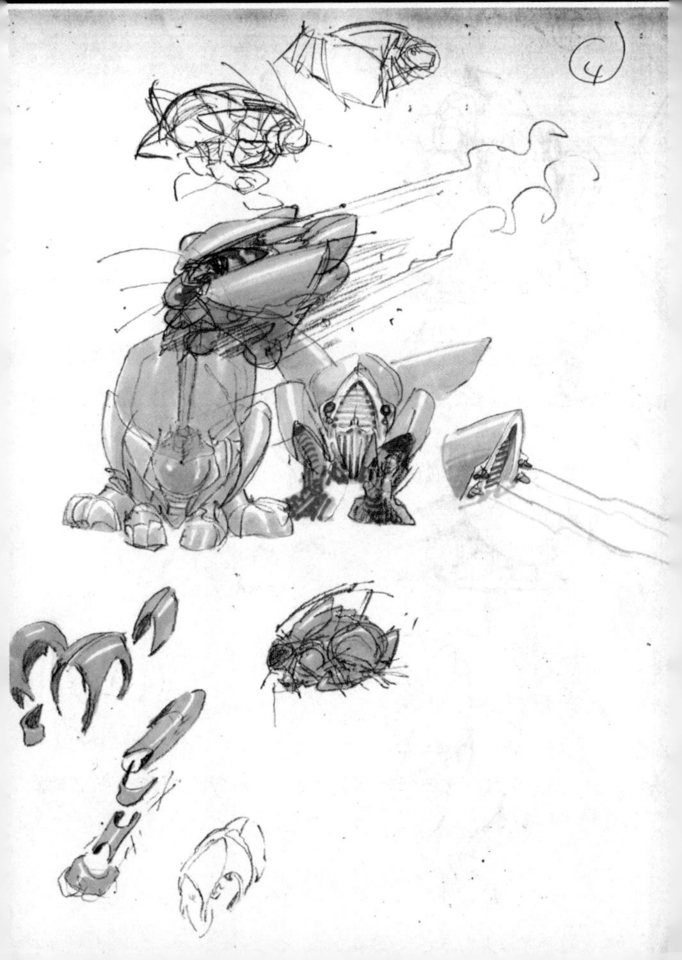

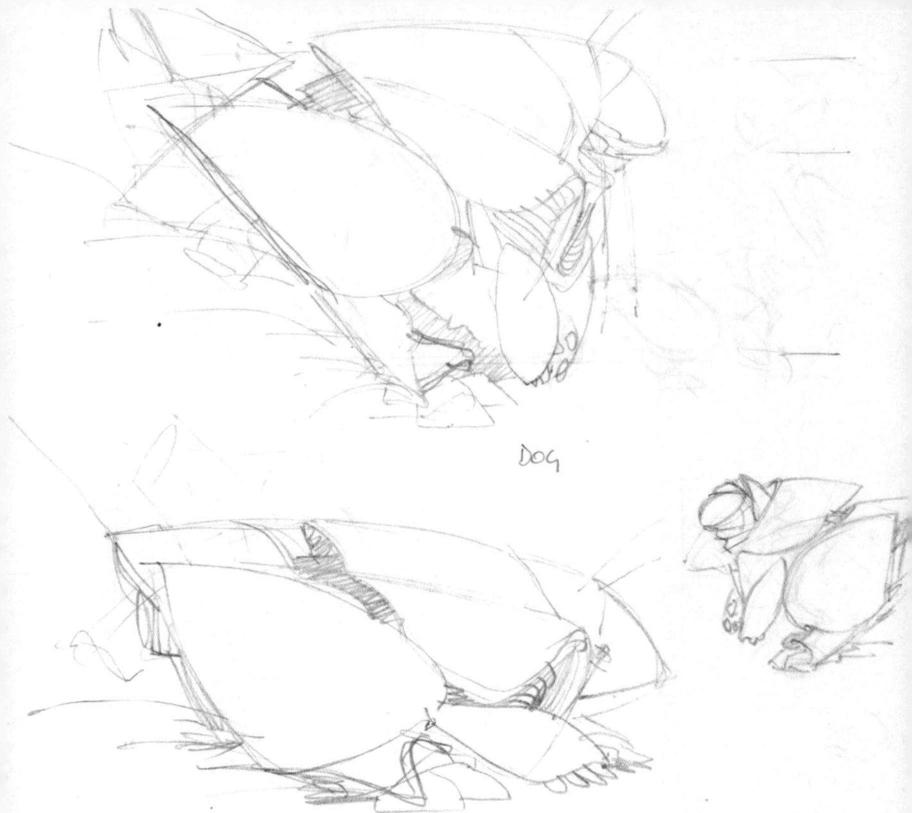
DOG

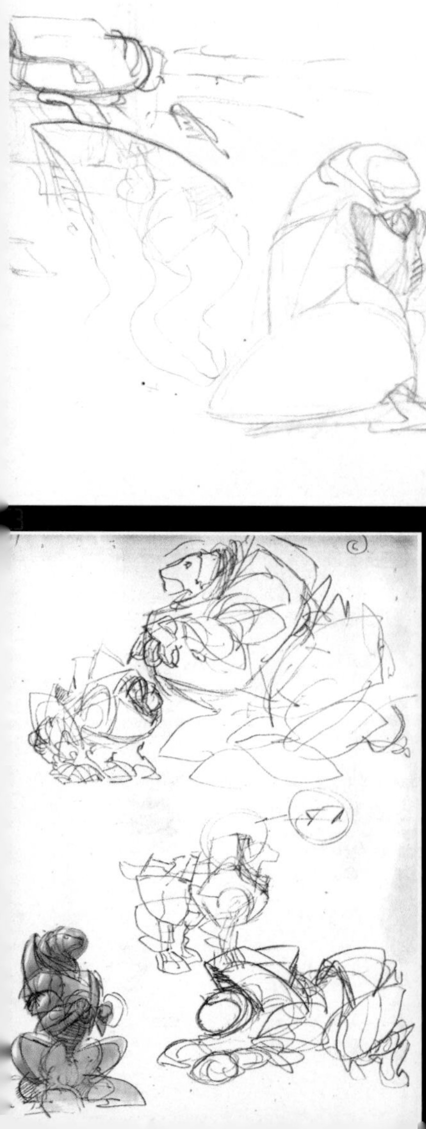

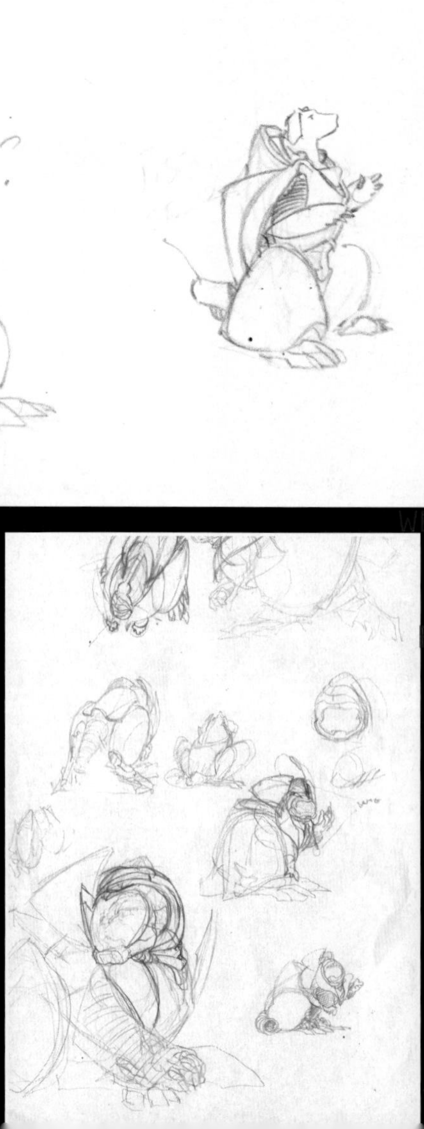

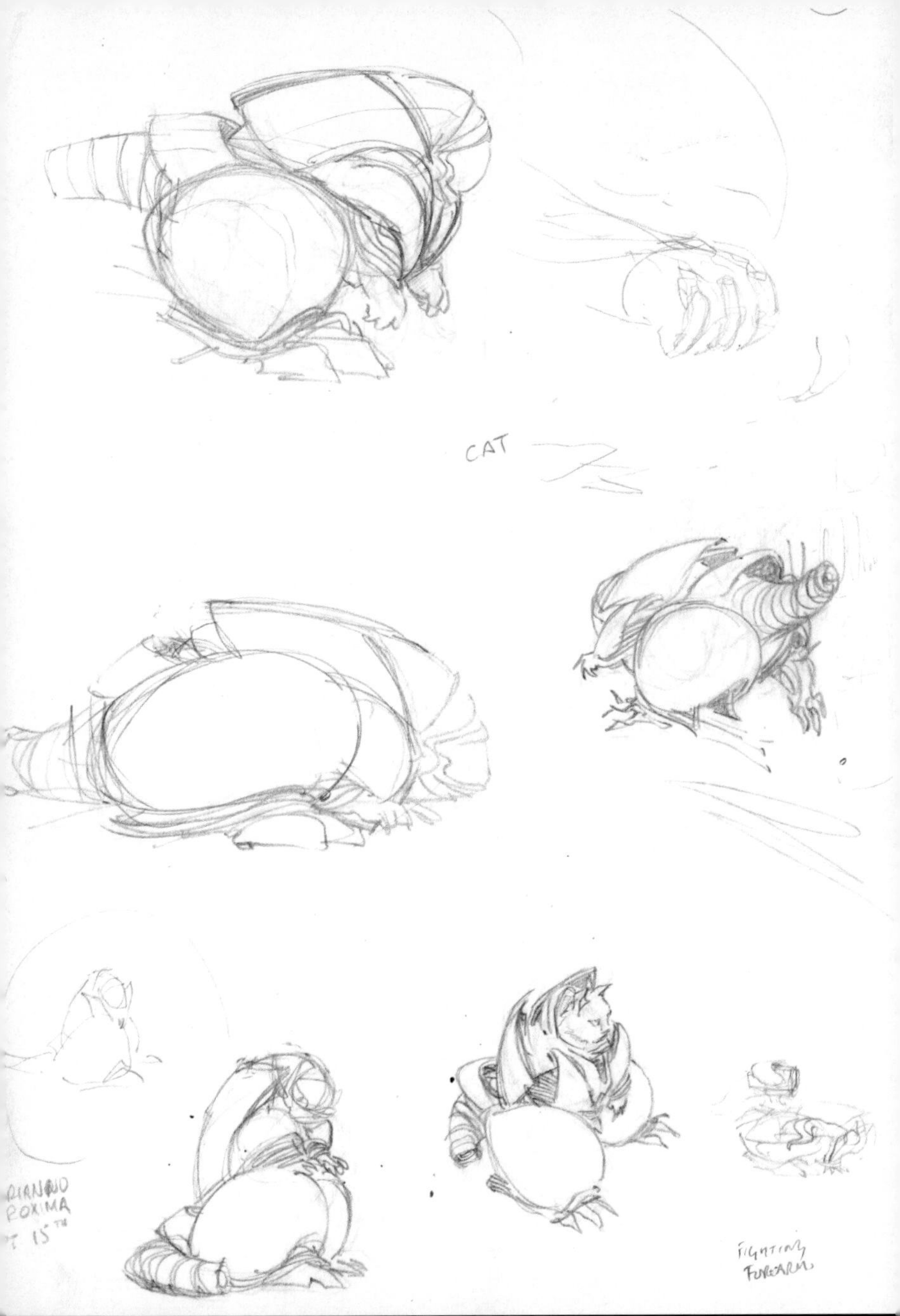
CAT
RIANNO
ROXIMA
T 15TH
FIGHTING
FOREARM

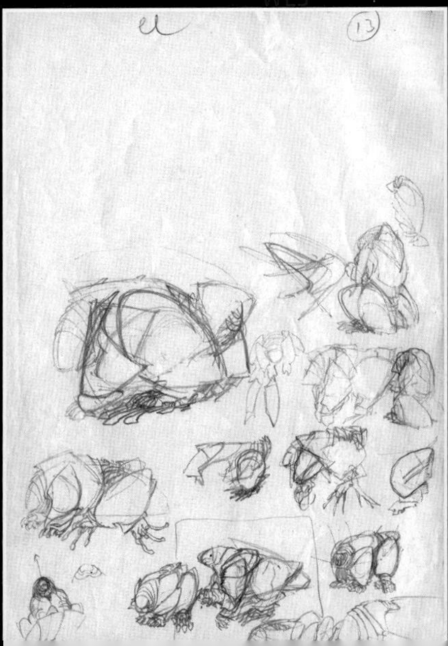
13

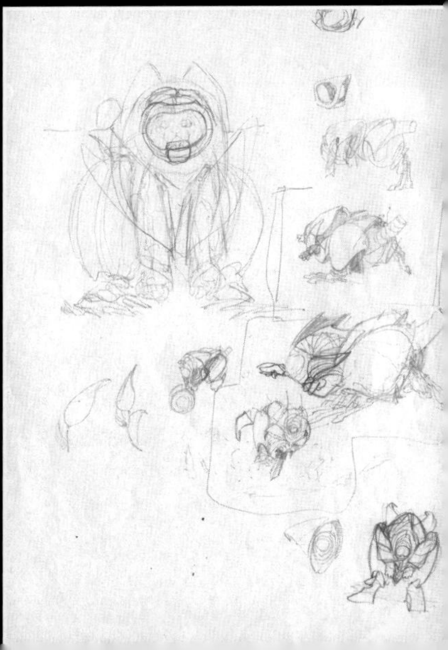

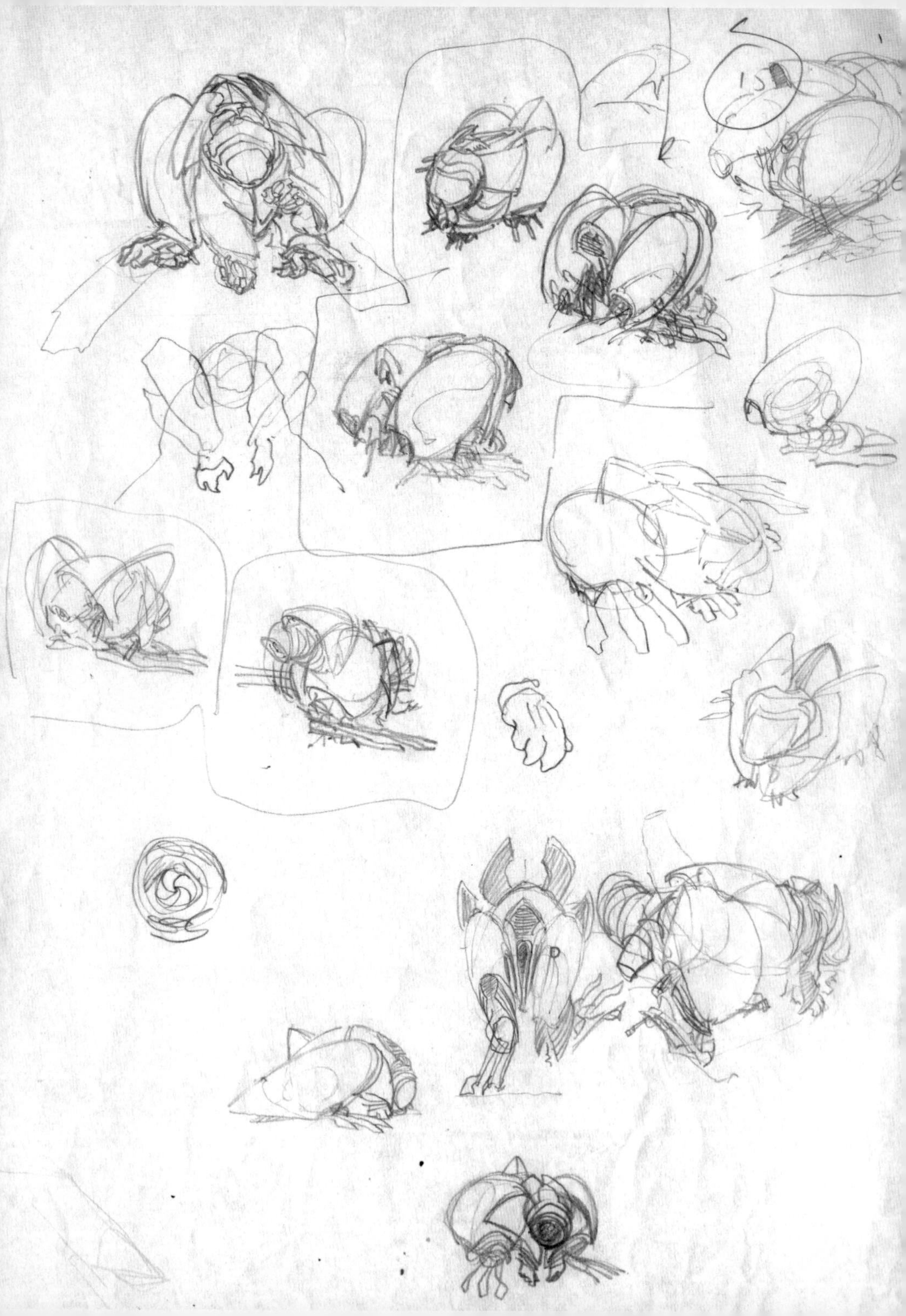

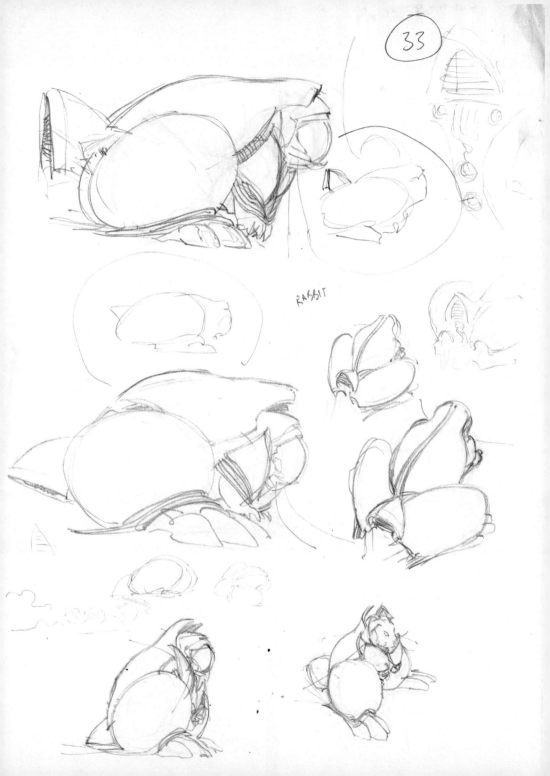

RABBIT

33

HEART SHOT SEQUENCE

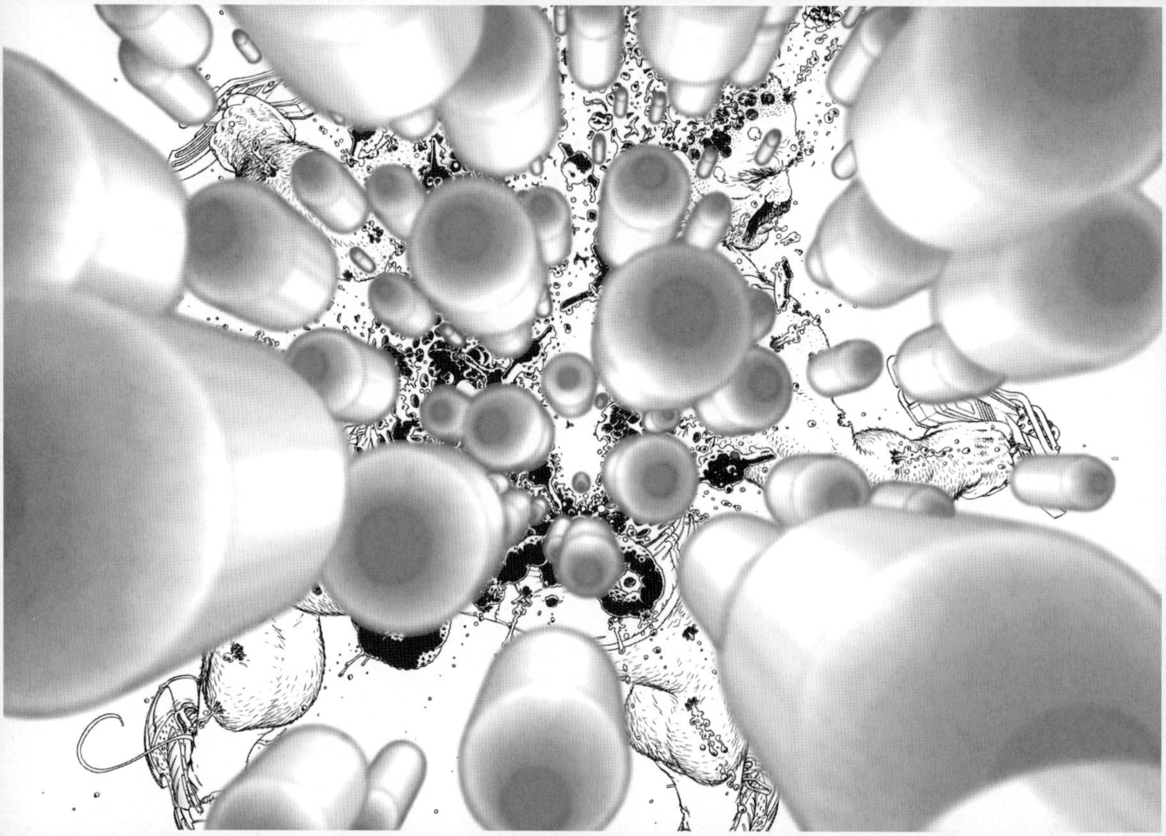

FRANK: I drew preliminary roughs for "shooting" this scene from two different angles — side-on, and from behind. In retrospect, I'm glad that Grant chose behind.

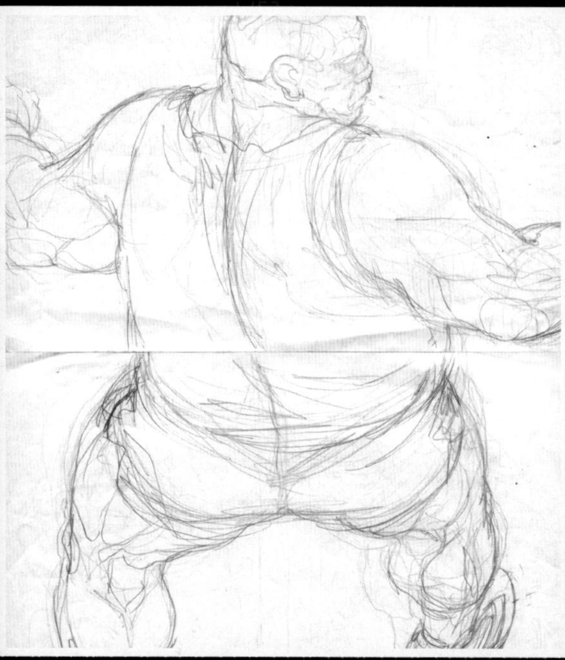

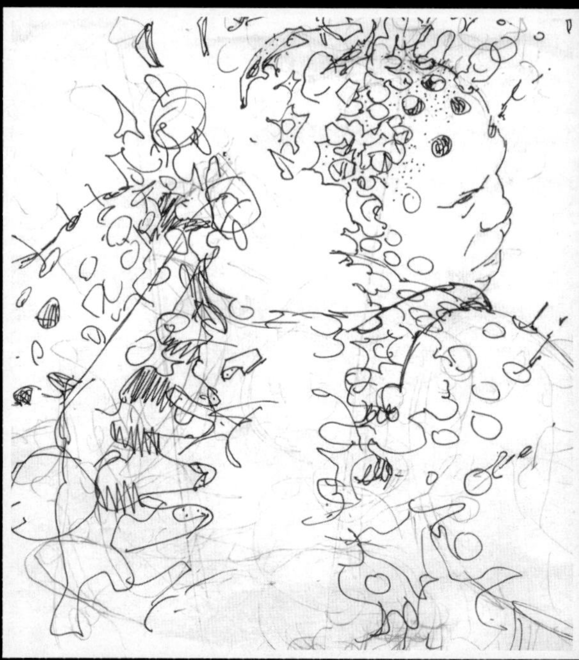

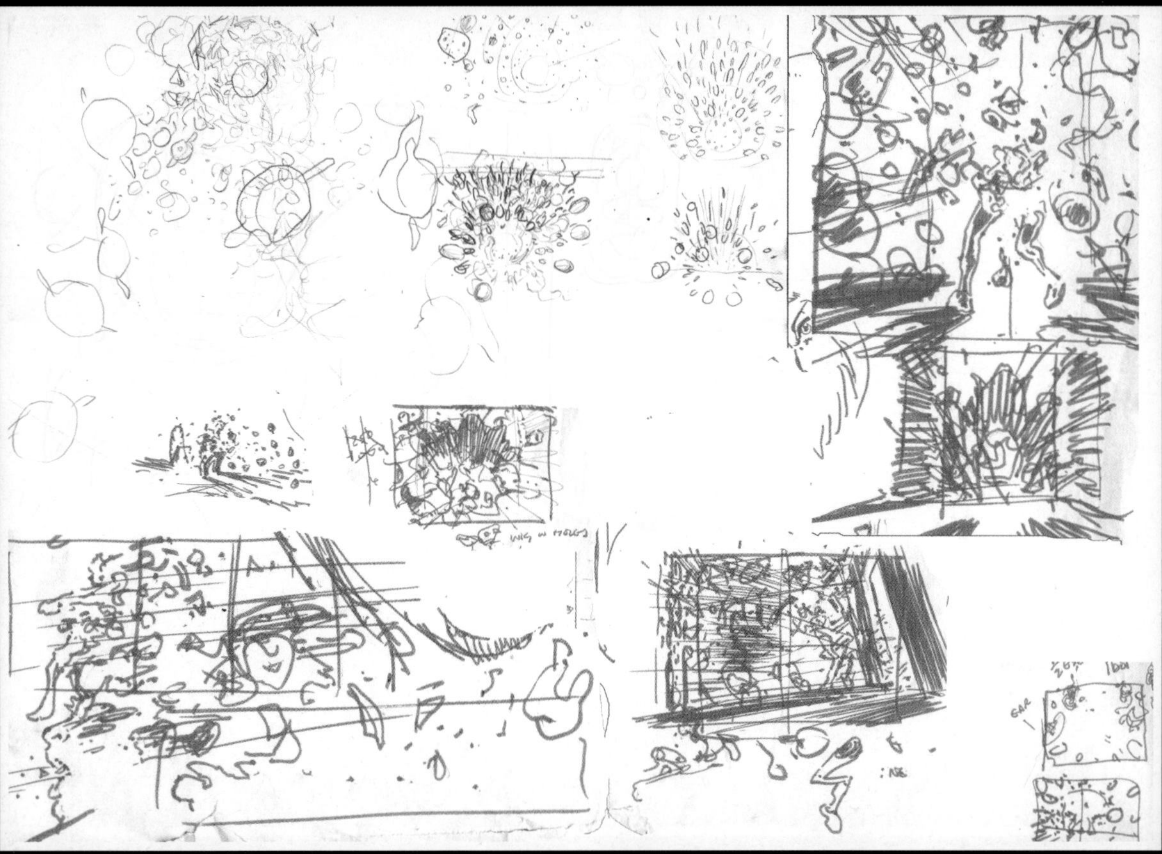

GRANT: This was the first big action shot in the book and an eye-popping demonstration of the "3-D page space" effects we'd developed — of which more later. Additionally, the explosive death of Señor Guerrera left readers in no doubt as to the levels of gore they would have to expect from this heartwarming tale of fluffy animals.

The visceral, forensic detail of the blood and guts in this book has often raised eyebrows, but we felt it was a necessary "red in tooth and claw" counterbalance to the sentimentality that's always hard to avoid in tales of plucky animal pals. Parents who may feel uncertain about exposing their little angels to anatomically detailed drawings of entrails and punctured eyeballs may not necessarily be surprised to discover that Quitely was relentlessly goaded to each fresh crescendo of grand guignol by his sons Vinnie and Joe, both under ten years old at the time.

SEQUENCE

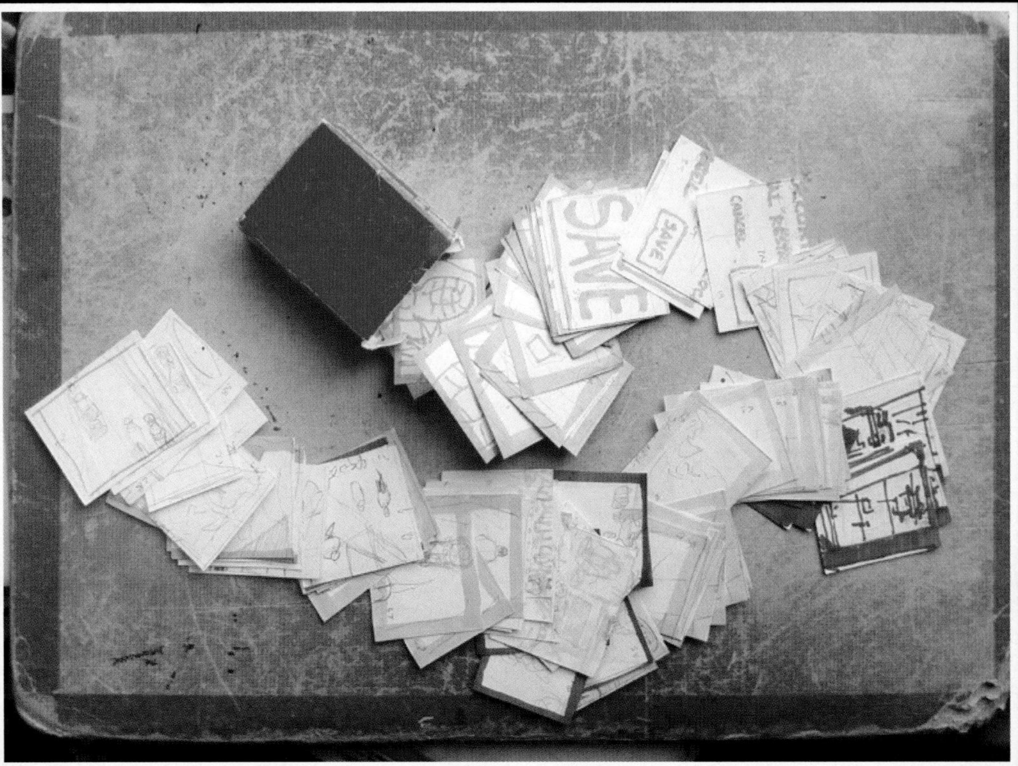
SAVE
SAVE

FRANK: All 108 panels for this 6-page sequence were drawn and cut out individually and color-coded for each camera involved — that way I could lay it out as per my roughs, and then easily see how any changes made would affect the sequence as a whole.

It took a lot of time to prepare, but it really made it easier to get the storytelling right. The cards can be arranged linearly, like dominoes, intersecting like a crossword, or concurrently but in separate sequences, like musical tracks.

I kept them in a small cardboard box, which became really beaten up after a while, and someone put it in the bin by mistake, but fortunately I rescued it before the bin was emptied.

GRANT: That little cardboard box is a genuine wonder of the world. It allows an entire sequence of events to be experienced in any order including backwards, forwards and sideways. You can even play the scene as a card game if you like! The original idea was to use CCTV screen images to create a kind of "cubist" version of an unfolding event as it might be seen from multiple fixed camera angles. Close study of the sequence will cause a curious 4-D object or map to appear in one's head! The tight repeated rhythm of the 18-panel grids creates a sense of tension and claustrophobia that is released by the lovely 2-page escape spread.

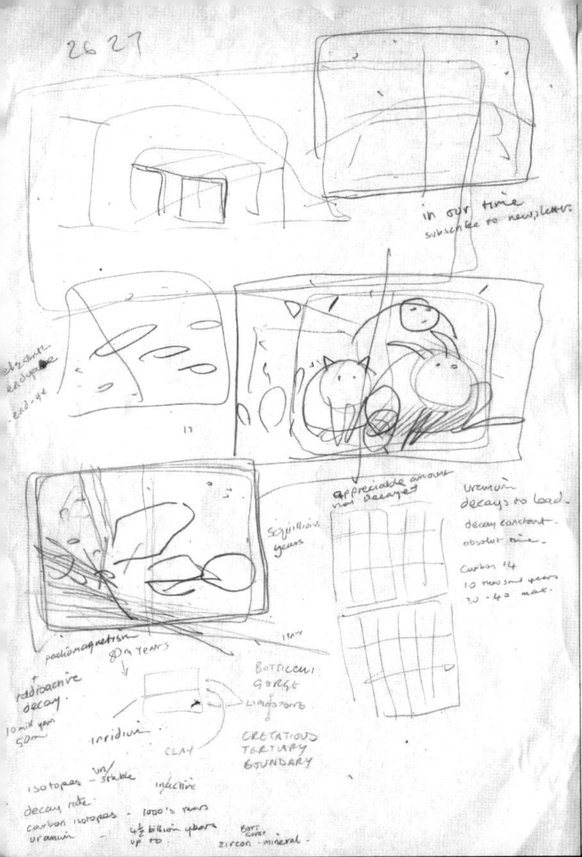
26 27
in our time
subscribe to newsletter
appreciable amount not decayed
uranium decays to lead
decay constant
absolute time
Carbon 14
10 thousand years
30-40 max
paelomagnetism
80m years
radioactive decay
10 mil years
50m
Botticelli Gorge
Limestone
iridium
CLAY
CRETATIOUS TERTIARY BOUNDARY
isotopes - un/stable
inactive
decay rate
carbon isotopes - 1000's years
uranium - 4½ billion years up to
zircon - mineral

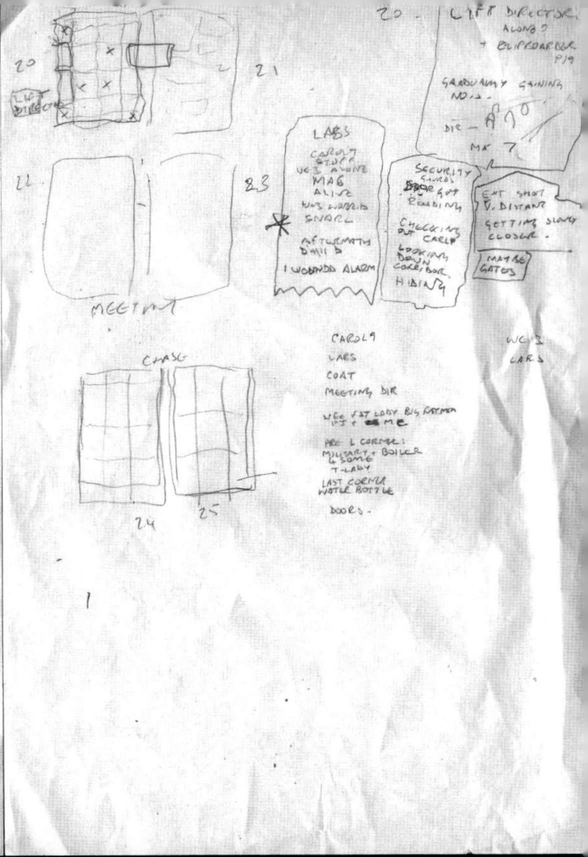
20
21
LIFT DIRECTOR
22
23
LABS
MAG
ALIVE
SNARL
AFTERMATH
WOUNDED ALARM
SECURITY
CHECKING OUT
LOOKING DOWN CORRIDOR
HIDING
EST SHOT V. DISTANT
GETTING SLOWLY CLOSER
MAYBE GATES
MEETING
CHASE
24
25
LABS
COAT
MEETING DIR
LAST CORNER WATER BOTTLE
DOORS

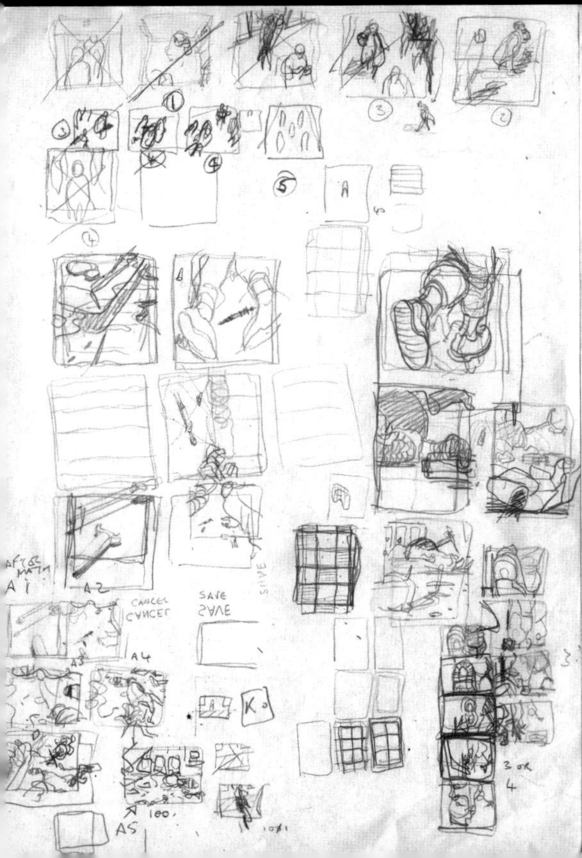
AFTERMATH
A1
A2
CANCEL
SAVE
A4
A5
3 or 4
100

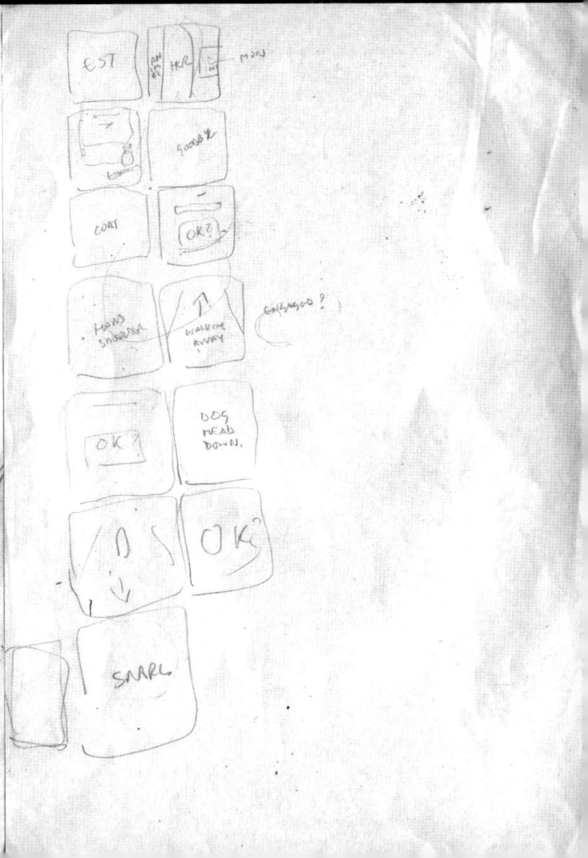
EST
HR
MON
GOODBYE
COAT
OK?
HAND SHOULDER
WALKING AWAY
ENGAGED?
OK?
DOG HEAD DOWN.
OK?
SNARL

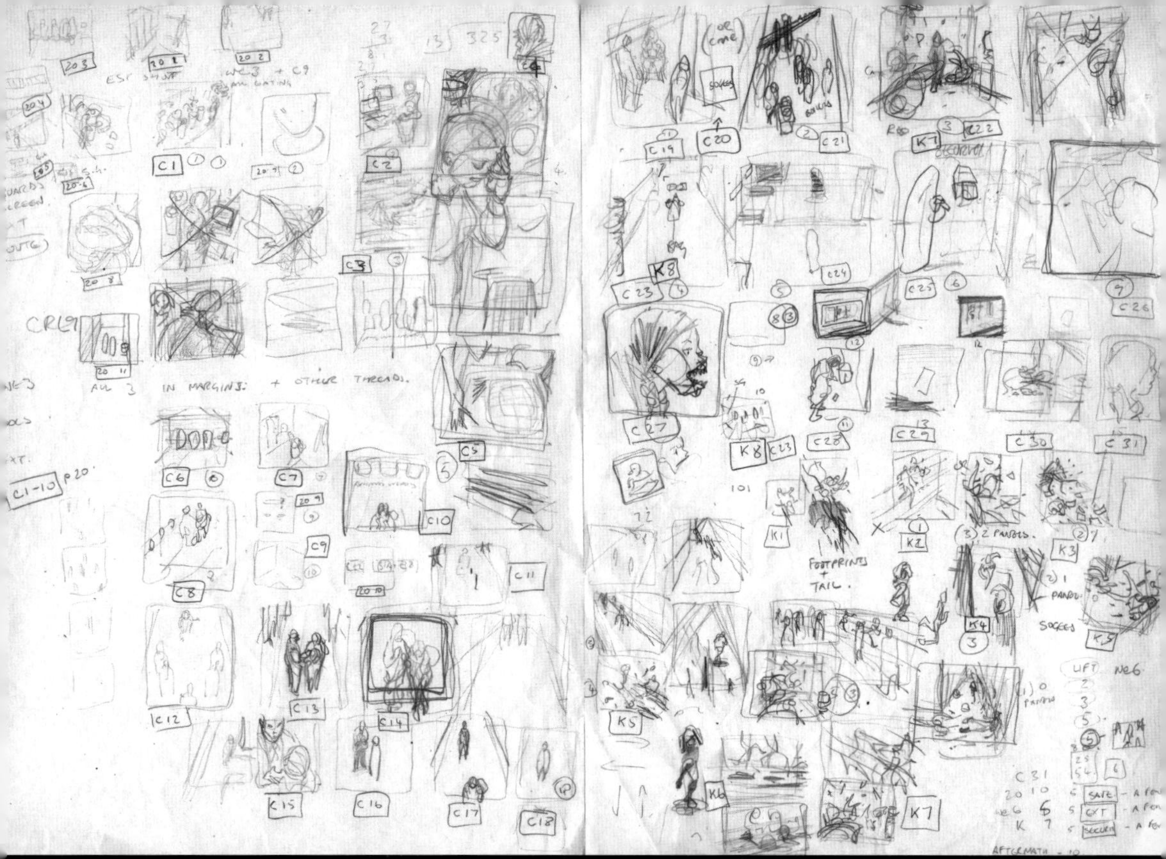

ALL 3 IN MARGINS + OTHER THREADS.
C1-10 P20.
CRL
FOOTPRINTS + TAIL.
(3) 2 PANELS.
SOGGES
LIFT
AFTERMATH

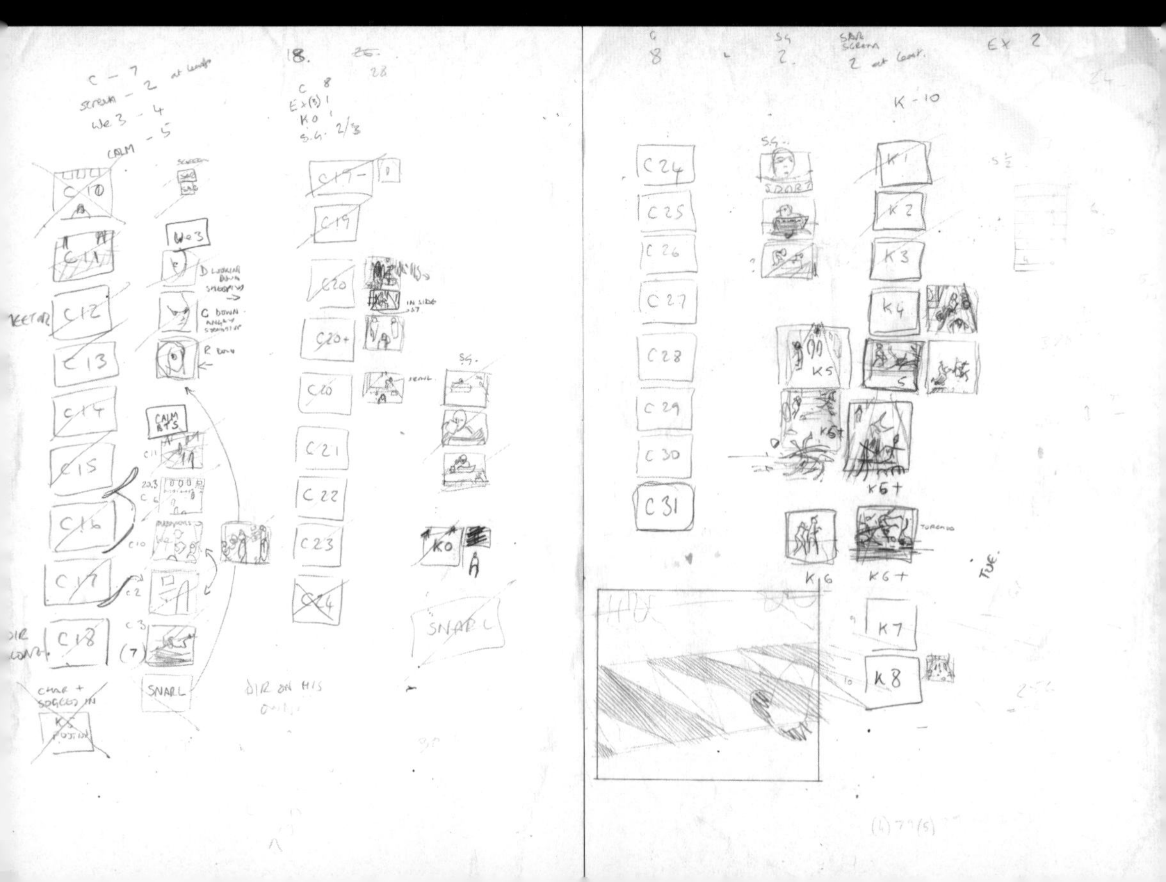

C - 7
SCREAM - 2
WE 3 - 4
CALM - 5
WE 3
CALM RTS
SNARL
DIR ON HIS
CHAR + SOGGES IN
K5 POISON
C 8
K0
SNARL
EX 2
K - 10
K6 +
K7
K8
C31

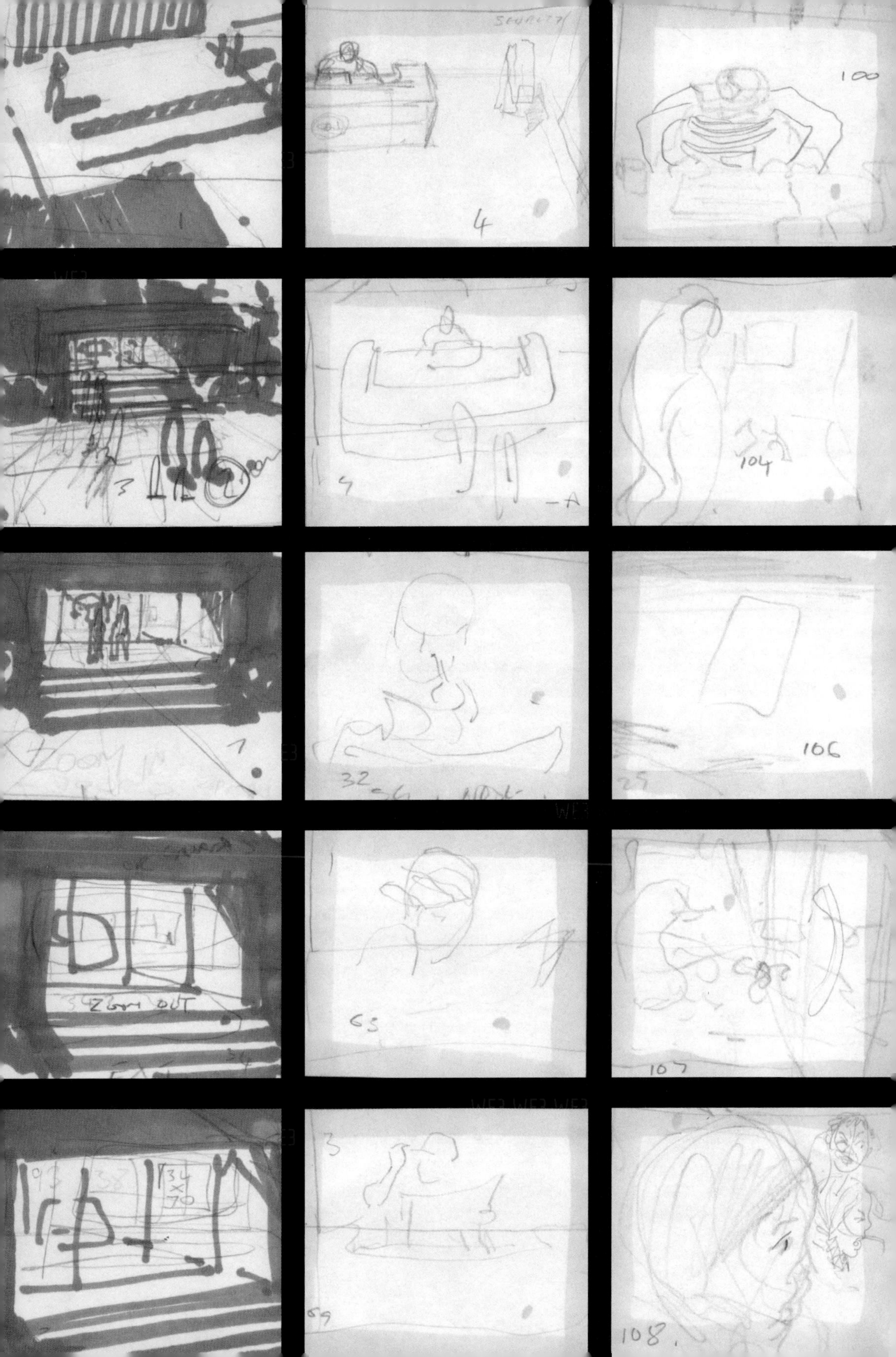

SECURITY
4
100
104
ZOOM
106
ZOOM OUT
65
107
34 x 70
108.

CAT AND DOG
ATTACK SEQUENCE

GRANT: At the beginning of the process of writing WE3, I described it as a story of "meat and motion
structured around the direct desires of three animals, it was intended as a very straightforward linear
narrative. The simplicity of the story freed us up to make the page layouts somewhat experimental
o Frank Quitely and I set about devising a different approach to the comics page that we hoped might
uggest non-human perception of time and space.

We chose to treat the page not as a flat 2-D surface upon which panels were "pasted" down flat but as a
virtual 3-D space in which panels could be "hung" and "rotated" or stacked one on top of the othe
According to scientists, small animals experience time more slowly, and we liked the idea of extending th
gutters around the panels to suggest the immense amounts of still "zen" time a cat might pass through betwee
the micro-seconds of human awareness.

Written before Frank and I worked out how this might actually look on the page, the following script excer
shows the first attempts to articulate the idea to editor Karen Berger and ends with a hopeful "... trust us, it
ook unbelievable." Fortunately, it did.

WE3: ISSUE 2

PAGES 6/7

Frame 1

This is the first of two big special effects action spreads which attempt to show time, space and motion from an
animals' POV instead of emphasizing human senses. To do this Frank and I are creating what I'm calling the "Pop-Out"
effect which is all about thinking past the apparent "flatness" of the 2-D page surface and instead visualizing the page
surface as having infinite white DEPTH — this allows for a new kind of "camera-eye" for comics — panels can "pop"
out of the page or sink into the page etc. It's all worked out visually and will change comics forever but beyond that to
explain more would be to spoil the surprise of seeing the pages. This is a completely new way of depicting high-speed
action which only comics can do.

Rapid cut to super-cool feline ultra-violence. The cats up in the topmost branches firing insane amounts of ammo.
Close up pop out panels showing microscopic 3-D detail on the needles. Or heat images. Pheromone frequencies.
Flash cut with receding panels of snarling animal faces. Dying men.

The dog leaps at the windscreen of the second jeep. We're right in there with the men as the monstrous cyborg comes
straight at us. Firing a single missile from its back cannon. These are not cuddly animals to fuck with, no sir! Pop-out
panels show impact wounds in forensic close up. Sound bursts. Close up animal reactions, sniffing noses. Fumes etc.
All sliding and shuttling around in the white depths of the page. Let Hollywood try to copy THIS stuff...

CAT:	SSSTINK
CAT:	BOSS
CAT:	DIE!

PAGE 10/11

Frame 1

The second of the "this is what you pay for..." super-effects "POP-OUT" effects spreads, this time with the pop-out
panels arranged on a different plane in page space... trust us, it'll look unbelievable. The big images here show the
Cat in super-strobe lapse slinking down and around a flaming tree, back onto the ground... shooting down the final
opponents. The Dog leaps from the second jeep as it crashes. The animals tumble down the bank. Flames take control.

Frame 2

DOG:	!?!
DOG:	GUD 2
DOG:	COME
RABBIT:	TAIL
RABBIT:	BAD
RABBIT:	TAIL

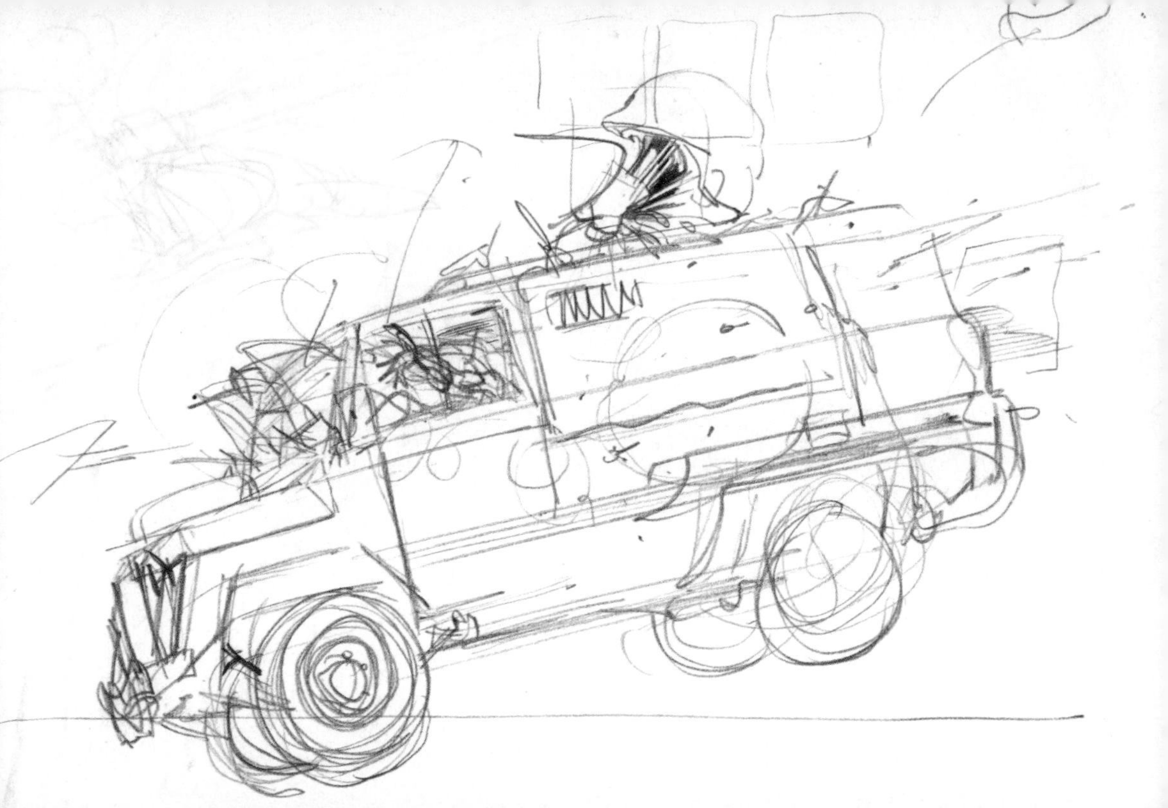

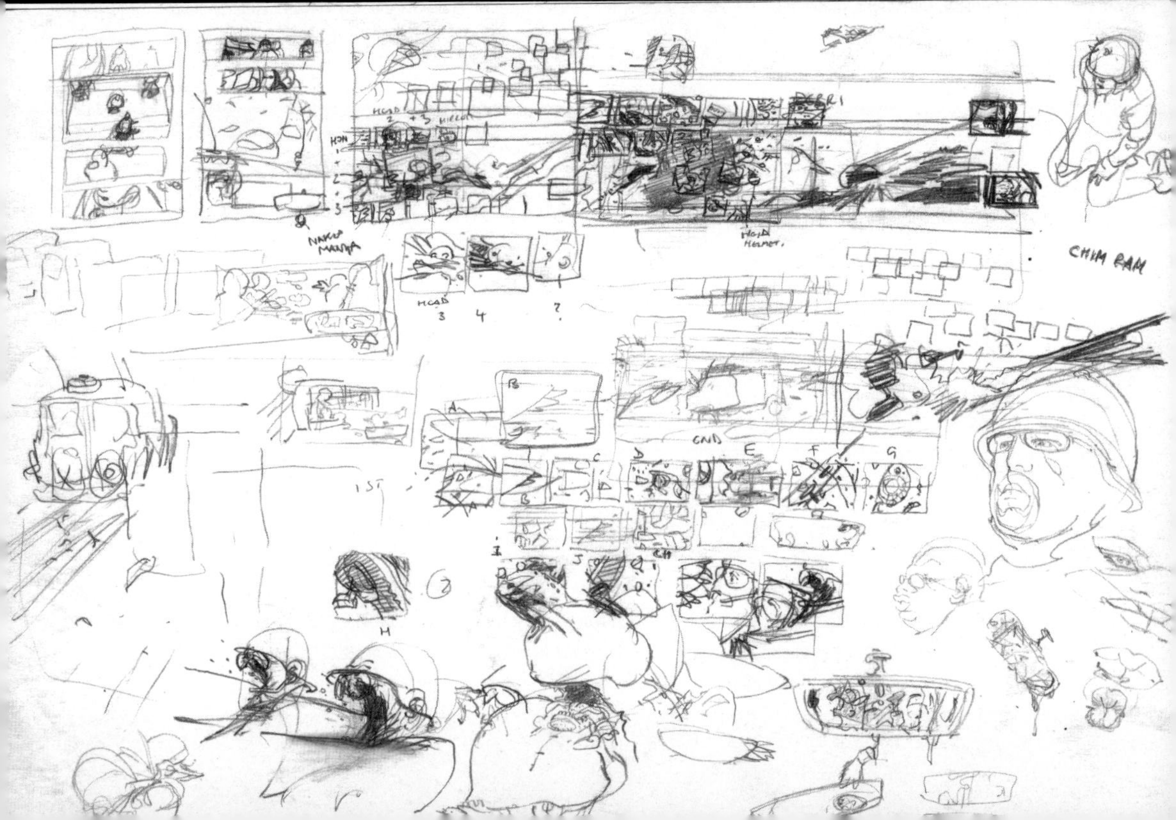
HEAD Helmet.
CHIM RAM
HEAD
3 4 ?
1ST
A B C D E F G
END
H
I J

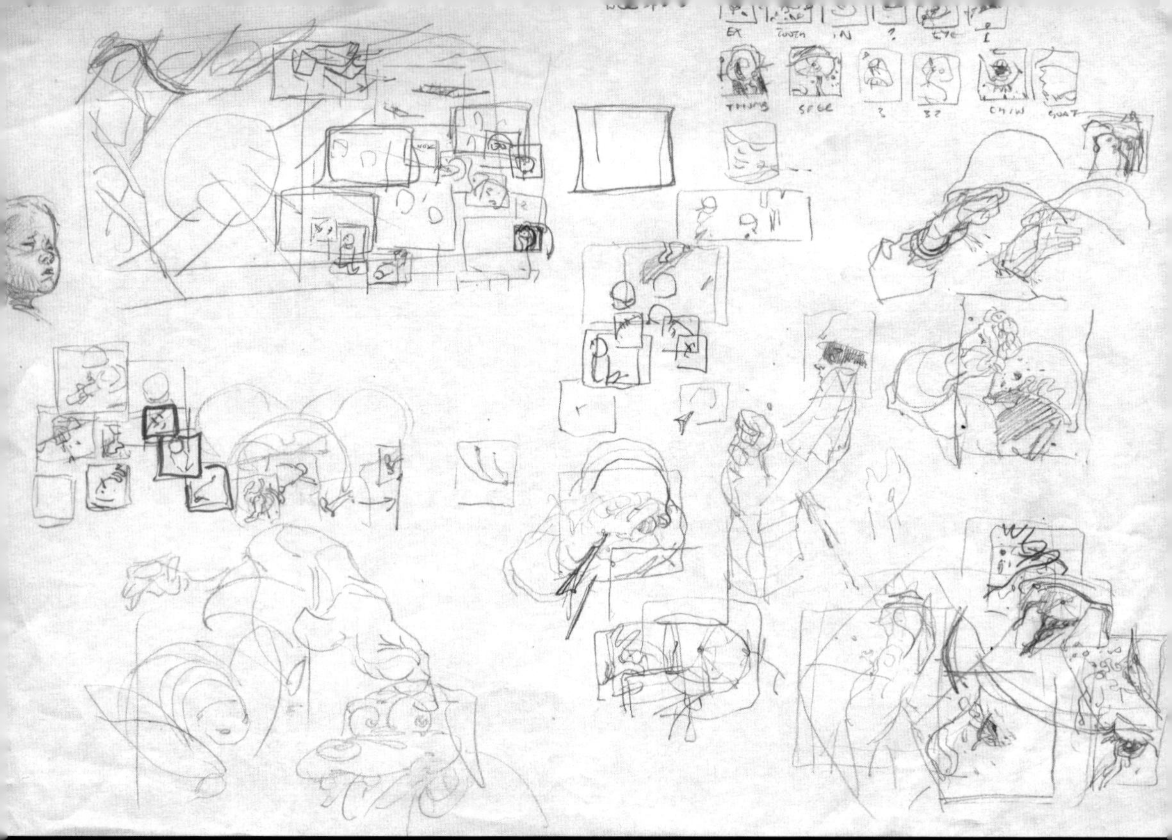
EX
TOOTH
IN
EYE
THUMB
SPEC
CHIN
GOAT

WE3

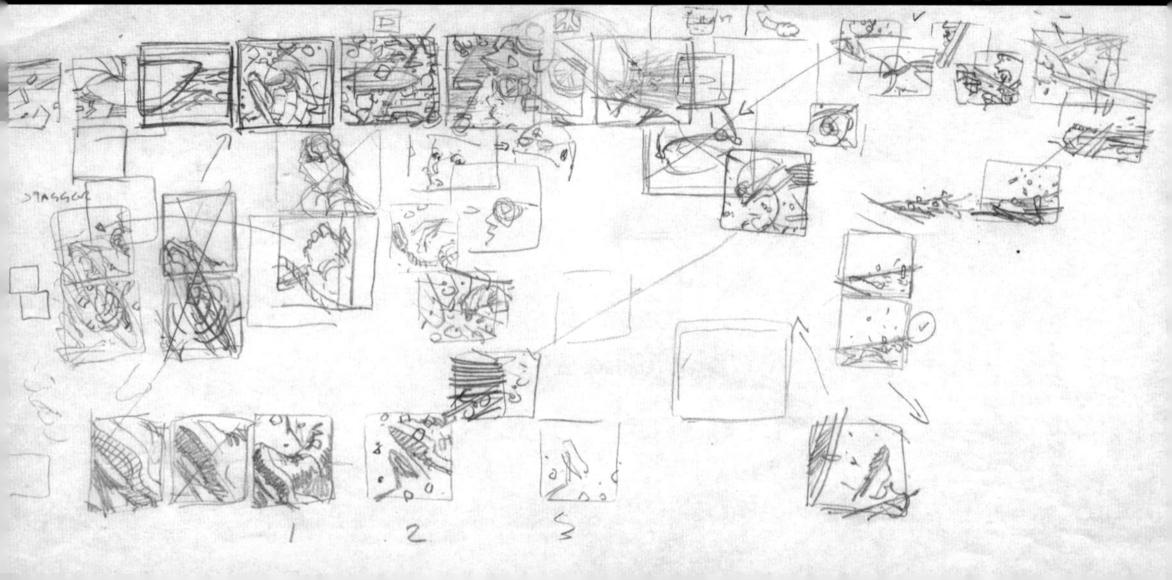
STAGGER
1
2

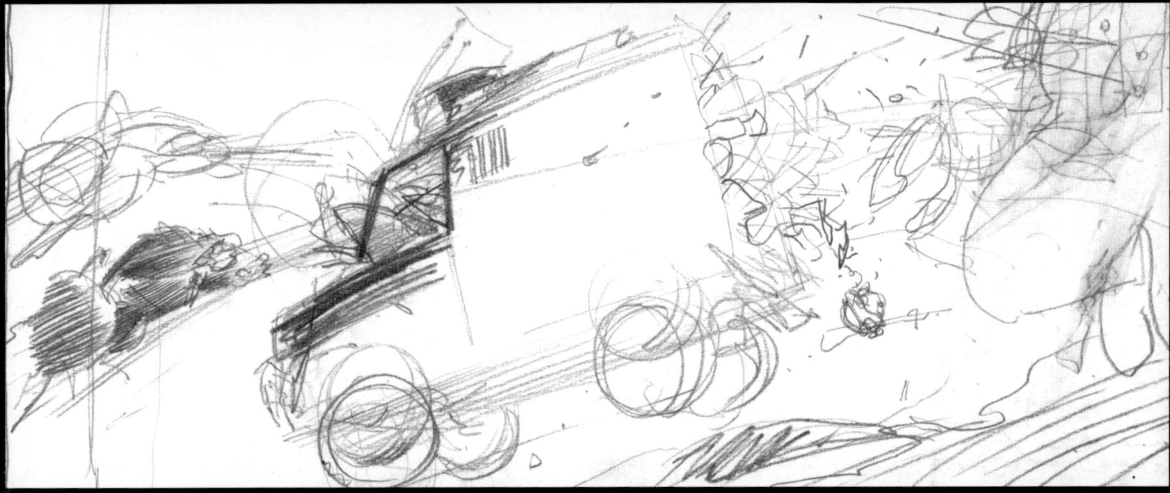

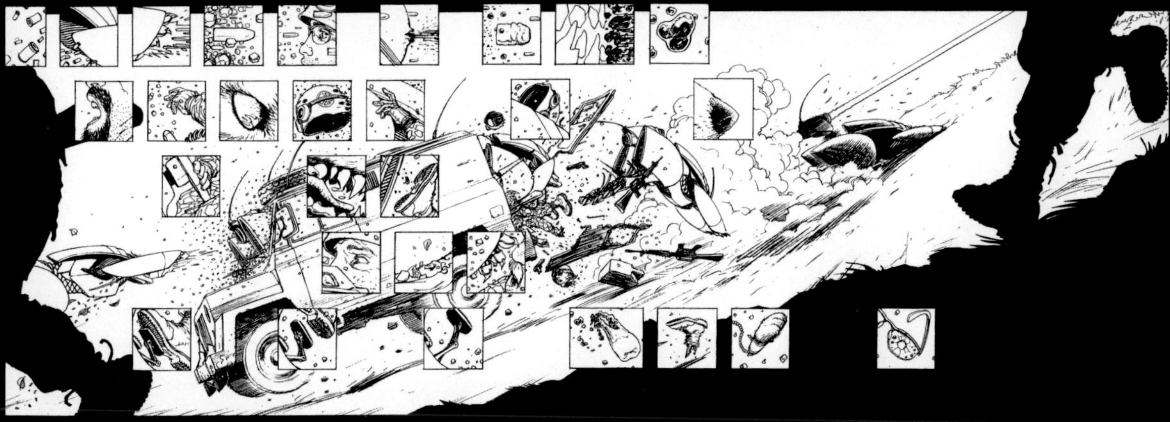

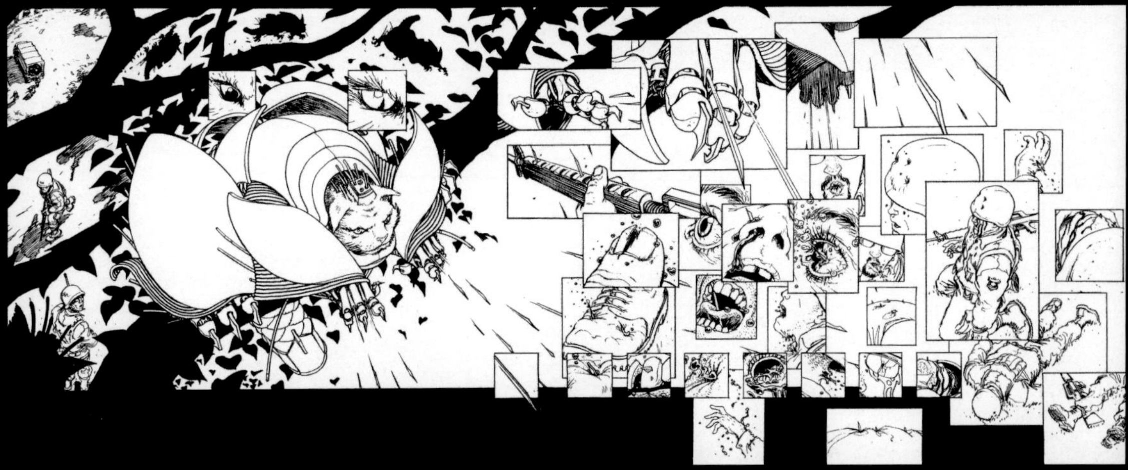

CAT FIGHT SEQUENCE

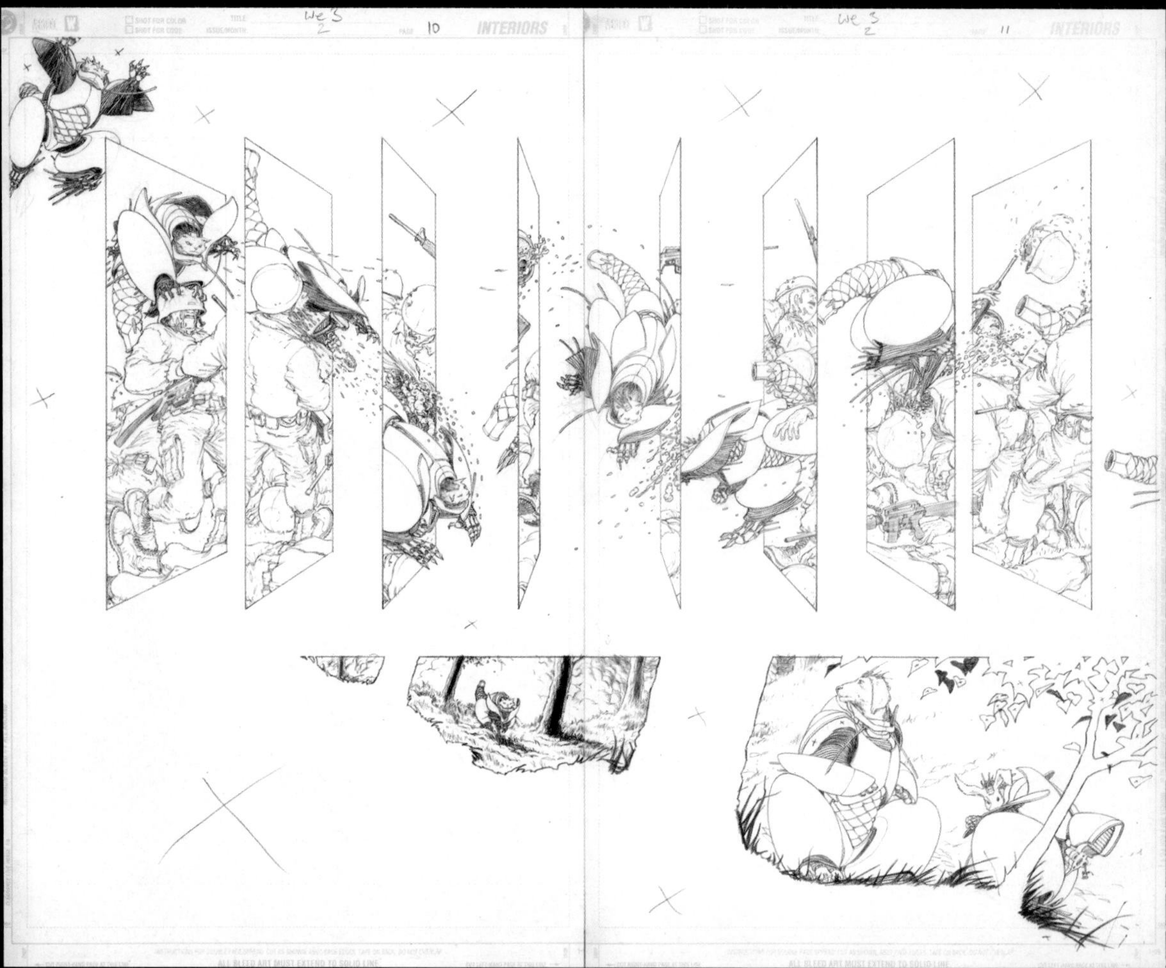

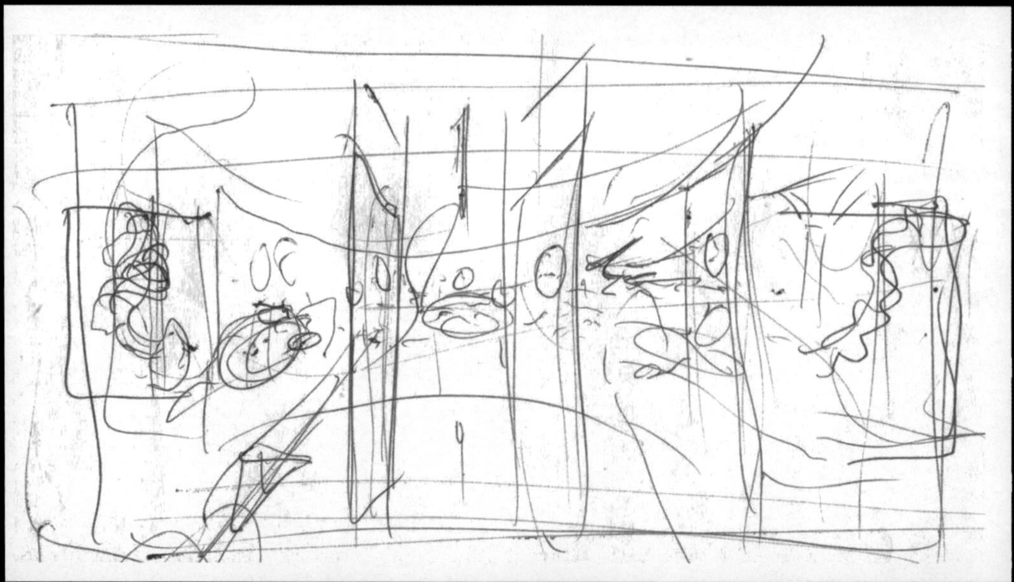

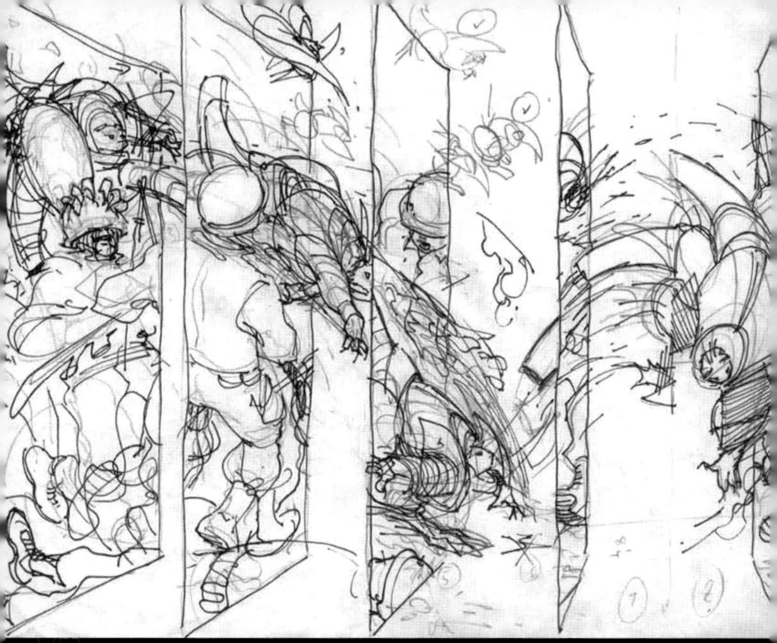

WE3

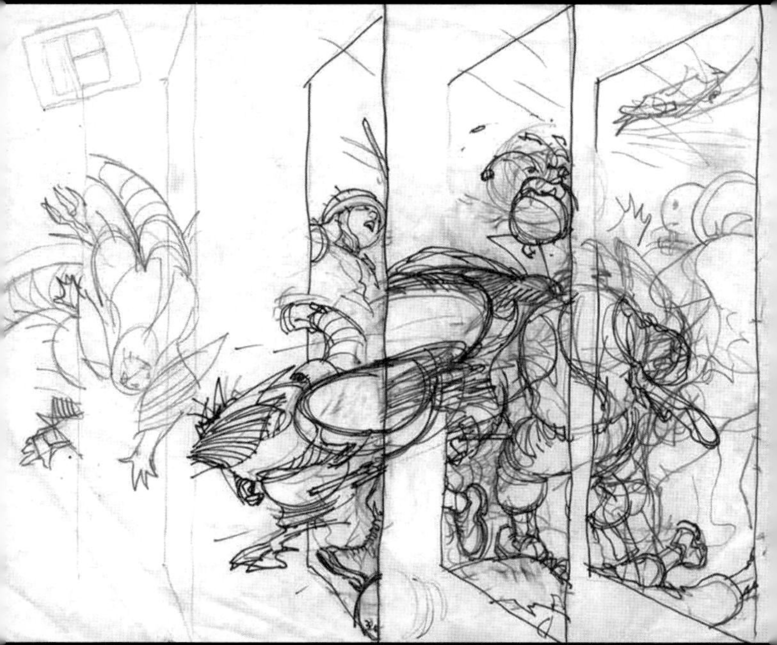

WE3

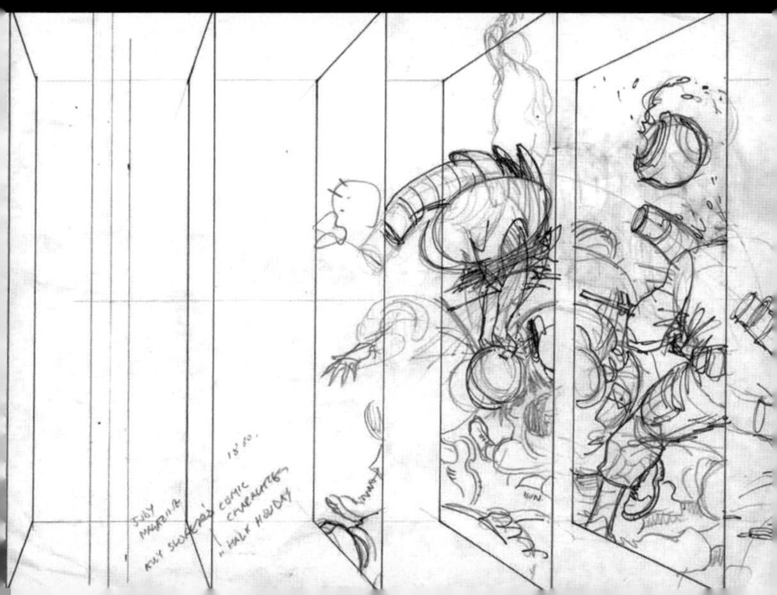
JUDY
MAGAZINE
ALLY SLOPER'S COMIC CHARACTERS
1880.
" HALF HOLIDAY

ORIGINAL MINISERIES COVER ART

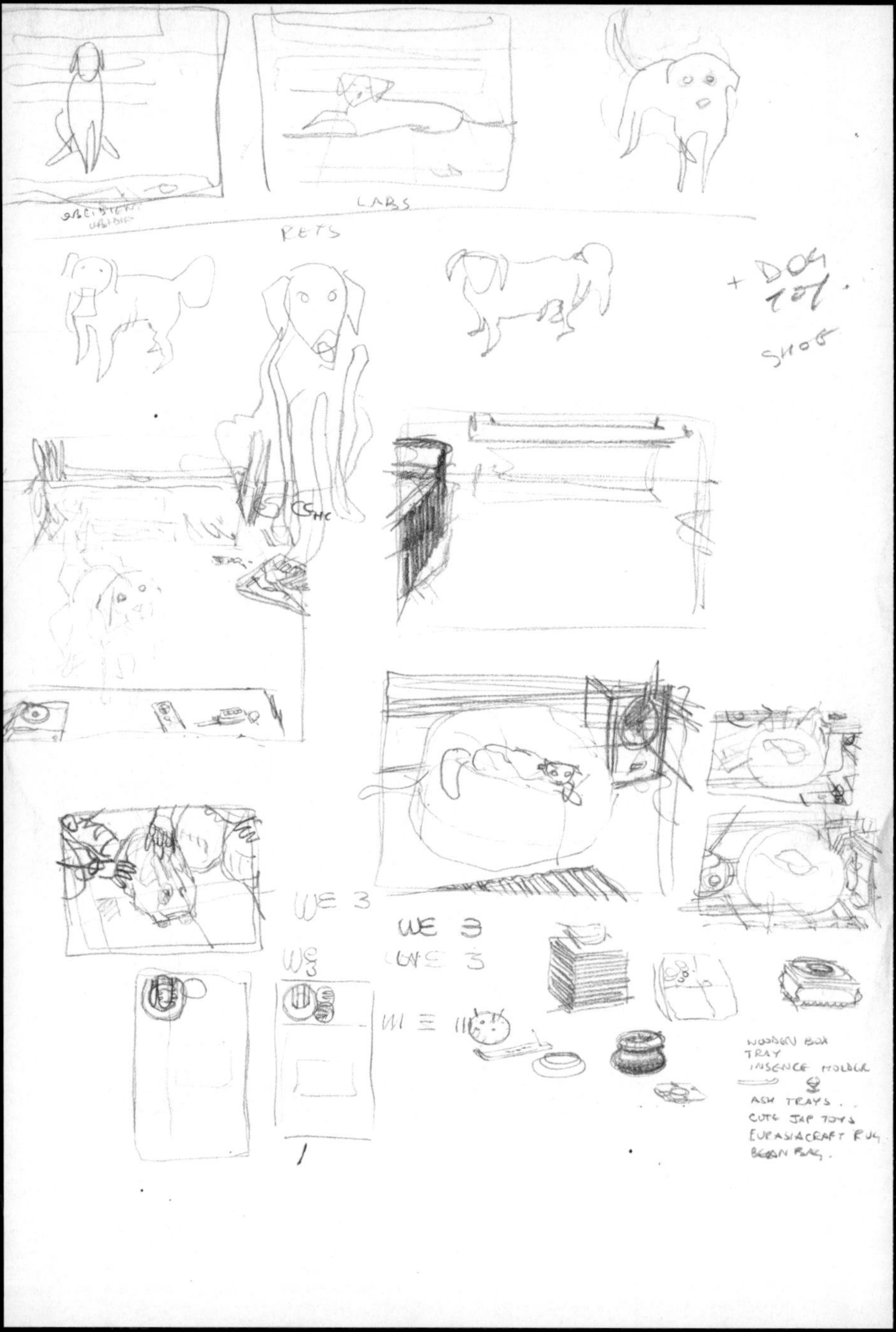
LABS
PETS
+ DOG TOY SHOP
WE 3
WE 3
WOODEN BOX
TRAY
INSENCE HOLDER
ASH TRAYS.
CUTE JAP TOYS
EURASIACRAFT RUG
BEAN BAG.

FRANK: The first cover for the original miniseries has an array of props from my own house at the time; the second has half the stuff I had in my bedroom as a teenager; and the writing on the third was done by my family — Johnny and Claire's by my kids, and Mrs. Mortimer's by my wife.

GRANT: The three covers were one of the first story elements that occurred to me. If we have hearts at all we've all had them broken by those sad, hopeful "pet missing" posters; those personal photos of beloved pets taken in happier times; the reward offers; the gut-wrenching fear and worry that haunts every handwritten, home-printed line. We wanted to emphasize what kind of story this was by engaging our readers' emotions straight away, and I think these covers do the job of not only introducing the three animals but making them immediately vulnerable and relatable.

his one page of logo ideas represents the entire process from initial discussion to enlisting bra
NYC to do the finished art.

We liked the idea of the logo being a literal dog tag, which would play with the double mea
and animals. The melting tag also suggested the way that the hard shell of military armor and t
reak down into more free-flowing unconfined natural shapes and responses after the animals e
tivity. And we wanted, I seem to remember, something that recalled the metallic logos on block
ovies.

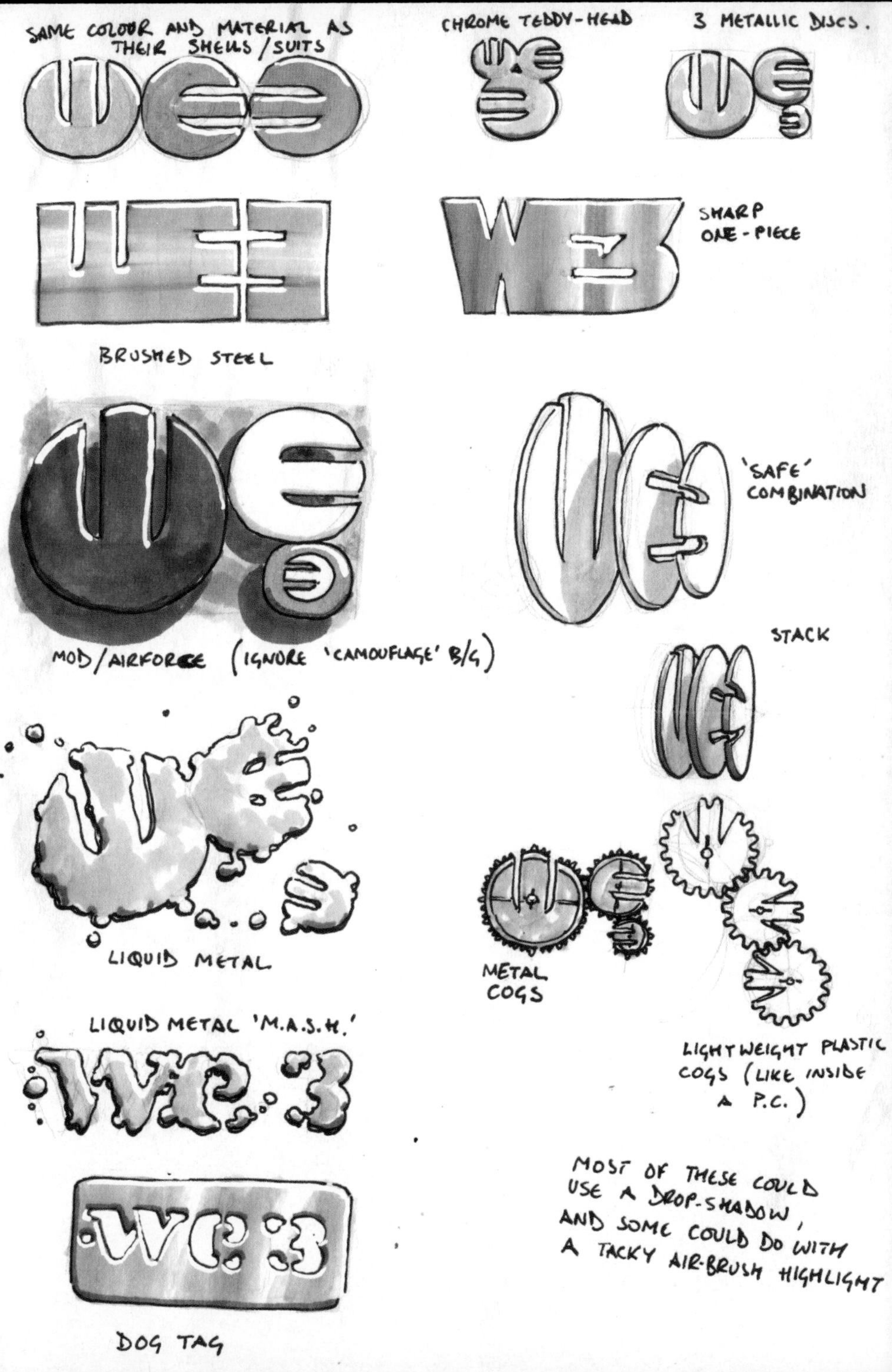

SAME COLOUR AND MATERIAL AS THEIR SHELLS / SUITS
CHROME TEDDY-HEAD
3 METALLIC DISCS.
SHARP ONE-PIECE
BRUSHED STEEL
'SAFE' COMBINATION
MOD/AIRFORCE (IGNORE 'CAMOUFLAGE' B/G)
STACK
LIQUID METAL
METAL COGS
LIQUID METAL 'M.A.S.H.'
LIGHTWEIGHT PLASTIC COGS (LIKE INSIDE A P.C.)
MOST OF THESE COULD USE A DROP-SHADOW, AND SOME COULD DO WITH A TACKY AIR-BRUSH HIGHLIGHT
DOG TAG

ORIGINAL TRADE PAPERBACK COLLECTION COVER ART

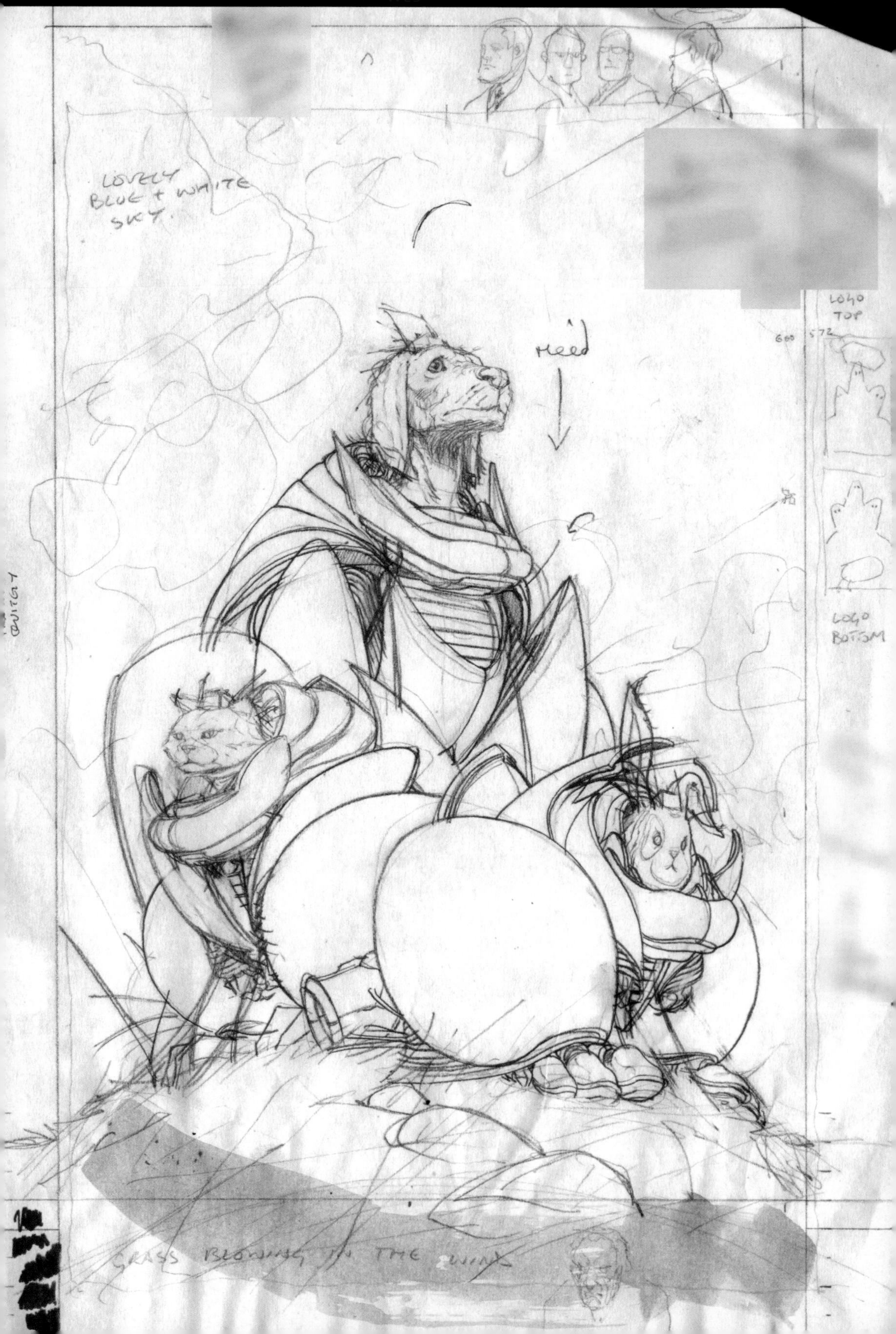
LOVELY BLUE + WHITE SKY.
HEAD
LOGO TOP
LOGO BOTTOM
GRASS BLOWING IN THE WIND

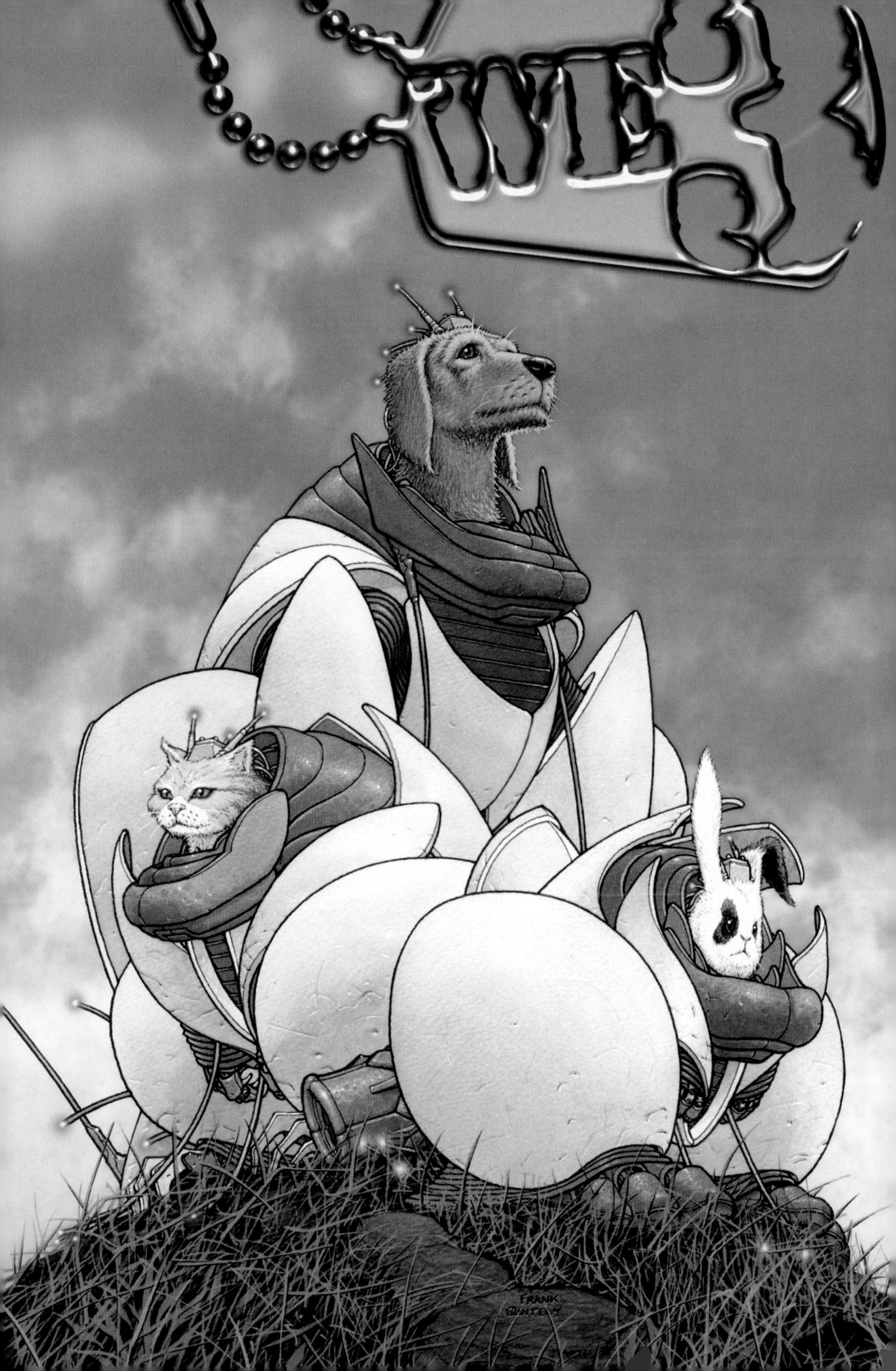
WE3
FRANK QUITELY

OVER ART

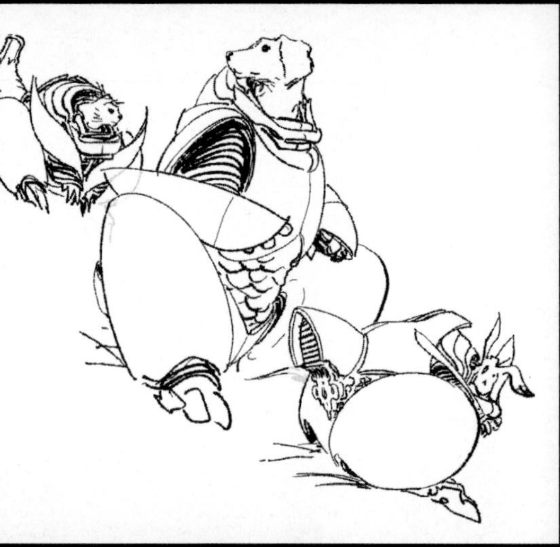

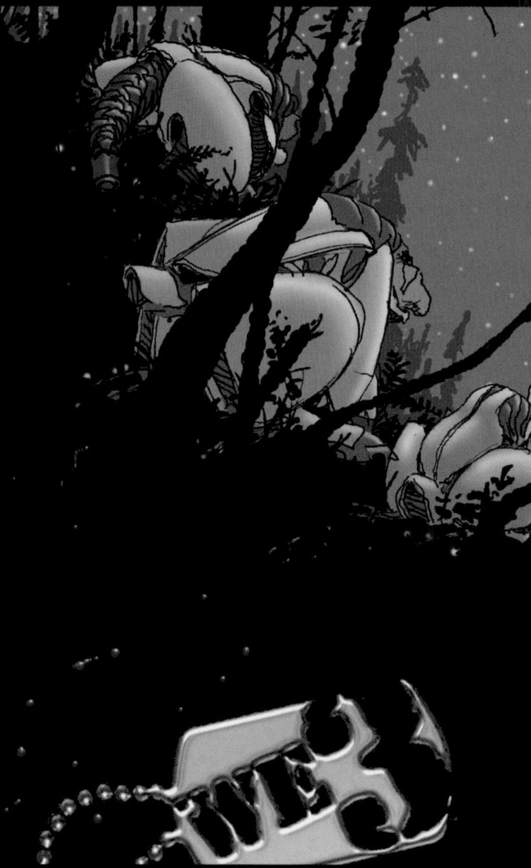

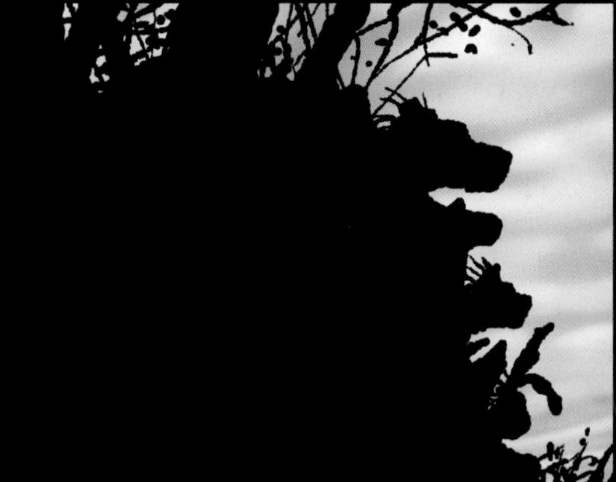

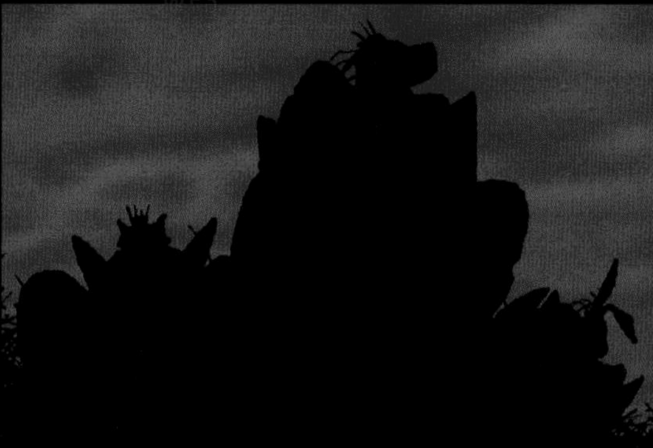

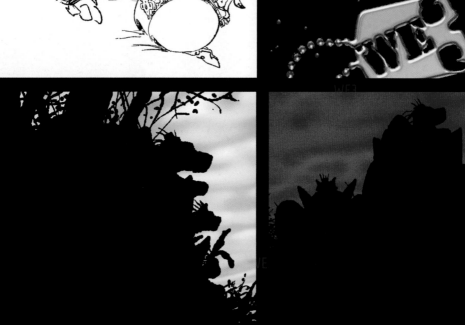

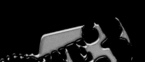